The
Future of
United States
Naval Power

The Future of United States Naval Power

James A. Nathan and James K. Oliver

Indiana University Press
Bloomington & London

For Carol and Mary

Library of Congress Cataloging in Publication Data
Nathan, James A.
The future of United States naval power.

Includes index.
1. United States. Navy. 2. United States—
Military policy. 3. Sea power—United States.
4. United States—Foreign relations—1974-
I. Oliver, James K., joint author. II. Title.
VA58.4.N37   359′.00973   78-9512
ISBN 0-253-12700-9   1 2 3 4 5 83 82 81 80 79

Contents

Acknowledgments

As "outsiders" seeking to understand conditions which might constrain the future of the Navy, we have incurred numerous obligations. We owe more than a modest debt to the handful of defense analysts who have recently begun to undertake a reexamination of the role of naval power in world politics. We have acknowledged this debt, as best we could, with the traditional accoutrement of citations and footnotes. We were also fortunate to be able to draw on the support and criticism of a small group of defense analysts and Navy professionals as this study progressed. None were more supportive than the staff, the members, and the Director of the Advanced Research Program of the Naval War College from 1974–1976, James King. The initial phases of our research were conducted under a grant from the Advanced Research Program. James King and his associates, especially Lieutenant Commander Kenneth McGruther, Professor F. G. "Bing" West, and Commander William Pettyjohn, provided insight and encouragement throughout the successive drafts of the manuscript. They have tried to save us from errors of fact and interpretation of frequently obscure and always rapidly changing naval doctrine. To the extent that errors remain, they are the responsibility of the authors alone. The interpretations and judgments contained in the study are solely the authors' and should not be taken as representing the views of the Naval War College, the United States Navy, or other government agencies.

The authors have also benefited from the commentary and criticism of the members of the Council on Foreign Relations' 1980's Project Study Group on the Future of the United States Navy, before whom a summary of the study's conclusions were presented in May and November of 1977. Professors Michael MccGwire of Dalhousie University, John Norton Moore of the University of Virginia, and Robert Osgood of the Johns Hopkins School of Advanced International Studies also read parts or all of the manuscript and kindly offered their comments. Ed Morse, as Senior Fellow of the Council on Foreign Relations, also supported and encouraged our work on the study.

Steven Llanso served as our research assistant during the first year of our research and provided us with a lucid introduction to many of the mysteries of U.S. Navy acronyms, jargon, and technology, and offered thoughtful and careful criticism of our work and the work of others. His assistance was essential in the early stages of the research, and without his time and professionalism the study could not have been completed. Finally, Carol M. Anderson, Mary Meyer, and Dorothy Shelton have cheerfully provided assistance with typing the many drafts of the study.

vi

The following acronyms are used with some frequency in the text. Other acronyms are used with much less frequency and are defined within the context of the discussion.

ASW: antisubmarine warfare

CSGN: nuclear-powered strike cruiser

CVN: nuclear-powered aircraft carriers of the large-decked classes, e.g., the *Enterprise* and *Nimitz*

CNO: Chief of Naval Operations

CVV: a proposed new class of smaller, conventionally powered aircraft carriers.

ICBM: land-based intercontinental ballistic missiles

197T: Between fiscal years 1976 and 1977, Congress changed the beginning of the U.S. Government's budgetary fiscal year from the traditional 1 July to 1 October. Funds for the "transition quarter" from July to October of 1976 were attached to the fiscal year 1976 budget and that year's budget was designated Fiscal Year 1976–197T.

PGM: precision-guided munitions

SLBM: submarine-launched ballistic missiles

SLCM: submarine- or sea-launched cruise missiles

SLOC: sea lines (lanes) of communication

SSBN: nuclear-powered submarines carrying submarine-launched ballistic missiles

SSN: nuclear-powered attack submarine

V/STOL: vertical/short takeoff and landing aircraft

Introduction

NAVAL POWER is perhaps the most flexible of all instruments of force. Its lethality is comparable to other branches of warfare. Its symbolic function is well known. It operates in a heretofore comparatively unambiguous legal medium. The Navy's capacity to perform strategic, symbolic, and supply functions as well as to project massive power at great distance, relatively cheaply, makes it seem particularly well chosen for an era where "economy of force" is an economic and political necessity of governance. The United States has placed a considerable wager on the continued viability of naval power: over 40 percent of current defense procurement costs. This study is an effort to assess the surety of that bet in light of the changing domestic and international "political ecology" of foreign policy.

For much of the period since World War II, foreign policy has relied on the use or threat of force. The Navy's place in this policy has not always been clear. Immediately after World War II, first the new Air Force and then the Army was the main element of the national security policy mix. The postwar 1940s saw the Navy lose out to the Air Force in a bruising struggle for control of the new strategic bombing mission.[1] Indeed, it took the Korean War to convince Congress that the demonstrated efficacy of naval air power

1

deserved a new generation of aircraft carriers. When the Korean War drew toward its indeterminate conclusion, a "new look" for American defense policy was proclaimed. Once again, the Air Force rapidly expanded its role in the defense budget at the expense of the Army. Although Navy modernization continued, its trajectory of growth by no means matched that of the Air Force.

The development of a modest Soviet strategic capability and the turbulence of the Third World in the late 1950s and early 1960s heralded a new debate and yet another adjustment in the American defense posture. Again the Navy, though it perhaps held its own, was not at the cutting edge of policy innovation. The need, it was contended by the Kennedy and Johnson administrations, was two-fold: an augmented capacity for intervention in the Third World and a more vigorous defense of Europe. The best means to support these two objectives, it was usually maintained, was through the use of an Army with new counterinsurgency and modernized conventional components.

Still, throughout all of these changes, the Navy played an important role, from exercises of brinksmanship in the Formosa Straits and eastern Mediterranean in the 1950s to America's involvement in Vietnam. Indeed, the use of naval power was pivotal in that climactic event of the Cold War, the Cuban Missile Crisis. Yet, seldom did concern about naval power and its use dominate policy debate during the 1950s and the 1960s. In contrast to the thousands of pages of public analysis devoted to the use of air and land instruments of force during these years, one finds little explicit consideration of naval power. American naval hegemony could be assumed. It was, it seemed, always "there." And when called on, for example, off China, Lebanon, Cuba, or Vietnam, it seemed to "work." But it was only when the Navy acquired a strategic mission during the 1960s that it began to bridge a budgetary and doctrinal salient otherwise held by the Air Force.

The current position of the Navy with respect to the strategic mission can be traced to technological change, bureaucratic politics, and congressional action in the mid- and late 1950s. The development of small nuclear reactors, solid fuel missile propellants, a masterful bureaucratic effort on the part of advocates of the fleet ballistic missile concept (and a "systems" concept equal to and ultimately superior to that of the other services) guaranteed the Navy's position at the forefront of strategic deterrence.[2] By the late 1960s, it was becoming apparent that only the submarine-launched ballistic missile system could continue to offer for the foreseeable future the requisite invulnerability to remain the unquestioned basis of strategic retaliatory capacity. Notwithstanding concern about breakthroughs in strategic antisubmarine warfare, the integrity of the manned bomber and the fixed site intercontinental ballistic missile—the other legs of the deterrent triad—were and remain more problematic than the ballistic missile launching nuclear submarine. Moreover, by the early 1970s one began to encounter references in technological literature and congressional hearings to changes in guidance and communications technology that could presage an expansion of the Navy's heretofore "assured destruction" strategic role into the realm of "flexible options," i.e., counterforce nuclear doctrine.

Nonetheless, the Navy's new-found prominence in the American defense budget of the early 1970s and in current debate about the uses of military force in the contemporary international system cannot be explained solely in terms of the undeniable appropriateness of the sea-based deterrent in the nuclear age. In fact, with few exceptions, the most recent debate about the present and future uses of sea power has tended to focus on aspects other than strategic deterrence. Moreover, apart from the admittedly expensive and significant modernization of the strategic fleet via the Poseidon missile and follow-on Trident system, the focus of Navy budget requests and executive-legislative debate has been on the surface fleet and its use.

Much of the new prominence of naval instrumentalities in contemporary analysis of military power and world politics is the result of the convergence of two trends. Both of these trends may prove to be unique, "one-time" circumstances. Specifically, the last ten to fifteen years have encompassed the onset of block obsolescence and subsequent retirement of about one-half of the United States surface fleet. As the American fleet has aged, the Soviet surface and subsurface fleets have been expanding to a point that very nearly all official and most nongovernmental analysts in the West would now regard the Soviet Navy as possessing global naval capability. Undoubtedly the juxtaposition of these two trends in the navies of the two superpowers is sufficient to set off considerable discussion and even alarm in the West. Indeed, most of the present debate in Congress and elsewhere about the future of American naval power is invariably prefaced by comparisons of the two naval establishments and their recent development. American naval decline and Soviet naval expansion seem to many to herald the end of American naval supremacy and the neutralization of the heretofore unchallenged last line of American defense. Certainly such an event would be grounds for new concern about the future not only of American seapower but, indeed, of American foreign policy as well.

At the same time, however, there is a body of opinion which holds that the American response to this situation will prove more than adequate to insure continued American naval superiority for the foreseeable future. Moreover, apart from the qualitative superiority of most new American naval units and the unchallenged supremacy of American sea-based naval air capability, American hegemony is assured because Soviet naval expansion has in fact peaked. Observers such as Michael MccGwire and George E. Hudson would suggest that current shipyard utilization in the Soviet Union as well as what evidence can be gleaned from the limited public discussion of military developments in the Soviet press can reasonably be construed as signaling a leveling-out of Soviet surface naval expansion.[3]

Though the argument that American and Soviet naval trends are not headed in convergent directions is, of course, challenged, even official Navy and Defense Department spokesmen generally agree that the United States Navy is now and, with current modernization programs, will remain equal to the tasks demanded of it. Caveats concerning the capacity of the Soviet Union to challenge American sea control—especially in the eastern Mediterranean and perhaps in the northern Atlantic—are invariably added. Seldom if ever, however, does one encounter an official forecast that the United States Navy would not ultimately prevail if challenged, albeit at higher cost than in the past.[4] Thus, the renewed concern for the future of American sea power is in some measure related to important changes in the balance of naval forces, though the dimensions and meaning of the new balance remain extremely controversial.

Other causes contributing to the new interest in the naval balance include the considerable and escalating costs of the new ships the United States Navy has requested of Congress during the last several years. As the costs of the "new" Navy have grown, attention has also been attracted to major questions about the kinds of ships the Navy should purchase and, even more important, the missions they should perform. So far, most debate and uncertainty have centered on the future of the aircraft carrier and the type of propulsion—nuclear or conventional—appropriate not only to the aircraft carrier but the entire surface fleet.

The future of the aircraft carrier, the future means of powering large ships, and the future of American sea power are closely linked. Virtually the entire American surface navy has been structured about the aircraft carrier task force since World War II. Furthermore, Admiral Hyman Rickover's zealous and skillful advocacy of nuclear power for all major naval vessels resulted in an increasingly nuclear navy during the late 1960s and early 1970s. Skeptics would point out, however, that it has also resulted in a smaller navy, due to the high procurement costs of large nuclear-powered ships. Thus, the Navy must now confront the tradeoff between fleet size and highly capable but very expensive surface combatants.

By the mid-1970s these multiple and intertwined issues had come to a head within the Navy and Defense Department, throughout the executive foreign and defense community and, inevitably, into Congress. Rickover seemed to have carried the day when Title VIII of the Defense Department Appropriations Act of 1975 was passed. Title VIII required that all future major combatants be nuclear powered unless the president could convince Congress that national security required otherwise. Almost immediately, however, the lack of consensus regarding the economics of nuclear propulsion within the Navy and the executive became manifest. No less a figure than Chief of Naval Operations James Holloway took issue with Admiral Rickover. Holloway argued publicly the necessity of a larger Navy. The clear implication of the CNO's position was that this might mean fewer, not more, large nuclear ships, although Admiral Holloway simultaneously asked for a fifth nuclear-powered aircraft carrier and a new class of nuclear-powered cruisers. Disagreement soon extended to Congress, where the House and Senate Armed Services Committees split on the continued feasibility of a Navy built around Title VIII. As the Ford administration came to an end, a major National Security Council study of the future of the Navy's force structure was completed. This study cast doubt on the practicality of the large modern aircraft carrier. Finally, the Carter administration, with campaign commitments to cut defense spending, seemed to be looking longest and hardest at naval spending. One of its first economies was to recommend rescission of a fifth nuclear-powered aircraft carrier and the new nuclear-powered strike cruiser and to reexamine lower-cost alternatives to the nuclear-powered aircraft carrier. Even more fundamental, however, has been the Carter administration's challenge in the late 1970s to the United States Navy's conception of its basic missions and role in the American defense posture.

The problems presented by Soviet fleet expansion, American block obsolescence, nuclear vs. conventional power, the future of the aircraft carrier, and fleet size all have led to a reopening of questions about the nature and future of sea power. Indeed, the bureaucratic and executive-legislative politics of ship construction aside, it is difficult to understand how the major questions concerning the future of the Navy's force structure and size could be resolved without resolution of broader underlying questions of policy.

In early 1974, a student of naval power lamented:

> At a time when a good deal of strategic studies has become, in the opinion of many critics, an over-intellectualized activity—too dominated by abstract theories and civilian analysts—it is rather striking that one ostensibly important area of it, namely naval analysis, has remained quite notably under-intellectualized. . . .
>
> In addition to being relatively under-intellectualized when compared with the rest of strategic analysis, naval analysis has also been relatively undercriticised. That is, while much of strategic studies has had to face criticism in recent years from a variety of standpoints, naval analysis, by and large, has escaped intact.[5]

As the late 1970s approached and planning for the 1980s began to assume more concrete form, however, the process of "intellectualizing" naval power and strategy was under way. Almost as Ken Booth, a British civilian defense scholar, was writing the words above, what had been a trickle of analysis turned into, if not a flood, then at least a rivulet of papers, studies, and symposia on the nature and future of sea power.[6] The intense debate growing out of Mr. Carter's first comprehensive budget proposals made it clear that these problems are of more than academic interest.

Beyond issues of the relative quality of the United States or Soviet Navy and questions regarding the efficacy and expense of various naval platforms and propulsion systems, much of the recent interest in sea power is related to ongoing attempts to resolve the dilemma of reconciling the perceived need for using force in an international system in which the use of force, at least between superpowers, has become increasingly, if not intolerably, dangerous. And force is not only at a discount in Soviet-American relations; now, American military power must be projected from a domestic environment that has proved as dangerous to American political leaders as the international environment, nuclear weapons notwithstanding. But if power is unwieldy in terms of Soviet-American relations and domestic constraints, it does not mean that power has been forsaken by American statesmen as an instrument of policy. Given some of the "new" inhibitions on the use of military force, most observers and policy-makers have eagerly seized upon the purportedly unique qualities of sea power. As Australian strategist Hedley Bull recently noted:

> As an instrument of diplomacy, sea power has long been thought to possess certain classical advantages *vis-à-vis* land power and, more recently, air power. The first of these advantages is flexibility: a naval force can be sent and withdrawn, and its size and activities varied, with a higher expectation that it will remain subject to control than is possible when ground forces are committed. The second is visibility: by being seen on the high seas or in foreign ports a navy can convey threats, provide reassurance, or earn prestige in a way that troops or aircraft in their home bases cannot do. The third is its universality or pervasiveness: the fact that the seas, by contrast with the land and the air, are an international medium, allows naval vessels to reach distant countries independent of nearby bases. . . .[7]

Sea power's attributes have been recognized for some time. But they have assumed new importance because of changes in the international and domestic political framework within which contemporary and future naval power is and will be used. There is, in short, an emerging consensus in the new literature on naval power that although "contextual" changes require considerable rethinking about both naval structure and use, naval power will be the most appropriate form of military force in the future.

But even as this "renaissance" of sea power has emerged and taken shape, there have been changes in the world which have been little touched on as yet by the new doctrine of naval force. Many analyses and, most important, new budgetary decisions on capital expenditure taken by Congress and the executive branch have been supportive of the classic advantages of sea power. Indeed, they came during the 1970s to rely increasingly on sea power in calculating the relationship between American power and American interests. Yet each of the purportedly unique advantages of sea power is now threatened by international political, technological, and legal change. An examination of these changes will be an important element of this book. For now, let us merely note that the emergence of the Soviet Union as an important naval rival reduces flexibility for both nations. The problem of carefully calibrating naval force is complicated when confronted by opponents with a capacity for sea denial. Currently, Soviet surface vessels are armed for a preemptive attack.[8] The Soviets are not the only actors competent to complicate the use of American naval power. Its persuasive potential may also be diminished if coastal states increase their stocks of precision-guided weaponry. Paradoxically, the proliferation of highly accurate fleet-damaging weapons is likely to occur because both the Soviet Union and the United States and its West European allies have pursued aggressive arms sales programs during the last decade. Arms now transferred to Third-World and other consumers are no longer merely the obsolete castoffs of the American, NATO, or Soviet military establishments, and they are now frequently delivered to these consumers even as similar or identical models are delivered to the vendor's own military forces. Finally, as the process of developing a new legal regime for the oceans continues, the likelihood is that, at a minimum, territorial seas will be extended. Furthermore, if some degree of sovereignty is appended to very large "economic zones," the pervasiveness of the American capacity to use "flexible" sea power could be correspondingly diminished. Legal enclosure of the oceans will probably not affect American and Soviet strategic submarines significantly. But the utility of surface fleets—the very essence of most conceptions of modern sea power— could well be circumscribed.[9]

To summarize: modern sea power, its classical advantages notwithstanding, does have limits. How fragile or flexible these limits are is by no means certain at this juncture. The implications of legal enclosure are especially perplexing in view of the rather uneven course of the United Nations Conference on the Law of the Sea. Technological change is similarly indeterminate in that changes in naval propulsion, i.e., the adaptation of nuclear power to ship propulsion sensor technology, and satellite communications would seem to expand naval flexibility, visibility, and universality. At the same time, new sensor and guidance technologies have had enormous consequences for weapons accuracy across the full range from strategic nuclear to tactical conventional naval armaments. Precision munitions would seem, therefore, also to constrain the flexibility, visibility, and universality of sea power.

The outcome of this interplay of forces is of course extremely important for the United States, which has staked a great deal on the continuing utility and flexibility of naval power. The present study offers a commentary on that commitment. Thus, we seek to identify and analyze the most salient constraints at work now and those that are likely to impinge on American naval policy in the foreseeable future. These forces and constraints can, we believe, be grouped into at least three broad categories: (1) naval forces, naval doctrine and U.S. foreign policy objectives; (2) domestic political and institutional constraints; and (3) the international system.

Hence, this book will explore the efficacy of naval power in a purportedly new international and American domestic political environment. The latter factor—American domestic politics and institutions—has not been generally considered in recent discussions of naval power. This omission is understandable in that an already immensely complicated analytical problem is thereby simplified somewhat for analysts not usually conversant with, for example, the technical details of congressional decision-making or the belief systems of the American public. Nevertheless, we feel that its inclusion is essential, for the very ambiguity of the future of domestic factors as they relate to the use not only of naval power but of all military power may constitute an important inhibition on the future efficacy of naval and military instrumentalities. To the extent that domestic factors are limiting rather than permissive in their effects, they may prove additive to emerging constraining changes in the international system. Domestic considerations, we shall argue, contribute to a more uncertain future for naval power than is usually portrayed in recent analyses.

United States Navy and civilian naval analysts have gone some distance in assessing and adapting the place of American naval doctrine in a world of change. Nevertheless, much of this analysis has been devoted to the attributes of naval power and its use rather than the environment—domestic and international—within which that power must be used. And a consideration of these "environmental factors" in which naval force operates suggests the need for some greater skepticism concerning the efficacy of naval power in the future.

PART 1

American Naval Power
and the International System

CHAPTER ONE

Foreign Policy and
Naval Power in the 1970s

THE 1970s have seen a "renaissance" of interest in sea power and its relationship to foreign policy. On both sides of the Atlantic, a growing number of strategic thinkers and practitioners have come to devote themselves to the problems of "power at sea."[1] No individual or school of thought has emerged that can lay claim to a commanding position astride contemporary sea-power theory. Nevertheless, the scope of analysis in the last decade has been broad. It includes macroanalytic efforts that seek to assess the totality of the contemporary linkage of sea power and foreign policy. There also are analyses of specific elements of the missions assigned to navies, including nuclear deterrence. And there is considerable interest in the presence mission as well as technological changes affecting sea power. Finally, of course, there are numerous studies of the Soviet-American naval balance and naval arms control.[2]

Moreover, this renaissance is not merely a phenomenon confined to academe, defense research institutes, and war colleges. For, during the last decade, the military establishments of the Soviet Union and the United States have seen significant changes. Specifically, both navies have claimed larger shares of their respective countries' defense budgets, especially with respect to procurement and research and development.

The changes in the Soviet Union's naval power have achieved considerable notoriety in the United States. Official and nongovernmental sources have in the past few years called attention to Admiral S.G. Gorshkov's pronouncements about Soviet sea power and maritime presence and their use in the future.[3] Many observers have taken Gorshkov's statements as heralding a revolutionary new phase in Soviet maritime and naval policy in which the Soviet Union has passed from insular, "coastal defense" thinking about the uses of sea power to one of "blue water," forward deployment in support of Soviet globalism. As evidence for this thesis, frequently alarmed notice is taken of the changes in Soviet naval force structure over the last decade, especially the increase in Soviet surface vessels, such as the heavily armed *Kara* and *Kresta I/II* cruisers and the *Krivak* class of destroyers. In addition, the deployment of three helicopter/ASW "carriers" in the last ten years is seen by some observers as providing the Soviets with a new capacity to project power ashore. Finally, the Soviets' attack submarine capability remains as a threat.[4]

Other observers, while granting that the Soviet Union's force structure is no longer that of a coastal defense navy, suggest that it by no means follows that the Soviet Navy is now launched on an ever-expanding globalist course. Thus, Michael MccGwire and his colleagues[5] note that Gorshkov's comments, when placed within the context of a decade of Soviet decisions on defense priorities, sound rather like those of a hard-pressed bureaucratic politician trying to protect hard-won naval assets from a Politburo that seeks a more prominent and potent Soviet naval presence but is nevertheless reluctant to pay for it. Moreover, it can be argued that recent Soviet deployments can be understood as reactive to expanding United States Navy nuclear submarine and carrier deployment. Finally, the rather small proportion of shipyards devoted to navy surface vessel construction and relatively lower (as compared to the United States) construction rates would not seem congruent with the image painted by more pessimistic commentators on the Soviet navy.

This debate over Soviet naval and maritime capability and its use has occupied a major portion of the energy devoted to and in some measure caused by the resurgence of interest in sea power. Far less attention has been focused on the emergence of the United States Navy as perhaps the dominant service in the American force structure of the early 1970s.[6] Indeed, the major concern of most commentators has been the declining size of the United States Navy in the face of the "block obsolescence" of that half of the fleet constructed during World War II. Nonetheless, the portion of the total defense budget consumed by the Navy has grown significantly since the turn of the decade, so that now that service is the dominant one in terms of its claim on American defense dollars. Undoubtedly, much of this apparent dynamism in the Navy's budget is a function of inflation and the inherently high cost of ship construction. Nevertheless, in the last decade, the Navy has introduced new classes of aircraft carriers, amphibious assault ships, cruisers, destroyers, attack submarines, and strategic submarines. Moreover, the Navy's claim on United States defense research, development, test and evaluation funds is most impressive and foreshadows continued growth.[7]

The reasons for this new prominence of naval power are numerous. The search for a stable deterrent relationship has resulted in greater emphasis on the nuclear submarine as an invulnerable platform for the bulk of one's retaliatory capability. This has clearly been the case in American defense planning; the percentage of nuclear delivery vehicles deployed on submarines increased steadily during the late 1960s and early 1970s. Such a trend is not so clear in Soviet strategic force deployment, perhaps reflecting the combined limitations of Soviet strategic submarines and missile technology.

The dominance of nuclear weaponry in the contemporary military environment has contributed to the new salience of sea power in a more abstract manner as well. To the extent that nuclear war and the concern about escalation of subnuclear conflict to the level of total nuclear war have constrained the use of force since 1945, some theorists profess to see the international system as having moved into a "regulatory phase" in the history of the relationship between force and order.[8] This phase need not involve a reduction in the incidence or intensity of the use of force in general, but it does include significant limitations on the use of force by the two super-powers against one another. Thus, in some measure, we have seen over the postwar period an attempt to identify and use those forms of military power which are both potent and at the same time responsive to the conjoined needs of the two superpowers—especially the United States. There has been an intense search for usable instrumentalities of violence, but instrumentalities which are nevertheless controllable—lest their use escalate into superpower nuclear confrontation and war.

The purported historical flexibility of naval power has proved, therefore, increasingly attractive to the superpowers. Not only does modern naval technology offer enormous lethality across the full spectrum of potential military force and conflict, but the platforms on which and from which naval power is based and projected have proved to be extremely versatile. Inasmuch as naval vessels operate in a medium historically regarded as open and free, and which also covers most of the globe, they can be moved readily into and out of areas deemed vital without the entangling commitments frequently incurred in the use of land-based power or forms of air power requiring overseas basing.

In the case of the United States, a number of other developments and factors have contributed to a renewed emphasis on naval power. Geopolitically, as American advocates of an expanded United States naval presence invariably underscore, the United States is dependent upon open sea lanes. Thus, although the economic constraints of interdependence tend increasingly to be multilateral and reciprocal, the spectre of embargoes, especially oil embargoes, has exercised a powerful hold on strategic planning in recent years. Moreover, as long as American security policy includes significant military and quasimilitary commitments to Western Europe, Israel, and Japan, "sea lines of communication" will remain central to

American policy and planning. The NATO and Middle East contingencies are especially important, because scenarios of anticipated conflict in these areas have served as primary determinants of American naval force structure and planning.

Naval power would seem especially attractive in a post-Vietnam global and, more important, American domestic political environment. The domestic constraints on the use of force are especially important given public concerns about the costs of any sustained intensive conventional involvements in the future. At the same time, however, the need for an American "presence" and the ability to project military power persists in view of outstanding American commitments and resource needs. Being technologically intensive in nature, sea power avoids the political liabilities associated with casualties invariably incurred with the use of land forces. Furthermore, its flexibility and visibility would maximize the ability of the United States to demonstrate will and support clients in the "gray areas" short of Vietnam-like involvements. Under these circumstances, naval forces and carrier-based tactical air power would seem to be a set of military instruments most appropriate to the demands of the retrenchment in foreign affairs begun during the Nixon years.

Notwithstanding these apparent advantages, however, the Carter administration has argued for a reduction of the Navy's role, especially regarding the projection of naval power directly against the Soviet Union within the context of a European war. The Navy's role in lower-risk areas remains unclear. Predictably, this reexamination of the role of the Navy has led to intense debate, and any assessment of these issues requires some consideration of the political framework out of which the Navy's current force structure and planning have arisen. Let us turn, then, to an overview of recent American foreign policy.

The End of Postwar International Relations

The Nixon-Kissinger stewardship of American foreign policy appeared to be a break with the historic tradition of American statecraft. As Nixon himself proclaimed, early in his first term, the "postwar period of international relations [had] ended." The rigid bipolarism of the former era would be replaced by a more flexible and pragmatic attitude toward the great Communist power. American commitments based on containment of Communism could, therefore, be reevaluated. No longer would the United States have to stand by all commitments equally. No longer would "world order" be considered a seamless web wherein a rent in one corner would cause a tear in another until the whole fabric was undone. Instead, it seemed to some observers, Nixon and Kissinger saw the necessity of looking at commitments on their merits and not as a reflection of the whole skein of global stability. Thus, Nixon declared, "We are not involved in the world because we have commitments; . . . our interests must shape our commitments, rather than the other way around." According to Mr. Nixon, the American effort to achieve a "structure of peace" would be part of a system of shared responsibilities where "we will help where it makes a real difference and is considered in our interest."[9]

Nevertheless, there was a paradox inherent both in Mr. Nixon's assertions and in his behavior. Although it appeared that commitments would be reexamined, none were willingly abandoned. The United States did not, in the Nixon-Kissinger-Ford years, relinquish any element of its postwar globalist posture, but strove merely not to get caught with the interventionist consequences which seemed implacably embedded in these commitments. Thus it did not abandon global presence as one of the pillars of its policy. At the time of the Angola crisis, for example, Kissinger resurrected the logic of containment and the domino theory:

> When one great power tips the balance of forces decisively in a local conflict . . . and meets no resistance . . . an ominous precedent is set . . . even if the intervention occurs in a seemingly remote area. Such a precedent cannot be tolerated. . . . And if the pattern is not broken now, we will face harder choices and higher costs in the future. . . . What will be the perception of leaders around the world . . . ? And what conclusions will an unopposed superpower draw when the next opportunity for intervention beckons?[10]

Not only, it was asserted, is there a domino effect to great power expansion in the Third World "for the first time in history," but there is also a reciprocal dynamic to this expansion that can lead to war. Thus, the Soviets were told by Helmut Sonnenfeldt, Kissinger's principal advisor on Soviet affairs, "when . . . perhaps marginal shifts occur in the power relationship, the other superpower is going to look for and find compensation . . . sooner or later there will be conflict."[11]

The apparent contradiction of a continuing globalism on the one hand and more limited commitments predicated on real interests along with the development of a more pragmatic relationship with the Soviets and the Chinese on the other could be resolved if one recalled that the aim of American policy remained stable, orderly relationships. The U.S. strategic relationship with the Soviets was based, beginning in the Nixon-Kissinger years, on the predictability of the behavior of both sides. Thus, Soviet interests as a "great power" were acknowledged, and, for that matter, conceivably tolerated. But instability and revolutionary movements that might favor collectivist solutions were still feared as upsetting the current great power equilibrium. If, for instance, a Third World state moved to the left, Nixon and Kissinger feared it would appear as if the Soviets had gained and the U.S. had lost and this in turn might embolden the Soviets themselves, thus further damaging global stability. The problem, in the Nixon-Kissinger analysis, was that revolutionary movements are unpredictable by their very nature. The fact that these movements are frequently not under the aegis of a great power means that they are rarely "manageable" by any outside power and, therefore, are unaccountable. Thus, a large effort was made to make the Soviets (and the Chinese, for that matter) assume responsibility for their clients. In countries where the Soviets or the Chinese were the most important benefactors it has been demanded that they maintain control over their clients, and in at least one case a nuclear alert ensued when they did not.

Further, America intervened against collectivist regimes in Chile, Thailand, and Portugal, and favored anticollectivist movements in

Italy and Spain. But the rationale for these policies was often based less on anti-Soviet fears per se than on fears of how the "loss" of these regimes would affect the predictability of a global equilibrium among major powers. Thus, ironically, one of "Kissinger's top aides" was widely quoted as having told European leaders that the "United States would rather see a 'Stalinist' Party in Italy than a truly liberal Euro-Communist one."[12] The United States feared that a successful independent European Communist movement might severely complicate the American commitment to Europe and, eventually, increase Soviet influence in the area if only through propinquity. As Kissinger noted, once in power, Western European Communists "would be tempted to orient their economies to a much greater extent toward the East. . . . [and] steer their countries' policies toward the positions of the nonaligned. . . . NATO would be inevitably weakened, if not undermined. And in this country, the commitment of the American people to maintain the balance of power in Europe, justified though it might be on pragmatic, geopolitical grounds, would lack the moral base on which it has stood for 30 years."[13]

Even if Soviet interests were resisted by a liberal European Communist movement, European politics would be less politically coherent and, perhaps, more dominated by German power. This, in turn, might resurrect some of the tensions that led to World War II. The Soviets also seemed ambivalent about the expulsion of the United States from Europe, knowing that German power would be a likely substitute. Indeed, *Izvestia*, in January of 1974, termed any discussion of an independent defense community in Europe "divorced from the present realities" and a "connivance" of China.[14] The Soviets also were plainly worried about the effect a truly liberal European communist movement would have on their own bloc, where several expeditions have had to be mounted against liberal tendencies in Hungary, Poland, and, most recently, Czechoslovakia. They feared the effect of liberalism not only on their clients but also on their own population.

Thus, the two countries seemed to approach, in part as a result of a deliberate policy of the Nixon-Kissinger administration, a realization that they shared a number of interests, not only in the strategic arena but also as great powers: a shared interest in stability, in the status quo in Europe, in the future ocean regime, in resource allocations between the developed and underdeveloped world, nonproliferation, and in some matters relating to terrorism.

For the United States, this has been no mean achievement. It appeared to represent nothing less than the historic desiderata of a mellowing of Soviet ambitions. Thus, if the Soviets were to be opposed in some areas and favored in others, it was now to be in an atmosphere less cluttered by the anti-Communist rhetoric that portrayed the Soviets as Lucifer's agents if not the Devil himself. As Kissinger explained: "We are at a point . . . where, for whatever reason, it may be that even the Soviet Union has come to a realization of the limits of its ideological fervor."[15]

Nevertheless, the United States and the Soviet Union had reached this point, it was believed, because the United States had successfully "contained" Soviet power in the past. Moreover, the redefinition of the American position would continue to depend on such an exercise of military and diplomatic power although now, because of changes in the military balance and the dangers inherent in the use of military intervention—in terms of both international and domestic political stability—the exercise would involve a much more fragile structure and deployment of political and military instrumentalities. How, then, were the Soviets to be "contained" in the "new" formulation of American foreign policy? The answer developed slowly during the eight years of Nixon-Kissinger-Ford stewardship of American foreign policy and consisted of three elements:

1. A redefinition and application of deterrence;
2. Exploitation, even exacerbation, of Sino-Soviet antagonism; and
3. Fostering a new balance of power that included Japan and Europe.

Deterrence: A New Look?

After the first check of American arms in Asia in this century, the United States developed a theory that emphasized the role of air power and strategic retaliation against the Soviet Union. The manipulation of the threat of massive retaliation appeared to work in ending the Korean War and, later, in the Formosa Crisis. But massive retaliation was increasingly unconvincing as its use came to appear so patently disproportionate to most of the contingencies American policy faced and as the Soviets, too, gained a credible intercontinental retaliatory force. But after the second failure of American arms in Asia, yet another effort was made to compensate for the obvious lack of enthusiasm on the part of the American people to commit men to the maintenance of far-flung commitments or to oppose Soviet power. The roots of this strategy can be traced to the late 1950s, when Kissinger wrote that "diplomacy which is not related to a plausible employment of force is sterile, it must be the task of our military policy to develop a doctrine and capability for the graduated force";[16] for the "refusal to run any risk would amount to giving the Soviets a blank check."[17] Therefore, Kissinger argued, it is incumbent on American statesmen to develop a "diplomacy which seeks to break down the special horror which now surrounds nuclear weapons." Of course, such a strategy may have its dangers but if a statesman has great ends in mind, then risks pale. Kissinger explained: "The very greatness of the statesman's conception tends to make it inaccessible to those whose primary concern is with safety."[18]

For a while, many in government resisted the logic of Kissinger's arguments for making nuclear war at least "plausible." As Daniel Ellsberg recalled:

> McNamara's tireless and shrewd efforts in the early sixties, largely hidden from the public to this day, [were to] gradually control the forces within the military bureaucracy that pressed for the threat and use of nuclear weapons. [He had] a creditable motive for proposing alternatives to nuclear threats. . . . In this hidden debate, there was strong incentive—indeed it seemed necessary—for the civilian leaders to demonstrate that success was possible in Indochina without the need either to compromise Cold War objectives or to threaten or use nuclear weapons.

Such concerns remained semi-covert for it was seen as dangerous to lend substance to the active suspicions of military staffs and their Congressional allies that there were high Administration officials who didn't love the Bomb. . . .[19]

But, not surprisingly, when one element of the mix of diplomacy and violence, counterinsurgent war, failed, then the other element, the threat of nuclear war—like Lazarus—again gained substance from the ghostly shadow of governmental and academic oblivion.

The reappearance of the nuclear threat was announced by Secretary of Defense James Schlesinger.[20] In July, 1975, he suggested that a conventional attack in Europe might result in a strategic nuclear attack against the Soviet homeland. In August of 1975, Schlesinger argued that the U.S. should be able to use strategic nuclear weapons against the Soviets as a "limited bargaining exchange if American missiles were targeted on Soviet missiles."[21] These echoes of a strategic policy considered and dropped in the early Kennedy years, though obliquely criticized by Kissinger as undermining his efforts at achieving strategic arms control, nevertheless served some purpose in his broader vision of superpower balance. Insofar as the changes in strategic policy advanced by Schlesinger represented a display of continued American willingness to stay the course of global involvement, they might serve to anticipate any desire to exploit American flexibility that might be lurking in the recesses of the Soviet bureaucracy. Also, the threat of the "hawks" in the Pentagon could be employed by Kissinger to prod those in the Kremlin whose commitment to strategic predictability and order might be flagging.

Schlesinger also demonstrated his apparent enthusiasm for the use of nuclear weapons in other situations, such as in response to a conventional challenge in Asia. In an official statement he conspicuously pointed to the American tactical nuclear presence in South Korea.[22] It was reported that he had sent out strategic "Nuclear Weapon Employment Policy" briefings regarding North Korean targets.[23] When three Americans attempting to chop down a forty-foot poplar in the North-Korean-administered DMZ were killed with their own axes by North Korean soldiers, Schlesinger retaliated by means of B-52s and nuclear-equipped F-4s and F-111s carrying out "practice runs,"[24] thus displaying his bold intentions for the "next time": "Rather than simply counter your opponent's threats, it is [now] necessary to go for the heart of your opponent's power. . . ."[25]

In sum, the Soviet-American strategic relationship was to be stabilized and even institutionalized by the process of Strategic Arms Limitations talks and their outcomes. But this process of making the strategic relationship more stable, predictable, and safe would be pursued against a backdrop of nuclear arsenal development, refinement, and threatened use. The latter was of course related to domestic and bureaucratic politics in both countries, but it was also a function of Nixon's, Kissinger's, Ford's, and Schlesinger's desire that the United States not appear to be negotiating from weakness. To appear so, it was thought, would threaten not only the developing Soviet-American relationship but the more comprehensive structure of world order which required continual American involvement—even intervention—and Soviet "responsibility."

Sino-Soviet Antagonism

The second element of the Nixon-Kissinger effort was to enlist the Chinese in a tripolar relationship that would in some measure "contain" the Soviets. This was, at first, a brilliant tactical success. Before Kissinger's surprise visit to Peking in 1971, it was not clear that the Chinese would respond to any American initiative, given the long-standing American security arrangements with Taiwan. But de facto American recognition of the Peking government served dramatically to reduce, even reverse, the effects of much of the bilious anti-Communist, anti-Chinese rhetoric in the U.S. and set a "normal" tone of moderation in Chinese-American relations. More important than tone was the ad hoc political military alliance directed at the Soviets which ensued. The U.S. and China both tried (and failed) to limit Soviet influence in Vietnam. The U.S. and China tried (and failed) in Angola. Chou En-Lai warned the leftist Thai government to be more supportive of the United States. The Chinese attempted to block the Soviet- and North Vietnamese-supported uprising in Thailand.[26] The Chinese supported the American presence in South Asia to the extent that they became visibly (and ironically) worried that the fall of Indochina would have a "domino" effect on the American position in the area. Thus, throughout 1976, the Chinese were noisily, although "privately," encouraging the United States to remain in Korea. One U.S. official reportedly related, "They even said we ought to expand our naval base at Diego Garcia" in the Indian Ocean.[27] Even Philippine President Marcos, who has been fighting a Communist rebellion for years, was warmly greeted in Peking by Chairman Mao. In Europe, the Chinese have repeatedly called for a strong NATO.[28]

This Chinese assistance to U.S. foreign policy has not been a one-way street. Three times in 1974, China received warnings from the U.S. that a Soviet attack appeared imminent.[29] And in the summer of 1976, Russia was warned publicly that an attack on China might invite American retaliation. The benevolence and necessity of these warnings are, of course, called into question when one realizes the stake the U.S. has in continuing Sino-Soviet animus.

As early as 1973, the Soviets began to suggest publicly that the United States and China had entered a military relationship. Chou En-Lai reportedly asked Kissinger, in November, 1973, for twenty jet fighters, and the Soviets broadcast a report that the U.S. had actually set up a tank and helicopter assembly plant on the Chinese mainland.[30] The U.S. did little to disabuse the underlying suspicion that if arms were not actually being supplied, this contingency was being actively considered. Thus, a few months before going to China, Dr. Schlesinger declared that military aid to the Chinese would "depend on the circumstances," but would not be rejected out of hand, "for the Chinese" were, he asserted twice, a "quasi" ally.[31] Later, a CIA analyst detailed some of the advantages of giving the Chinese military assistance.

1. It would be a "concrete" "pay-off" for establishing a working relationship with the U.S.
2. It would give the Chinese a stake in U.S. defense technology and "preserving good relations" with the U.S.
3. It would help the Chinese deter a Soviet attack which could jeopardize world peace.
4. It could draw more Soviet military assets away from U.S. allies.[32]

The advantages of a military supply relationship with the Chinese seemed persuasive to many. And the midsummer, 1976, approval of a sale of a multimillion dollar computer eminently adaptable for military use to the Chinese by the U.S. seemed to indicate United States military sales to China were more than conjecture. Indeed, they made a great deal of sense, if the assumption about a stable level of Sino-Soviet antagonism was granted.

But is the latter assumption entirely warranted? The Peking-American axis is not without its problems and since 1974 is, according to some observers, increasingly fragile. Beginning on November 7, 1974, the Chinese began to admit that their border dispute with the Soviets might be soluble. They accepted the Soviet offer of a nonaggression pact if the Soviets accepted Chinese border claims. The Chinese claims are, of course, enormous, but the Soviets have repeatedly told the Chinese that they would be willing to make "minor adjustments" if the Chinese gave up their demand for "preconditions."[33] Following the November 7 note, Kissinger and Ford met Soviet leaders in Vladivostok to discuss strategic arms issues. Not only did the discussions themselves nettle the Chinese, but the location of the meeting, thirty-five miles from the Sino-Russian frontier in an area ceded by the Manchu dynasty in an "unequal" treaty with the Russians, undoubtedly was viewed as thoughtless at best. The failure of the Ford administration to disengage from Taiwan as promised by President Nixon increasingly exasperated the Chinese to the point of treating the disgraced Mr. Nixon as if he were, in fact, a figure of continuing significance when they sent a plane to fetch him from San Clemente in mid-1976.

Nixon was honored by a long talk with Mao; Kissinger, a few weeks later, was not.

In the beginning of 1976, the Chinese returned a Soviet helicopter crew captured two years earlier and stayed to hear some innocuous remarks about global affairs at the state dinner celebrating the Soviet Revolution—usually an occasion for symbolic acrimony. After Mao's death, the Soviet Union, according to Victor Zorza, began "using every argument it [could] find . . . to make Peking seek a reconciliation." Kissinger attempted to counter these incipient signs of Sino-Soviet reconciliation by approving the sale of computer technology and by issuing a warning to the Soviets not to attack the Chinese.[34] A Sino-Soviet rapprochement could, after all, hardly bode well for a policy forthrightly designed to pit the two countries against each other so that American interest might predominate.

In summary, the Chinese are not really a military power in the same league with the United States or even the Soviets. They could hardly be a pole of "equivalent power," in Mr. Nixon's words, given their crude atomic arsenal. More than eleven years have passed since the Chinese exploded their first atomic device, and they possess, in the words of the Chairman of the Joint Chiefs, General George Brown, yet to be deployed "limited range" ICBMs of modest numbers and "obsolescent and cumbersome" IRBMs as well as "old and vulnerable" bombers housed in caves.[35] As Harvard's Jonathan Pollack wrote of General Brown's testimony: "These findings raise serious doubts about any incipient triangularity in the strategic relations among China, the United States and the Soviet Union. . . ."[36]

A New Global Balance?

The third and most problematic means of containing Soviet power, yet leaving the option of condominial cooperation, was the notion of a new global balance of power analogous to the "classic" eighteenth- and nineteenth-century balance. As President Nixon told *Time* Magazine on January 3, 1972: "The only time . . . we have had any extended periods of peace is when there has been a balance of power. So . . . I think it would be a safer world and a better world if we have a strong, healthy United States, Europe, Soviet Union, China and Japan, each balancing the other, an even balance."[37]

The nature of the Sino-Soviet antagonism assured Mr. Nixon that there could be at least a semblance of a tripolar relationship in East Asia. In an effort to effectuate a more comprehensive balance, Mr. Nixon actively and even brutally pressed the Japanese to expand the definition of their interest and thus become another "pole" in a pentagonal balance of power. The Japanese had relied on the American nuclear umbrella and had imitated the rigid American posture toward mainland China (in the face of much internal opposition and historic interest). When Nixon reversed American policy on China with virtually no prior consultation with the Japanese, it was taken not only as an insult, but also as a humiliating incentive for Japan to elaborate an independent course toward China. A similar shock occurred when the Nixon administration sought unilaterally to force the Japanese to reverse their trading position with America by realigning the value of the dollar. The heavy-handed import tariffs, quotas, and embargoes, combined with the temporary withdrawal of the dollar from the role as a medium of international liquidity, were seen by the Japanese as another indication that they should start to make their own way. American policy under Mr. Nixon undermined the paternalistic relationship that had evolved from Japan's wartime defeat. This rather brusque treatment of Japan—a country where saving face is a national priority—served to vitiate the surety of the American "nuclear umbrella." The humiliation of the Sato government had its desired effect. As Professor Robert Osgood related, "Official statements suggest that Japan's nuclear abstention [has been] contingent upon a confidence in the credibility of America's nuclear deterrence, which it no longer automatically takes for granted."[38] Apparently, however, this was an intended result of the Nixon policy that sought to promote "regional balances of power."

The Japanese, after several "Nixon shocks," began to undertake large-scale development schemes in China. Indeed, China loomed as potentially Japan's largest supplier of oil. But the underlying vulnerability of Japanese power to economic constraints, as shown by the oil crisis and by growing Japanese interest in Chinese oil and Russian resources, hardly made Japan appear as a great independent "pole" capable of real flexibility in the context of a pentagonal balance. Indeed, at least one Japanese observer, while accepting the inevitability of a quadrilateral balance in East Asia, has nevertheless rejected the wisdom of a future for Japan which involves becoming part of a "cynical balance-of-power game."[39]

Nuclear deterrence had a certain prima facie appeal as a means of containing Soviet power. So, too, had the manipulation of the Sino-Soviet antagonism. But a five-polar balance of power was always less convincing, perhaps because it was uncertain how Europe could fit into this new equation. In early 1973, the Nixon administration announced that the next twelve months would be the "Year of Europe"—a year when the Europeans could be convinced to act as a regional unity cooperating for purposes "not necessarily in conflict" with the U.S., "but in the new era, neither are they identical." The separation of the aims of the Europeans and the U.S. was a function of their relative power. For "the United States has global interest and responsibilities," explained Dr. Kissinger, while "our European allies have regional interests."[40]

Nevertheless, the reality of a Europe pursuing separate interests pointed to the underlying fallacy of any new pentagonal balance. Somehow it was assumed that the European component of the new five-power balance, even if it did not work parallel with U.S. interests, would not actively oppose them. But when West Germany refused, during the October 1973 Mid-East crisis, to permit ships carrying war goods from Europe to leave West German ports, and when virtually every NATO country except Portugal forbade American planes destined for Israel to refuel on its territory, the vapidity of the notion of Europe playing a munificent role in some near-term future balance of power was revealed. According to the nine-page report of a December 6 meeting with some of his former Harvard colleagues, Kissinger displayed extreme anger at the Europeans' Arab policy, calling their behavior "craven" and "contemptible."[41]

There were a number of problems inherent in the apparent Nixonian resurrection of the golden age of the balance of power, beyond Secretary Kissinger's disgust with the errant Europeans. Not the least of the difficulties with the concept was that it was an extrapolation of political and military trends not yet materialized. Perhaps more important, it did not appreciate the complex political and economic dependencies that constrain European diplomatic maneuvers.

In the abstract, one can certainly conceive of an independent or quasi-independent European security force replete with at least a finite nuclear deterrent capacity. Perhaps an essentially European defense of the central front would be possible through a marriage of tactical nuclear weapons and precision-guided conventional weapons. But such cooperation on security issues presupposes a degree of European political coordination and a willingness to shoulder the costs of the security burden not now foreseeable in Western Europe. In the meantime, therefore, Europe will remain dependent upon the United States for its security in both a military and economic sense.

Moreover, European economic dependency is more complex than a "simple" Atlantic relationship. The oil crisis of 1973–1974 and the embarrassing Daoud* affair demonstrated that European dependencies extend across the Mediterranean as well. Hanns Maull, in an analysis of the use of the "oil weapon" in 1973–1974, has concluded that its greatest effect was on the Japanese. Nevertheless, Maull's observations on the effects of the crisis for the Europeans raise serious questions concerning the viability of any notion of global balance involving a European actor:

*Daoud was a well-known Palestinian terrorist picked up by French police but quickly released for "lack of evidence."

The core of the disagreement in the Western alliance and the European community was the issue of security. During the Israeli-Arab war, the United States pursued a policy which took account of American concern for the global balance *vis-à-vis* the Soviet Union and aimed to prevent any shift in Moscow's favour. The European countries, however, were primarily concerned about their oil supplies, and were not prepared to see their economic security put at risk. . . . European governments therefore preferred to take a neutral attitude and to appease the Arabs. . . .

Within the European Community a basically nationalistic approach prevailed. . . . the political damage to the idea of European solidarity was considerable: the EEC had to face the hard truth that national interests still had priority over European solidarity.[42]

There is an additional hard truth implicit in the 1973–1974 crisis: "Europe" is unlikely to serve for some time—if ever—as one among several poles of world political, military, and economic power. Ministerial-level consultations on foreign policy notwithstanding, Europe is still in the making.[43] Even if a politically united Europe with political and strategic independence did arise, its interest would probably be, as the Nixon administration did not hesitate to point out, too narrow to serve as much more than a regional balance constraining Soviet power. But, perhaps as plausible, a new Europe might accommodate Soviet power. More likely, however, is a continuance of a fractured alliance, dependent on the underlying strength of American economy *and* Arab oil for its prosperity, fearful of German economic power, susceptible to cycles of boom and bust, and churlishly insistent that America attend to European security interests while keeping a European nuclear deterrent looming as a kind of foreboding backdrop to the rather farfetched eventuality of a final separation of American and European interests.

Some Implications and Problems for Naval Power

In the final analysis, therefore, American foreign and security policy during the early years of the new era of international politics heralded by the Nixon administration remains centered on the

Soviet-American relationship. European and Japanese "poles" in a new balance of power are at best nascent, and the manipulation of Sino-Soviet antagonism, though undoubtedly somewhat useful in ending American involvement in Vietnam and perhaps in encouraging the Soviets to adopt a more flexible position in arms control negotiations, may now be of diminishing tactical utility. In short, the distinct political dynamics of East Asia and Europe and the American relationship to each cannot be facilely linked to the central Soviet-American relationship. That there are linkages involved is clear; what is less clear is how these can be juxtaposed in some sort of tensional balance of power as a basis for inducing Soviet responsibility and restraint and hence the fulfillment of the postwar American vision of global order without extensive (and expensive) American conventional military involvement.

Thus, by the end of the Nixon-Kissinger-Ford years American diplomacy was increasingly dependent upon the uncertain dynamics of the tattered, officially renounced, but still recognizable policy of detente. Kissinger's view of detente was probably always more limited than the expansive vision that Mr. Nixon allowed to develop in the service of his own domestic political ends. It is doubtful that Kissinger ever saw detente as more than a difficult attempt to establish a more predictable strategic environment and process of strategic arms development. Simultaneously, by extending economic, technological, and agricultural rewards, he sought to develop a more comprehensive Soviet-American relationship of sufficient benefit to the Soviets that they would not find it in their interests to threaten either by "irresponsibility" at the strategic level or in other areas where American and Soviet interests might come into conflict. But these were long-term objectives; the immediate need was for a more orderly strategic relationship.

In the meantime, potential Soviet-American conflict at the substrategic level and especially outside the European theater would have to be dealt with by increased United States military assistance and arms sales in pursuit of regional surrogates for American military intervention. Accordingly, during Mr. Nixon's tenure, American defense posture shifted from the nominal two-and-a-half war force structure of the Kennedy-Johnson years to a posture that provided for "full" war capability in Europe but at most "half" war capability elsewhere. At the same time, however, this force structure was to maintain the capacity for air support for regional counterrevolutionary efforts.

The implication for the United States Navy was and is fairly straightforward: the maintenance of naval "presence" as well as the capacity to establish and maintain local sea control in support of resupply efforts, and, if necessary, actualize American intervention through the projection of power ashore—if not land power via the marines, then certainly tactical air support. Moreover, if liabilities implied in maintaining large on-shore bases were to be minimized, then no major reduction of United States global naval presence was conceivable. Indeed, force structure modernization and even expansion were implied.

Finally, concerning the one "full" war capability vis-à-vis Europe, a major naval role was also implied. Insofar as conflict scenarios for Europe continued to center on the notion of a fairly protracted military struggle with consequent need for significant resupply and projection of power on the Southern and Northern flanks of NATO, then clearly the Navy's sea-control mission was paramount. Moreover, continued American commitment to Israel implied the indefinite extension and perhaps even expansion of the American naval presence in the Eastern Mediterranean. Indeed, the necessity for such a presence seemed all the more compelling in view of increased Soviet naval activity in the area and the demonstrated unreliability of West European basing during Middle East crises.

On balance, therefore, the diplomacy of the new era of international relations anticipated by the Nixon doctrine and Mr. Kissinger's concept of detente assumed the continuation of tension requiring the manipulation of threats of and, on occasion perhaps, the actual use of force. Preferably, the use of force would be undertaken by American surrogates backed up by American presence and support, a substantial part of which could be provided by American naval power. Nevertheless, the question remains what the American response would be in the event that such support proved to be inadequate and a local defeat seemed imminent. Earl Ravenal has posed the question and succinctly suggested one implication: "The basic question is whether the Nixon doctrine is an honest policy that will fully fund the worldwide and Asian commitments it proposes to maintain, or whether it conceals a drift toward nuclear defense or an acceptance of greater risk of local defeat."[44] Ravenal's query was a precocious augury of events. For by 1976, it had become clear that Kissinger was only prepared to concede "local defeats" when mandated to do so by Congress. At the same time, if the Korean case is illustrative, the drift toward nuclear defense seems to have been accelerated, thereby confirming Ravenal's observation that "the 1-1/2 war strategy provides the President with fewer alternatives and renders the resort to nuclear weapons a more compelling choice, as well as making nuclear threat a more obvious residual feature of our diplomacy."[45] Mr. Nixon's rhetoric seemed to support these inferences as he resurrected a modified version of the Dullesian formulation of "massive retaliation" that emphasized the new options now available in the American nuclear arsenal: "having a full range of options does not mean that we will necessarily limit our response to the level or intensity chosen by an enemy."[46]

But it is by no means self-evident that the threat of nuclear war, limited or otherwise, in fact resolves the dilemma of marrying force and the preservation of order in the contemporary international system. Indeed, Enthoven and Smith have suggested that the presumed flexibility provided by a refined strategic and tactical nuclear weapons inventory has proved illusory: "The trouble with this concept is that it rests on faulty assumptions (for example, that civilian casualties and collateral damage can be kept to low levels); it ignores a basic lesson that the leaders of the U.S. Government in all cold war crises have learned—that when faced with the decision to start a nuclear war, almost any other alternative looked better;

and it is too risky to serve as the foundation for a preferred strategy."[47]

If it is uncertain that the American strategic and tactical arsenals can be managed in such a way as predictably to induce the Soviets to control their clients and temper their own ambitions, it is in part because of the apparent decline of the relative utility of force in international relations. Military power in the form of nuclear weapons is so enormous that it is difficult to relate its use to political objectives short of strategic attacks. United States nuclear capability makes it by far more powerful than a North Korea, Vietnam, Rhodesia, or a group of Angolan insurgents, and essentially equivalent to the Soviet Union. But because this power is so difficult to threaten convincingly at a substrategic level—in the past because of the disproportionate relationship between the threat and the purpose of the threat—any meaningful calculation of what might be termed actualizable power necessarily discounts nuclear threats. Moreover, the United States, by threatening power which cannot be used and by pouring resources into these weapons, may serve to enervate itself in fact, if not always in appearance. For by threatening these weapons in theory and practice, but, because of their nature, not being able to use them, the United States may have upped the ante necessary to effect what was once referred to as "extended deterrence." Not only will more vociferous threats have to be uttered "next time," but, perhaps also, the U.S. will have increased the psychological incentive to use these weapons so as to prove, once and for all, these weapons' credibility.

In Europe, military policy may become even more constrained because the nature of conventional weapons may become more ambiguous with introduction of a generation of precision-guided weaponry which could be conventionally armed but nevertheless targeted on Soviet missile silos and/or command and control. So armed, the use of "conventional" weapons becomes almost imperceptibly linked to "strategic" weapons which may invite a "strategic" response from the Soviets, or, at a minimum, push them to heightened levels of reaction. In fact, some contemporary discussion of the tactical effects of PGMs suggests that "area" weapon nuclear preemption of NATO defenses is not only "tactically" plausible from a Soviet standpoint, but essential from their perspective in the event of conflict.[48]

Thus, policies relying heavily on military power are confronted with a novel paradox of contemporary international society. Indeed, the paradox seems most confounding in those instances where the apparent differences in military capacity are most pronounced. As Professor Morganthau notes, there are reasons why, today, the strong have difficulty in coercing the weak: "(1) The moral climate . . . is hostile to attempts at the revival of open colonial relationships. (2) Furthermore, this moral climate favors guerrilla wars on behalf of decolonization. (3) Military issues . . . run a more or less immediate risk of getting countered by . . . [a] nuclear power."[49]

But paradox has by no means induced paralysis among analysts and practioners of military policy. As noted previously, part of the response to the dilemmas posed by recent American policy and a changing international environment has been a renewed interest in the nature and applicability of naval power to the contemporary situation. The Nixon doctrine, we have suggested, certainly implied a major, perhaps overarching, role for naval power in its search for military means appropriate to a continued global role for American power less the political costs of sustained conventional intervention. The United States Navy, as we will note in the next two chapters, has moved to define its missions and adapt its force structure to the changed circumstances of American policy and international conditions in the 1970s. What remains, however, is the problem of the place and kind of naval power in future decades. If the dynamics of domestic and international politics in the 1970s worked so as to complicate prohibitively the use of most American military instrumentalities except naval power, what might the future environment of domestic and international politics hold for naval power, its relative success in the environment of the 1970s notwithstanding? Indeed, is it not possible that the apparent success of the Navy in the

1970s may constitute an important constraint in the future? That is to say, the adaptations in doctrine and force structure undertaken in the face of the exigencies of the 1970s may well prove inappropriate in the future international and domestic environment. The chapters to follow seek to shed light on this question by summarizing and placing the doctrinal and force structure outcomes of the turmoil of the last decade in the context of conceivable future domestic and international political constraints, technological change, and possible alteration of the legal regime affecting the oceans.

CHAPTER TWO

The "Official" View

In his Annual Defense Department Report for 1976, former Secretary of Defense James Schlesinger stated the general assumptions which he had used as a guide in preparing the report. They all reflect what Schlesinger felt to be the basis for DOD claims to national resources:

—The United States is inescapably the leader of the non-communist world; there is no other country to fulfill our role if we abandon it.
—Grave challenges face the industrialized nations of the West, and they are as much external as internal.
—If we are to realize our dreams of domestic progress, we must first stay alive and free.
—National defense . . . provide[s] an indispensable public good that is the basic duty of this Republic to its citizens.[1]

These basic assumptions mirror those of virtually every Secretary of Defense since 1947. They fall within the consensus on American defense policy that emerged from the turmoil of the late 1940s and remained more or less free of challenge until the late 1960s and early 1970s. Thus Schlesinger affirmed that the effort at building and maintaining world order in the face of grave external threats must remain essentially an American task.

Predictably, United States Navy spokesmen emphasize the purportedly unique attributes of naval power and the presumed advantages it provides American policy-makers in the present international system.[2] Moreover, the special place of naval power in the American defense posture is also confirmed by the twin necessities—unfailingly underscored by sea power spokesmen—of importing by sea substantial amounts of strategic raw materials and petroleum,[3] and of providing the underpinnings for an alliance system of global scope. Not surprisingly, therefore, virtually all postwar Navy spokesmen have concluded that the global strategy of the United States must be a "forward strategy." Chief of Naval Operations James Holloway's language is typical: "It is clear that support of U.S. allies, as well as attacks against the United States, must be overseas operations. In essence, our forward strategy uses the oceans as barriers for our defense, and avenues to extend our influence abroad."[4]

During the late 1960s and early 1970s the Navy derived four seemingly distinct missions from this conception of naval power and American foreign policy: strategic deterrence, sea control, projection of power ashore, and presence. More recently, Admiral Holloway has lumped these missions into two broad and interrelated mission areas or "functions": sea control and projection. Sea control assumes prominence not only for the Navy but for the entire defense establishment in that it is viewed as "a prerequisite of all other naval tasks and most sustained overseas operations by the general purpose forces of the other services." Sea control capability provides "secure areas" from which naval combat and combat support operations are carried out as well as protecting commercial shipping when necessary. Projection, on the other hand, involves "projecting power from the sea" by means of war-fighting capability in the form of everything from the strategic submarine force to naval gunfire, but also the projection of political influence through the presence of naval power off shore.[5] Thus, down through the Ford administration, the Navy had come to view the missions of sea control and projection as functionally interrelated. With the arrival of the Carter administration, however, fundamental questions have been raised concerning the sea control-projection relationship.

In this and the following chapter we shall identify the Navy's conception of its role and the force structure appropriate to those missions as they had developed through the mid-1970s. On the whole, therefore, the following synopsis is based on the Navy's "official" view of itself. However, comment will be offered and questions raised concerning mission-force structure relationships and where appropriate—especially in Chapter Three—we will take note of the important conceptual and practical differences that have arisen between the Navy's view of the future and that reportedly held by the Carter administration.

Strategic Deterrence

U.S. Navy officials have tended to place strategic deterrence and sea control at the top of their mission priorities. Although sea control is now viewed as "fundamental" and a "prerequisite" to other mission areas by Admiral Holloway, he has referred to the strategic submarine force as "the highest national priority."[6] Throughout the late 1950s and the 1960s, the "assured destruction" element of the strategic deterrence mission was clearly dominant. The limits imposed by warhead accuracy, missile range, and command and control seriously constrained the ability of the United States to anticipate a controlled response role for much of the strategic force structure. Sea-based systems were the most constrained of these forces and tended to be viewed as the last line of invulnerable strategic forces whose mission entailed the destruction of an aggressor's cities and industrial targets. The invulnerability of these sea-based systems insured the central role of submarine-launched ballistic missiles (SLBM) in a strategic force structure that viewed assured destruction as the organizing concept of strategic policy.[7]

This emphasis on assured destruction has in no way diminished in the 1970s and seems unlikely to change during the 1980s. However, changes in technology have complicated strategic policy. Former Secretary of Defense Schlesinger concluded that these factors "make some of the earlier views of nuclear deterrence totally obsolete. Clearly, our requirements in this realm are for strategic forces capable of providing more than the simple response of a limited or wholesale destruction of cities."[8]

The implications of this situation for sea power are as yet ill defined, but recent official discussion of these changes in strategic doctrine and sea-based deterrence platforms points to a greater controlled nuclear response role for the strategic submarine (SSBN), attack submarine (SSN), and perhaps surface platforms as well. Regarding the strategic submarine, movement in this direction would require a combination of improved missile accuracy and improved command, control, and communications capability. The latter will perhaps have been achieved with the advent of the Trident submarine. What is less clear is whether the warhead technology available for the Trident I missile will have sufficient accuracy to undertake a counterforce role.[9]

Current planning calls for the deployment of Trident I on board the new *Ohio*-class submarines as well as on ten of the thirty-one remaining Polaris/Poseidon boats. During the next decade, therefore, the capacity of the SSBN fleet to engage in controlled flexible nuclear responses will be increased through improvements in boat design and missile range, but must be regarded as ultimately somewhat problematic in view of warhead accuracy limitations. Between 1985 and 1995, however, these uncertainties could be reduced significantly if the deployment of the more accurate and longer-range Trident II missile proceeds according to current projections.[10] Fifteen, twenty, or twenty-five-year forecasts are clearly risky. Nevertheless, if warhead accuracies continue to improve, the task of the sea-based deterrent force may expand to encompass more of the strategic deterrence mission, including some of the flexible counterforce options.[11]

Navy planners are also moving to extend the capacity of the attack submarine (SSN) into areas of the strategic deterrence mission formally reserved to the strategic submarine.[12] Whereas previously the SSN seems to have been thought of almost exclusively as an antisubmarine warfare (ASW) and anti-surface ship platform, the advent of the sea-launched cruise missile (SLCM) now raises the possibility that the SSN can be given a strategic offensive capability.[13] In the past, the mission of attack submarines was based on a combination of factors, including: (1) the location of Russian SSBN, (2) the location of the Soviet surface fleet, and (3) the need of the American SSBN force for a degree of deceptive screening or "interference" by American attack submarines in order to complicate and/or evade detection by Soviet attack submarines at the beginning of patrol. Now with the development of greater tactical capability, the SSN becomes even more versatile. With the acquisition of the *Harpoon* missile in concert with the 25-mile-range, wire-guided Mk 48 torpedo, for example, the SSN might in some cases be an escort or serve as a screen for naval task forces or even escort convoys. The development and deployment of a tactical SLCM will extend the SSN's flexibility even further. Moreover, the deployment of strategic SLCM on attack submarines would confound any simple classification of these platforms as a tactical as opposed to strategic weapons system—a point recently underscored in the Strategic Arms Limitations talks.[14]

The extent to which the mission of the SSN will be transformed by the SLCM and other new systems which will become available during the next decade is, therefore, indeterminate. Nevertheless, it would appear that incipient technological changes in the near future could lead to a rethinking of the missions and deployment of the nuclear attack submarine, a weapons platform whose mission and place in the Navy's force structure has been fairly stable for over a decade. In his 1978 posture statement, for example, the CNO noted that the "planned capability" of the SSN now includes the use of nuclear and conventional warheads mounted on SLCM to provide the attack submarine with both a nuclear and a conventional strike capability.[15]

Finally, it should be noted that Admiral Holloway has hinted that the mission expanding effects of the strategic SLCM may even extend to surface platforms. In his fiscal 1977 statement before the House Armed Services Committee, for example, the CNO observed with respect to the TOMAHAWK, the Navy's version of the cruise missile: "The strategic TOMAHAWK, being developed to add a new dimension to the power projection function, has the potential to supplement the weapon capabilities of the attack submarine as well as some cruisers."[16] By fiscal 1978 the "potential" of the SLCM had become part of the "planned capability" of surface combatants.[17]

It is not inconceivable, therefore, that the Navy will have available some counterforce capability before Trident II becomes available. Limitations will remain. The cruise missile now being developed will have a range of only 1,300 to 2,000 nautical miles in contrast to the more than twice that range envisaged for Trident I and II. But its relatively low cost, its capacity for low-altitude approach (less than 200 feet, thereby bringing it in under radar), and its highly accurate terrain-matching guidance system will[18] provide the Navy with an almost irresistible opportunity to capture part of the force structure implied by current strategic doctrine.

In early 1974 when he announced the shift in American strategic policy, Schlesinger reasoned:

> Assured destruction must remain an essential ingredient in our overall deterrent strategy. However, under certain hypothetical circumstances, if the use of U.S. strategic capability were required in response to an act of aggression, we might well reserve our assured destruction forces so as to deter attacks against the American and other free world cities into the wartime period—what we call intrawar deterrence.
>
> The emphasis in the new retargeting doctrine is to provide a number of options, selectivity, and flexibility, so that our response, regardless of the provocation, is appropriate rather than disproportionate to the provocation. I think that understanding of this will serve to shore up deterrence.[19]

The reaction of some former members of the defense policy-making community during the 1960s suggests that not everyone would agree.[20] This debate aside, it is now apparent that the quest for intrawar deterrent capability has raised serious doubts in the minds of the Soviets concerning American intentions.[21] Thus reports have circulated that the Soviets have begun intensified research on a cruise missile of their own.[22] More important, these new weapons have become a central concern of the Soviets in the current round of SALT. The consequences of the weapon's deployment on future strategic arms limitations agreements remain speculative, but the arms limitations problems raised by the SLCM are readily conceded by the Navy:

> *Question* (Senator Symington): Can you tell us how you would propose to constrain the large scale deployment of submarine launched cruise missiles once a long-range cruise missile capable of being fired from a torpedo tube has been developed? . . .
>
> *Answer* (Secretary Middendorf): Constraint of submarine launched cruise missiles has been essentially economic. The only form of meaningful constraint thus far seriously discussed in SALT is to prohibit or limit cruise missiles beyond a given range. Limiting the launchers is not a feasible option because launchers are reloadable, and the actual numbers of cruise missiles in the inventory cannot be verified. . . .[23]

Notwithstanding these arms control difficulties, the Navy seems intent on acquiring the SLCM in both its tactical and strategic variants. From a bureaucratic perspective this is certainly understandable. Moreover, as in the case of Polaris two decades ago, prevailing strategic doctrine reinforces the bureaucratic political dynamic in that the doctrinal framework now calls for counterforce as well as assured destruction capability. The deployment of SLCM would allow the Navy to claim quite logically (bureaucratic rationales aside) a major portion of this new spectrum of strategic missions. At the same time, however, the Soviets' reaction to these developments suggests that, politically, the advent of the sea-launched cruise missile is proving most closely analogous to MIRV in that its imminent deployment by the United States has led to a significant hiatus in the strategic arms control process as the Soviets seek and perfect their own strategic cruise missile capability (or countermeasures) in order that they might redress a perceived imbalancing of strategic parity. One suspects that given the peculiar difficulties of surveillance in the suboceanic environment, the next plateau of parity between the United States and the Soviet Union will be even more difficult to recognize and institutionalize than that reached in the late 1960s and early 1970s.

Sea Control and Power Projection Defined

The objectives and forces deemed relevant to the mission of strategic deterrence have traditionally been regarded as distinct and very nearly self-evident in nature and function.[24] In contrast, the missions of sea control and projection have undergone considerable redefinition during the last few decades and stand today as the focus of debate concerning the future of the United States Navy. We will examine first the Navy's concept of sea control and projection as it stood in the mid-1970s and then take note in this and subsequent sections as well as in the next chapter of the differences between the Navy's view and that of the Carter administration, especially as they relate to the Navy's future force structure and its use.

Sea Control and Projection in the Mid-1970s

A combination of America's geographic position and global security commitments provides the strategic basis for the Navy's claim in the mid-1970s that the protection of sea lines of communication is the prerequisite of virtually all of American foreign and economic policy. Accordingly, sea control came to be viewed as "the fundamental mission of the U.S. Navy. It is a basic prerequisite for the projection of power from the sea against hostile shores. A credible sea control capability permits the achievement of national objectives through the use of naval presence forces during peacetime; and is essential to support our diplomacy in crises short of major war. It also enhances the survivability of our strategic deterrent SSBNs."[25]

During much of the period after World War II, American naval superiority was such that in the event of war, the United States

Navy could very nearly totally deny the use of the seas to its enemies while asserting its own exclusive use. By the late 1960s, however, the growing presence of a Soviet threat in the air, on the
surface, and below the seas had compelled a rethinking of the tactical implications of sea control. Out of this has come a more tem-
porally and spatially circumscribed concept "to connote more realistic control in limited areas and for limited periods of time. It is
conceivable today to temporarily exert air, submarine, and surface
control in an area while moving ships into position to project power
ashore or to resupply overseas forces. It is no longer conceivable,
except in the most limited sense, to totally control the seas for one's
own use or to totally deny them to an enemy."[26]

Tactically, therefore, the Navy's concept of sea control entails the
use of offensive and defensive capability to secure an area encompassing air, surface, and subsurface dimensions. The purpose of this
control might involve protecting a convoy or securing coastal and,
perhaps increasingly in the future, deep-sea commercial activity.
Clearly, however, the Navy has been and continues to be most concerned with the interrelationships of sea control and the projection
of power ashore in one or more of its many forms, including strategic nuclear response, offensive carrier-based air strikes, naval
bombardment, amphibious assault, or the projection of influence
via naval presence.[27]

The Perils of Projection

The projection mission has become the focus of much of the criticism and uncertainty surrounding the Navy's future. Initially, skepticism emerged both within and outside the defense establishment
concerning the use of amphibious assault as a means for projecting
power ashore in the face of increasingly lethal and more readily
available defensive systems. While he was Secretary of Defense, Dr.
James Schlesinger observed: "An amphibious assault force . . . has
not seen anything more demanding than essentially unopposed landings for over 20 years, and . . . would have grave difficulty in ac-
complishing its mission of over-the-beach and flanking operations
in a high-threat environment."[28]

Schlesinger spoke before the Tang Island assault, but the hundred or so casualties involved in the *Mayaguez* affair pointed up the vulnerability of the amphibious assault force to concerted defense armed with even the most basic of modern weapons. There is debate concerning the adequacy of planning for the Tang Island operation. Nevertheless, important questions remain as to whether helicopter and assault landing craft possess the requisite speed or defensive capability to defend themselves against precision-guided missiles, aircraft or shore-based missilery, and guns. Amphibious assault has always been a costly venture and the costs have escalated.

An even more fundamental challenge to the Navy's conception of the projection mission has been advanced by the Carter administration. The elements and implications of this challenge will concern us throughout the following pages. For now it is sufficient to note that in its initial guidelines for long-term Defense Department planning, and in its Five-Year Shipbuilding Program, the Carter administration is seeking to reorient the Navy away from its traditional notion of power projection especially with respect to the Soviet Union. Indeed, projection by naval forces would now be confined to relatively low threat areas where less expensive, conventionally powered vessels could serve. Beyond this much scaled-down concept of projection, the primary role of the Navy would become that of sea control in the narrowest sense of keeping sea lanes open for communication and resupply or commercial purposes.[29] Apart from the bureaucratic and political implications inherent in the predictably bitter charges from within the Navy that Mr. Carter's proposals will reduce the Navy's role to that of a rather mundane police force,[30] the consequences of such a redefinition of the sea control/projection missions will be most evident in the evolution of the force structure dedicated to those missions.

Sea Control and Projection Force Structure

As the Ford administration came to a close, the U.S. Navy was in the midst of a general purpose force structure modernization program designed to maintain United States superiority over the

Soviet Union especially in the area of surface combatants. The purpose of this modernization was to expand significantly the Navy's capacity to wage war against the Soviet Navy and to reinforce the linkage of sea control and projection as interdependent and inseparable missions.[31] However, disagreement and criticism concerning major elements of this force structure have introduced great uncertainty concerning the future of the surface Navy. This uncertainty reached a peak during the last days of the Ford administration and especially at the outset of the Carter administration. First, the Carter administration reaffirmed a late decision by the Ford administration to shelve a proposed new nuclear-powered strike cruiser (CSGN) as well as go forward with the deployment of the new Aegis air defense system on a conventionally powered platform (a modified *Spruance*-class destroyer DD-963, now numbered DDG-47). At the same time, the new administration agreed to the modification of a *Virginia*-class nuclear-powered cruiser as an Aegis platform. Most important, however, was the emergence of major debate within the Carter administration concerning the future of the large-deck aircraft carrier.[32] There followed in the fiscal 1979 budget request the elimination of a fourth nuclear-powered aircraft carrier of the *Nimitz* class that had been proposed by the Navy apparently in favor of the development of a new smaller class of conventionally powered carriers (CVV) embarking V/STOL aircraft.

The Aircraft Carrier

The aircraft carrier and especially the large-decked nuclear-powered class of carrier has for some time been the target of criticism from within and outside the government. A recent nongovernmental critique emphasized that carriers face four threats: (1) precision-guided munitions, (2) satellite and long-range aircraft reconnaissance, (3) improvements in submarine sensing and attack capability since World War II, and (4) the inevitability of some air defense failure in a sustained attack. All of these militate against the aircraft carrier as a weapons platform in a high risk environment. This would especially be the case, it is contended, if the carrier is used in its projection mission and is therefore required to remain in a relatively confined area.[33]

Some governmental critics of the large nuclear-powered carrier are somewhat more sanguine concerning the utility of aircraft carriers per se but not the large *Nimitz*-sized ship. The *Nimitz* class is criticized because they concentrate large numbers of naval aircraft (ninety to one hundred planes) on a small number of very expensive platforms, thus compounding the risks. Moreover, the *Nimitzs'* vulnerability to new reconnaissance and weapons technologies complicates their use in high-threat areas. Consequently, what is needed, it is argued, is a new generation of smaller (50,000–60,000-ton), conventionally powered ships which would deploy perhaps half the aircraft available to the *Enterprise, Nimitz, Eisenhower,* or *Vinson* and operate in lower risk conditions. These smaller carriers (CVVs), it is pointed out, would cost less than a nuclear-powered carrier and therefore larger numbers of platforms—two or perhaps three—could become available in the late 1980s and early 1990s as replacements for the *Midway*. The deployment of such ships would presumably be confined to areas where the threat of sustained high-intensity combat was lowest, i.e., "small" wars or the more limited sea control mission foreseen by the Carter administration.[34]

United States Navy spokesmen do not deny that carrier attrition will be significant—perhaps 30 to 40 percent—under certain conflict scenarios, especially those involving the Soviet Union. However, as Admiral Holloway testified recently, although "carriers are vulnerable, our other surface ships are vulnerable also, and furthermore, without carriers all of our other surface ships become a great deal more vulnerable. Without carriers we feel that we would have to revert to a Coast Guard type of Navy. *We would be unable to conduct forward open ocean major force deployment and operations.*"[35] The carrier remains, in Navy thinking, therefore, the crucial element in the general purpose force structure, combining the "distinctive operational characteristics" of air power at sea, mobility, complete support, and flexibility unavailable to any other general purpose ship or combination of vessels.

The aircraft carrier is the major striking element of our general purpose naval forces. As such, it serves to insure our free use of the world's oceans. The nuclear-powered carrier can respond quickly to areas of tension, moving in international waters, and providing local superiority wherever it goes. Its wide range of capabilities permits a precise response in any distant situation. The aircraft carrier provides today's margin of capability between the U.S. and Soviet Navies.[36]

Admiral Holloway's emphasis on "forward open ocean major force deployments and operations" as a primary use of the carrier would seem to be a clear extension of his belief that the sea control mission will be the primary war fighting mission of the United States Navy in the foreseeable future. Thus the Navy maintains that no other ship shares the offensive *and* defensive capability possessed by the modern large-deck carrier and its attendant task force. Colossal target it may be, but, carrier advocates maintain, it carries on its decks the armament necessary to keep its attackers at arm's length at least as well if not better than *any* surface ship can.

The core of the carrier's capability is, of course, its complement of aircraft which vary in number from eighty to one hundred depending on the size of the carrier. The mix currently includes: (1) twenty-four fighter/interceptors—F-4s and/or F-14; (2) twenty-four to forty-eight attack aircraft—A-7Es and A-6Es; (3) a mix of perhaps four tankers (KA-6Ds), four airborne early warning, four electronic countermeasure, and three reconnaissance aircraft (E-2C, EA-6B, and RA-7); and (4) about eighteen antisubmarine warfare aircraft—S-3s and SH-3s. Their hypothetical use in sea control and projection of power missions has been described recently by Vice Admiral William Houser (Deputy CNO, Air Warfare). In the sea control situation

air, surface, and submarine units threatening sea lines of communications are challenged by a carrier. Advance warning is provided via real time data link from an E-2C. EA-6B aircraft jam enemy radar and communication frequencies; fighters, under control of the E-2C, are vectored to intercept enemy aircraft and cruise missiles. Attack aircraft (A-6 and A-7's) strike enemy surface combatants; while S-3 aircraft search for and attack enemy submarines. The modern CV wing can conduct effectively all phases of war at sea from a single carrier.[37]

Deployed in the projection mission, these same aircraft (minus perhaps the S-3) might be used in the following manner:

> Reconnaissance aircraft obtained up-dated information pertaining to the target complex. E-2C's provide early warning for the task force. The strike group, composed of A-6 and A-7 aircraft, proceeds to the target. Fighters (F-14's and F-4's) are assigned to protect the strike aircraft. The EA-6B, accompanying the strike group, jams enemy missile radars and communication frequencies. Some of the attack aircraft carry antiradiation missiles (ARM), which home on enemy missile control radars.[38]

Under mid-1970s projections the F-4s would be gradually replaced by F-18s and current tanker, ECM, and reconnaissance aircraft, and perhaps ASW helicopters would be followed by new aircraft. However, if the CVV concept proves feasible it is likely that new V/STOL aircraft will find their way into future aircraft inventories as complements to the F-18 which, according to some reports, could be deployed on CVVs.[39]

Deployment of the aircraft carrier and its attendant forces had been predicated upon: (1) a 1-in-3 rotation sequence that saw a carrier in port and one training for every one on station and (2) a perception of NATO and Pacific commitments requiring two carriers in the Mediterranean and three in the Pacific. By 1977, however, U.S. carrier force levels were down to thirteen, one of which had no assigned air wing. The consequences of this situation were described by former Secretary Middendorf as follows: "With a total of only 12 routinely deployable carriers, including one home-ported overseas in Japan, only four can be continuously deployed forward on a normal peacetime basis. Accordingly, we plan to reduce our routine carrier deployment in the Western Pacific from three to two in FY 1976, and to continue for the present the deployment of two carriers in the Mediterranean."[40]

By the late 1980s, however, the *Forrestal* and *Kitty Hawk*-class carriers will begin approaching thirty years in service, and the *Midway* will be more than forty years old. To maintain the twelve-carrier deployment from the mid-1980s on, the Navy therefore requested $30 million in fiscal 1978 to initiate a "Service Life Extension Program" (SLEP) for the four *Forrestal* carriers to extend their service lives to forty-five years and advanced procurement for a fourth *Nimitz*-class carrier, the CVN 71, as a replacement for the *Midway*. The Carter administration went along with the extension program and rejected the CVN 71 as a replacement for the *Midway*, proposing instead the development of a 60,000-ton conventionally powered carrier. Congress overrode the administration on the nuclear-powered carrier and has not acted on the smaller conventionally-powered carrier proposal. If, as the Navy desires, however, any smaller carrier is introduced as a two- or three-for-one exchange for retired large-decked carriers, it is not inconceivable that the number of carriers—albeit some of them smaller and less capable than those now deployed—could actually *increase* by the end of the century. In any event, the Navy seems likely to deploy at least the equivalent of a twelve-carrier navy throughout the remainder of the century.

The introduction of an aircraft carrier with lower capability than the large-decked carriers now deployed or delays in the deployment of the CVV could introduce some new problems into the deployment equation; we will return to these questions below. No less important, of course, are the projected changes in the use of a Navy still dependent in large measure on the aircraft carrier for the bulk of its offensive strike capability. For, whatever the significance of the proposed doctrinal changes advanced by the Carter administration, the force structure with which it must work will remain much more difficult to change. Nowhere is this more evident than with respect to the large numbers of surface combatants now available to and planned by the Navy.

Surface Combatants

In the past, the surface combatant force structure has been in large measure keyed to the defense of the carrier. Airplanes have and will continue to provide certain of the defensive elements. For others, cruisers and destroyers, depending on their antiair and antisubmarine capability, have been used. For example, at some distance from the aircraft carrier, one might find one or more cruisers and destroyers responsible for early detection and engagement of enemy forces as well as controlling defensive aircraft launched by the carrier. If there is a significant submarine threat there may be an intermediate station of destroyers responsible for neutralizing the threat but also able to serve as an intermediate air defense station. Finally, in the immediate vicinity of the carrier there may be one or more cruisers and several destroyers screening the carrier which is itself launching combat air patrols to cover the task force especially in the area of the outermost cruisers and destroyers.[41]

The advent of the *Harpoon* missile will change this picture of surface combatant deployment and mission. Fleet defense will by no means disappear, but Admiral Holloway has made it clear that the concept and configuration of fleet defense will change. The attack range of antiship missiles is such that the threat must be checked at considerable distance from the carrier. Thus, cruisers and destroyers comprising the task force will be more widely dispersed around the aircraft carrier than in the past. Moreover, the offensive capability of these ships vis-à-vis enemy surface ships is to be greatly enhanced. Consistent with this view, the Navy has begun planning for a force structure encompassing extensive deployment of the *Harpoon* missile on new surface combatants and attack submarines as well as those already in the fleet.[42] Table 1 shows the projected deployment of the *Harpoon* missile in early 1977.

Central to this conception of the general purpose forces has been the cruiser. In the short run, this led the Navy to redesignate (on 1 July 1975) the major frigates as cruisers and to begin planning for a new nuclear-powered strike cruiser (CSGN). The weapons system for the new cruisers (as well as older and redesignated ones where

Table 1

Anticipated Harpoon Missile Deployment, 1977

FF-1052		46
CG-10/16/26		20
CGN		9
DDG-2/37		33
DD-963		30
FFG-7		50
PHM		6
CSGN		10
DDG-47		13
	Surface Ship Subtotal	217
SSN-594		13
SSN-637		37
SSN-688		14
SSN-700		24
	Submarine Subtotal	88
	Fleet Total	305

Source: U.S., Congress, Hearings before a Subcommittee of the House Committee on Appropriations, *Department of Defense Appropriations for 1978*, Part 4, 95th Cong., 1st sess., 1977, p. 727.

practical) might include *Harpoon*, helicopters, at some future time V/STOL aircraft, perhaps cruise missiles, and the new Aegis air defense system. At the moment, Aegis is only in development and testing, but expectations are quite high:

> The Aegis area air defense system should provide marked improvement in the capability to counter the current threat and provide the growth potential needed for the future as well. Aegis offers reduced reaction time, better resistance to jamming, and most notably, greater missile firepower to counter high density attacks. More important, however, Aegis as a command and control system will permit the task force commander to coordinate all his air defense assets much more effectively. Against the threat of the 1980s and 1990s, Aegis will also

provide the core around which we could tailor defenses as necessary to counter the threat as it materializes. Missile and launcher technology is promising, and Aegis will be compatible with developments in these areas.[43]

The size and sophistication of its phased array radars, computers, and firing controls limit the number of platforms which can mount it and remain stable. To install it on most classes of cruisers now in the Navy would require substantial reconstruction,[44] but in the meantime the Navy has gone forward with planning for a new conventionally powered Aegis platform, the DDG-47, which will be a modified DD-963. The DDG-47 encountered initial congressional opposition from those who favored strict adherence to the Title VIII mandate that ships of the size and mission of the Aegis platforms be nuclear. Nevertheless, the Carter administration supported the concept of a cheaper, conventionally powered Aegis platform.

A second important element of the Navy's plans for its fleet modernization program, the CSGN or nuclear-powered strike cruiser, encountered decisive opposition in the Carter administration. The Navy's Five-Year Shipbuilding Program developed during the Ford administration called for eight DDG-47s by fiscal 1981, and long-range planners noted that the Navy hoped ultimately for sixteen conventionally powered DDG-47s to complement a planned eight Aegis-bearing strike cruisers or CSGNs, displacing 12,000–13,000 tons, two of which were planned for fiscal 1981. In addition to Aegis, the CSGN would have been equipped with the *Harpoon*, Standard (SM2), and Sea Launched Cruise Missile Systems.[45] The DDG-47 would also mount the *Harpoon* but not the SLCM. With the arrival of the Carter administration, however, the more expensive CSGN's future became problematic. The administration eliminated the money for the procurement of long-lead-time items for the first CSGN in its rescission message to Congress in early 1977. Not surprisingly, the House Armed Services Committee put some of these funds back into its authorization bill, thereby signaling that congressional nuclear navy advocates will be a source of difficulty for the administration's naval program if it ignores Title

VIII.[46] Nevertheless, Mr. Carter's FY 1979 budget did not include funds for the strike cruiser.

The CSGN/DDG-47 mix was central to much long-range planning concerning the future role of the Navy's Hi-Mix surface combatants. Indeed, the Navy seemed to be anticipating a role for the CSGN related to that once performed by the battleship.[47] In summary, the CSGN (and *Harpoon*) represented for the Navy a means for perhaps modifying the thirty years of dependence upon the aircraft carrier as the basis of its offensive capability. Throughout this period the capability of surface combatants as well as the testimony of Navy spokesmen made it fairly clear that the optimum deployment of these ships was within the framework of the integrated carrier task force. In such a deployment the extensive—indeed, very nearly exclusive—antisubmarine and antiair capability of the surface combatants could be married to the flexible offensive strike capacity of the carrier.

In view of the likely demise of the CSGN, however, and until the CVV concept is refined and tested, the offensive capability of the Navy will remain confined largely to the large-decked carrier and carrier task force. The deployment of *Harpoon* will certainly increase the offensive capacity of ships possessing it, but it seems unlikely that this will lead to the departures in the deployment and operations of surface combatants foreseen for a Navy that included CSGNs. Indeed, in view of the Carter administration's challenge to the Navy's entire concept of projection and hence the aircraft carrier, the role of surface combatants is unclear. The Navy's general purpose fleet and plans for its modernization have been oriented to the concept of the carrier task force which was ultimately dedicated to the projection of power ashore. The task force was to secure "sea control" but such control was to be the basis for power projection. Now it appears that the meaning of these fundamental concepts will undergo perhaps considerable redefinition. Notwithstanding the outcome of what promises to be an intensely bitter struggle over the future meaning of "sea control" and "projection," however, the general purpose fleet of the Navy remains and will continue to be a product of an era dominated by the large-decked aircraft carrier.

Summary and Some Force Structure Implications

The Navy's conception of its missions in the mid-1970s intersected virtually every conceivable use of force in the contemporary international system. Its strategic deterrent mission was firmly established and seemed likely to grow, given likely changes in strategic weapons technology and the strategic environment over the next decade or two. The military and political costs associated with amphibious assault had led to some official skepticism concerning this traditionally significant portion of the Navy's general purpose mission, but for the most part the Ford administration did not fundamentally challenge the Navy's concept of sea control and projection as the basis for force structure planning and expansion in the late twentieth century. Indeed, the Navy's missions seemed essential in view of a national security policy that held:

> If we are to take our strategic concept seriously (not only for force planning purposes, but also for the realistic implementation of collective security and deterrence), we should maintain military deployments in Europe and Asia. To ensure these deployments, we should be in a position to control the approaches to the Atlantic and the Western Pacific. In addition, for quite obvious reasons, we should be able to make our presence felt in the Mediterranean and the Indian Ocean.[48]

The comprehensive scope of the missions of American naval power seemed to follow quite logically from this globalized notion of "collective security and deterrence." Moreover, the expectations concerning what such deployments could do were equally comprehensive:

> With deployments of this general character, we are in a position to:
>
> —contribute immediately to collective security and the deterrence of attack in critical strategic areas;

—lay the groundwork for reinforcements and provide a strong initial defense in the event of an attack;

—prevent major losses of territory and the terrible human and material costs of taking the counter-offensive;

—keep the nuclear threshold high;

—project power into other areas so as to deter or respond to unforeseen contingencies;

—stabilize relationships in these areas because of our presence as one of only two superpowers, and because of the great potential that lies in back of our presence.[49]

Such broad missions and expectations ultimately depend upon weapons systems and platforms in significant numbers. But with the arrival of a new administration in the late 1970s, the Navy's missions were subjected to closer scrutiny than at any time since the great struggle over control of the strategic retaliatory mission in 1949. Admiral Holloway had earlier outlined his conception of an adequate general purpose force structure built around four to six CVNs. Assuming that task forces accompanying such carriers would also be nuclear, the basic task force complement would include: 2–3 nuclear-powered cruisers (2 Aegis platforms *or* 1 Aegis—presumably one of the planned new strike cruisers—and 2 additional nuclear cruisers) and 1–3 attack submarines. Overall such task force planning would require 12–18 nuclear cruisers ("immediately") for a Navy of about 570 ships which would also include 90–95 SSN-688s, 30 DD-963s, and approximately two DDG-47s for each CSGN built.[50] However, the same budgetary considerations that moved the Carter administration to question the fifth CVN have also led to the cancellation of the CSGN and compelled the Navy to think in terms of the DDG-47 as the primary platform for Aegis or somehow modifying newer CGN-38s* to receive Aegis. Moreover, if the CVV is introduced, the appearance and deployment of the general force structure will be even more uncertain.

---

*These are Virginia-class "cruisers" originally constructed as "frigates" (DLGN-38), but cosmetically upgraded in mid-1975 to CGNs.

The conventionally powered CVV is seen as operating primarily in open ocean sea control deployments and not in high-threat areas within 1000 to 1500 nautical miles of Soviet air bases, i.e., *not* in the Norwegian and North Seas, the Baltic Sea, the Eastern Mediterranean, the Sea of Japan, and much of the Western Pacific. In time, these high-threat areas are seen as expanding to include some of the North Atlantic and Central Pacific Oceans as well as the Western Mediterranean.[51] The mission foreseen for the CVV in those areas where it does operate "does not demand large numbers of offensive aircraft. It would emphasize air defense while providing sufficient offensive capability to engage any Soviet surface ships that are deployed in the open ocean. The smaller number of aircraft required for the sea control mission permits construction of small carriers. Reduced emphasis on strike missions for these ships precludes the need for nuclear propulsion."[52] The emphasis on air defense implies in turn the presence of Aegis platforms, but the Navy is not yet firm in its estimates of what this means in terms of the total number of Aegis ships or how they would be used with respect to the CVV:

> No decision has been made yet on a precise programmed force level, because that decision will depend in large part on how effective Aegis proves to be when actually introduced into the fleet. For planning purposes, we estimate that 18–24 ships with the Aegis system would be sufficient. This number would provide two Aegis ships with each carrier operating in conditions of higher threat, one with those carriers in the open ocean and a few additional ships to provide flexibility to our operational commanders. When CVV's enter the fleet, we would anticipate an Aegis ship would operate with them depending on the threat.[53]

It is, therefore, difficult to predict in detail the shape and deployment of the Navy's general purpose force structure at this time. Budgetary constraints would seem to be pushing the Navy in the direction of V/STOL technology, which is as yet still in the planning stage, and a platform for its deployment, the CVV, which would not appear in the fleet for several years. Moreover, these same budgetary considerations have forced the Navy to accept the conventionally powered DDG-47 as its primary means for getting the new Aegis air-defense system—itself only now entering the test phase—to sea in the 1980s. Finally, contemplation of an 11-carrier navy,[54] the appearance of the Service Life Extension Program for the *Forrestal* class carriers (estimated cost for the U.S.S. *Saratoga:* $300–500 million and 2–3 years per ship), and a planned six-year $3.2 billion modernization program for the 23 *Charles F. Adams* (DDG-2) class destroyers suggest that the Navy has begun preparing for a late twentieth century force structure scaled down from the expectations of a 600-ship fleet advanced by Navy spokesmen in the early and mid-1970s.

At the same time, Navy spokesmen maintain a strategic conception predicated on forward deployment and a sea control/projection capability against the Soviet Union notwithstanding the rather different view held by some in the Carter administration. But in the meantime, Admiral Holloway, when asked to advance his

> personal and professional views concerning our Navy's force structure over the next 20 to 30 years, as well as a related ship construction program . . . used, as an objective, a force structure which achieves acceptable levels of risk in carrying out a strategy which will enable the United States to fight a NATO-Warsaw Pact conflict in Europe and the Atlantic approaches, and at the same time support our allies and territories in the Pacific, and maintain the security of our strategic sea lines of communication to those other areas of the world such as South America and the Persian Gulf which are of continuing and vital concern to our fundamental national interests.[55]

In sum, sea control/projection remains the most "fundamental" mission for a Navy that sees itself serving a foreign policy predicated upon the forward and global deployment of military capability. And the aircraft carrier remains, in Navy thinking, the single most flexible and capable weapons platform for those missions. Sea control/projection and the aircraft carrier are, therefore, more or less synonymous in Navy thinking today and for the foreseeable future.

But it is no longer clear that the official U.S. Navy vision of its missions and roles developed over the last two decades within and based on a globalist American foreign policy will any longer shape the Navy's force structure and its use. For some within the Navy and the defense policy-making community, the mainstream U.S. Navy position outlined above, because of its fixation on the sea control/projection mission vis-à-vis a presumed Soviet adversary, ignores many of the problems posed by a rapidly changing international political system. Thus some would argue that in an era in which parity and detente are controlling between the superpowers, the emphasis on war-fighting missions and forces may be misplaced. In addition, it is argued, the ambiguous but increasingly salient political uses of naval power require much more careful attention than they have been given in the past. Much of this skepticism concerning the mainstream conception of United States naval power and missions has centered on the definition and force structure implications of the so-called presence mission, and will occupy us in the next chapter.

CHAPTER THREE

Naval Force: Changing Missions for a Changing World

IN THIS chapter, we will review the dialogue and debate concerning naval missions especially as they relate to current U.S. Navy doctrine and forces. Our first section will constitute a brief overview of the prevailing conceptions of the relationship between military force and the dynamics of world politics. The remainder of the chapter will review naval theory and missions as they have evolved within the context of changing international political circumstances.

The Expansion and "Regulation" of Military Force

For at least two decades the "state-centric" conception of international politics has been the prevailing metaphor for understanding world politics. This metaphor has encompassed both a description of reality and a prescription for prudent behavior within the described reality. The description of reality includes as "givens"

(1) More or less discrete national units.
(2) The units—the nation-states—pursue their respective and independently derived national interests.
(3) The pursuit of interests occurs within the most loosely integrated of systems of interaction. Thus, it is held, the international system is anarchic.

(4) Therefore, the only consensus in an "anarchic international society" clusters about a marginally normative set of rules (international law) which legitimize the principle of self-help. The ultimate means of helping oneself in the system is the threat and use of force.[1]

Hence, in its very nature war is "endemic" to the international system.

A central problem in such an environment has been the establishment and maintenance of a condition of minimal order in which states might find some modicum of security; for without some kind of order the opportunity to pursue interests beyond mere survival are obviously diminished. In the absence of any overarching set of institutions which might insure this minimal level of order, nation-states have resorted to the exploitation of force in pursuit of "security." For the last three hundred years of international history the nation-state, pursuing "security," has arrived at a condition of greatly expanded capacity to deploy force and military power.

As the potential volume of violence available to states expanded, "the dimensions, forms, and impact of force, both in war and short of war, were drastically altered, and many of the potentialities of modern military power for disorder but also for order became manifest."[2] This kind of paradoxical "order" has been embodied in that quintessential prescription for prudential behavior in an international political system based on the inevitability of war—the balance of power. Inis Claude has written: "The concept of the balance of power is relevant to the problem of the management of power in international relations. In this context, it must be considered as a system, an arrangement within which independent states operate autonomously, without the controlling direction of a superior agency, to manipulate power relationships among themselves. It is thus a decidedly decentralized system; power and policy remain in the hands of its constituent units."[3] Concerning war in such a system, Claude notes: "The implications of war should be serious enough to stimulate preventive measures, but mild enough to enable statesmen to invoke the threat, and on occasion the actuality, of force in support of policy. War should be imaginable, controllable, usable."[4]

In essence, then, the balance of power concept "is not a formula for perfect peace, but rather for reasonable stability and order with no more than moderate use of violent techniques by the states involved in the system."[5] Thus, the balance of power as prescription for systemic order is in fact a pragmatic attempt to moderate and then institutionalize the status quo of the state of war, albeit at a lower level of violence.

To many observers, however, the thirty years of international chaos ushered in by World War I and culminating in the skies over Hiroshima and Nagasaki at the end of World War II marked the inevitable outcome of this kind of thinking and practice. The exploitation of war must, it was argued in some quarters, fail as an approach to the management of force and disorder in international politics.[6] Stability could not forever rest on the paradoxical threat and use of instruments of war. Since, it was held, at the heart of the balance of power was the ultimate exploitation and development of the technologies of violence—nuclear weapons—the extent of the dangerous inconsistency could now be clearly seen. Could it not be said, therefore, that the historic expansion of war and the exploitation of military power had now been discredited?

The answer of the post-World War II "realist" school of thought has been a considered negative, for the realists could now envision— "with as much conjecture as hope"[7]—the initiation of a new "regulatory" phase in world politics.

> In many ways this phase is a response to the culmination of all the major trends in the evolution of force in the earlier phases. It raises the question whether the very same developments that account for the expansion of military power and the tendency of this power to become an autonomous and disruptive force beyond political control may now enable states to bring force back under control as a rational instrument of policy and order under radically different conditions.[8]

The basis for this optimism was to be found in the belief that the *threat* of war had now replaced the *use* of war as the central fact of international life. Moreover, the conviction grew during the period after World War II that a new approach to the management of the security dilemma could be constructed on the "uses of military power short of war."[9]

Like latter-day Madisonians of international politics, the realist-optimists have sought to use the nature of the system against itself. Madison's domestic order rested on the institutionalization of the inevitable interplay of countervailing ambition. Similarly, the balance of power manipulated and exploited war to facilitate "order" and now the realist-optimists would seek to build an international order on the fear of war because war, at least between superpowers, had become too violent and all-consuming to "use." There has followed, of course, the development and application of a large body of deterrence and limited war theory built around what Thomas Schelling has termed a "strategy of conflict" or the "diplomacy of violence." In terms of American foreign and defense policy, the generic analog (and precursor) of most of these precepts is the notion of containment. As long as the United States possessed a functional monopoly of the potential for nuclear war, the use of the threat of war as the basis for policy (and hence the *pax Americana*) took on a fairly simple form—massive retaliation. With the nuclear monopoly broken in the late 1950s and early 1960s, doctrines of limited war gained currency and were incorporated into American policy by the Kennedy and Johnson administrations in the form of "flexible response."

Vietnam suggests that the application of these doctrines of controlled threat and violence can become frightfully expensive if they fail and the actual use of even conventional force becomes necessary. Moreover, within this purported regulatory phase, the expansion of force continues. Sophisticated conventional weapons technology has become so diffused throughout a conflict-ridden non-Western world that some non-Western countries must now be counted as at least regional powers. Even more disturbing for the regulatory vision is what some observers are now referring to as the second phase of nuclear proliferation driven by the spread of so-

called peaceful uses of nuclear technology.[10] The dialectic of negotiations and arms racing that has marked the development of an
ambiguous set of partial strategic arms limitations agreements lends
some warrant to the notion of a purposefully regulated military
environment. But even between superpowers—presumably those
actors most sensitive to the needs and exigencies of regulation—the
persistence of older reflexes and the uncertainties of the new relationship may prove more important constraints than formal agreements or "unilateral" interpretations. Charges of "cheating," the
continued momentum of technological development, and former
Secretary of Defense James Schlesinger's refinement of the "strategy
of conflict" through the development of "limited nuclear options"
are all ambiguous markers on the road of regulation.[11]

With all, however, the attempt to develop and refine the uses of
military power short of war goes forward. The reopened debate
within the American foreign and defense policy community over
deterrence theory and policy is perhaps the most visible manifesta-
tion of continued interest in what Osgood has termed the "art of
coercion short of war and on the brink."[12] But the last decade underscores the possibility that perhaps the most difficult political and
military linkage remains the uses of conventional military power
short of war. Indeed, it is only at this level that deterrence has
failed. With the costs of that failure driven home and the subnuclear
applicability of the new strategic deterrence remaining problematical, there is renewed concern with less explicit forms of military
pressure—that "copious arsenal of discussion, persuasion, compul-
sion, and intimidation."[13] Nowhere is this preoccupation more
apparent than with respect to the uses of sea power short of war.

Naval Force as a Political Instrument

The evolution of sea power and, more specifically, American
naval theory can be understood within the more general framework
and gradual acceptance of Mahan's conception of the relationship
between national power, foreign policy, and sea power. Yet,

Mahan's comprehensive notion of command of the sea was not fully realized for the United States until World War II when the "overbearing power" of a "great Navy"[14] did indeed drive the Japanese Navy from the Pacific seas even as, earlier, the German U-boat's *guerre de course* of late 1939 through early 1943 had been suppressed. Immediately after World War II, after some initial ambivalence, American foreign policy moved to its now familiar globalist posture. Thus, the United States Navy retained and even enlarged during the 1950s the preponderate position it had held at the end of the war. By 1960, it had successfully competed with the Army and the Air Force for a piece of the strategic deterrence mission. When added to its existing capacity for tactical air war, command of the sea, and amphibious war, it was clear that the United States Navy was composed of a multifaceted and versatile set of military instruments and seemed particularly adaptable to the demands of a foreign policy that required an American global presence and interventionary capacity to "bear any burden, meet any hardship, support any friend, oppose any foe, to assure the survival and success of liberty . . . [to] do all of this and more." In sum, it was the embodiment of the expansion of military power in the twentieth century and at the same time admirably suited to the flexible response and the "strategy of conflict."

On the other hand, although the Navy has served at midcentury as among the most flexible agencies of American foreign and military policy, it is no less susceptible to some new constraints now affecting U.S. policies. One constraint is the cost of high technology weapons systems. Although recent congressional naval appropriations remain supportive, Navy planners must at least be as concerned as their counterparts in other services about the receptivity of the American people to the rising costs of military technology. A recent analysis of major systems development underway reveals that Navy technology is now far and away the most expensive technology being purchased by the Pentagon. And, with the possible exception of proposed mobile ICBMs, the Navy may continue to have the most costly technology for the foreseeable future.[15] Moreover, the apparent growth in skepticism on the part of the American public toward combat intervention of any substantial intensity and length of time may undercut the willingness of political leadership to exploit that portion of the Navy's force and mission profile devoted to the projection of power ashore.[16] Finally, changes in the very structure of the international system reflected in some measure in potential changes in the legal regime of the oceans, technological change, e.g., precision-guided weapons, and the general growth of Soviet naval power have all contributed to growing official and nongovernmental concern about the position of the U.S. Navy. Indeed, perhaps the most dramatic manifestations of Soviet military expansion have been in terms of their naval capability, which many analysts would contend effectively consigns the Mahanian doctrine of "command of the sea" to history.

Conceptual Change and Constraints

One consequence of these closing domestic and foreign constraints has been some reconsideration of U.S. naval missions. Recent years have seen somewhat closer consideration to what has been termed the "war-deterring" as opposed to the "war-fighting" misisons—although, clearly, the latter have not lost their prominence.[17] Former Chief of Naval Operations Elmo Zumwalt's definition of U.S. Navy missions[18] and his subsequent requests for ship construction, weapons, development, and procurement funds included and emphasized the Navy's war-fighting capability. Nevertheless, much of his rationale for this war-fighting capability was framed in the language of war-deterrence and the political uses of naval force. Similarly, more recent views of the presence mission are rooted in what a recent Secretary of Defense regarded as an axiom of international relations in a "world of competition and conflict." In such a world "it is generally accepted that forces in forward visible deployments make an important contribution to nonnuclear deterrence."[19]

The notion of deterrence is also central to Admiral Holloway's conception of presence: "The United States historically has used presence of naval forces to deter actions hostile to our national interests, to provide visible assurance of our commitments to allies and friendly nations, and to project a stabilizing influence during crises. The crisis management role of naval forces is one of their most important during peace-time."[20]

The crisis management potential of naval presence and power is seen by Navy spokesmen as lying once again in the unique flexibility of naval power. Admiral Holloway articulates a theme that runs throughout a growing literature[21] on naval presence: "Of our overseas military deployments, naval forces are least affected by diplomatic constraints, base rights, overflight privileges and other factors not under U.S. control. Forward-deployed naval forces allow us to demonstrate U.S. interest while retaining the flexibility to change force visibility and composition as required by the situation."[22]

Two kinds of tactics have been identified by Admiral Turner as relevant to this issue area. The first is preventive deployment. The primary intent of this peacetime activity is to signify U.S. interest in a region and to assert a determination to provide defense in the event of an adverse action by a rival. Turner observed that forces embarking on a preventive deployment "should be relevant to the kind of problems which might arise and clearly cannot be markedly inferior to some other naval force in the neighborhood, but can rely to some extent on the implication that reinforcements can be made available if necessary."[23]

Former Secretary of Defense Schlesinger emphasized that the need for preventive deployment of U.S. naval forces does not mean only fixed deployment, but might also include changing the mix of forces from time to time or moving large numbers of naval vessels into an area for crisis management purposes.[24] This "surging" of naval capability into an area to establish presence would constitute a strategy of deployment in reaction to events. Such reactive deployment should possess, Turner states, "an immediately credible threat and be prepared to have its bluff called."[25]

The credibility of the presence deployment is the final but nevertheless central component of the presence mission. Admiral

Holloway notes in passing that naval force can carry out humanitarian assistance, but at the basis of the presence mission as conceived by the Navy is the capacity for war-fighting. Thus sea control and projective capability are linked to the presence mission, in that the credibility of naval presence is viewed as inextricably a function of the war-fighting capacity of the naval forces in question.[26] In Holloway's view, therefore, sea control and projection of power remain the fundamental missions of the Navy. Yet Holloway also accepts the fact that the U.S. Navy is dealing with a very different world than that of the 1890s, or even the 1950s and early 1960s.

Naval Presence and Projection of Influence

If naval presence and projection of influence seem appropriate to contemporary international society, surprisingly little systematic thinking has centered on what exactly the substance of the mission is. The appointment of Admiral Turner to the presidency of the Naval War College in 1972 was, therefore, perhaps more than mere coincidence. As president of the War College from 1972–1974 Turner revamped curriculum and encouraged research oriented toward the exploration and understanding of the political constraints impinging on the U.S. Navy of the future. In his final report on his two years at the War College, Turner took explicit note of what he regarded as prevalent inadequacy of contemporary sea power theory as well as of the professionals responsible for using that power, saying that American naval preponderance in the years after World War II had led to complacency and even indifference among Navy professionals concerning the political uses of naval power.[27] Subsequently, while Commander in Chief of Allied Forces in Southern Europe, he expanded upon this theme:

> I believe that the essence of the deterrent peacetime function is to have many different types of ships, capable of orchestrating the right kind of action in many different places. But do we know enough about orchestrating? . . .
>
> Further, I think that we who exercise naval presence do not know enough about how to fit the action to the situation: how to be sure that the force we bring to bear when told to help in some situation

is in fact the one most appropriate to the circumstances. I would also suggest that in an era of detente we are likely to see much more competition between the Soviet and free-world navies in the field of presence.[28]

Ken Booth has gone so far as to assert that the Admiral's complaint might be directed not just at the analysis of the presence and political influence mission but at the entire literature on naval analysis.[29] There does exist, however, some analysis of the concept of presence specifically, and, more generally, of the role of naval force as an instrument of political influence.

James Cable's work is one of the most extensive treatments of the presence function. Presence is equated with the concept of gunboat diplomacy and limited naval force in that it involves the threat or use of limited naval force short of an act of general war.[30] To Cable, one can separate this kind of action from limited war because "limited naval force" is restricted in its execution to obtaining a political goal not extending (necessarily) to punishment. The range of this concept is enormous. But Cable's comprehensive definition of gunboat diplomacy and his relatively small number of categories diminish somewhat the analytical strength of his effort.[31] Notwithstanding these impediments, Cable does usefully point out that the limited use of naval force is becoming more salient.

Commander Jonathan Howe[32] has outlined some of the diverse context of the presence mission in his description of two events in which the U.S. Navy played a role—the resupply of Quemoy in 1958 and the more nebulous actions of the Sixth Fleet in 1967. Among the considerations that affected the U.S. response in these crises were the estimated intentions of the Soviet Union to intervene, defense estimates of U.S. capability, congressional and public opinion, and the degree of dependence on British support. Howe traces the effects of each factor (and combinations of two or more) on U.S. response to these crises. His attempt is notable because he treats naval presence as an integral part of U.S. foreign policy.

Howe draws other conclusions that are useful and—in light of recent events—prescient. He notes that crises such as the two he analyzes often blossom suddenly and public opinion does not rise in significance with them. In other words, dissent suffers a lag and gives breathing room for responses. This is certainly the case in the *Mayaguez* affair in which naval power was employed quickly and successfully. It was not without its cost (a total of 41 killed, 50 wounded, and the loss of several helicopters), but these costs have not included public outrage. This stands in contrast to the Tonkin Gulf incident which was initially also greeted by public and congressional support. Later, however, when gunboat diplomacy and naval presence were revealed to be the initial stages of a broader escalation and intervention, public support was withdrawn.[33]

Almost all analysts of the presence mission point to the flexibility of the naval force in contrast to the use of, for example, ground forces. The latter are not easily withdrawn once in place and logistics support established. Placing troops on alert or calling global strategic alerts very nearly exhausts the repertoire available to non-naval forces. In contrast, as Kenneth McGruther notes in a recent review of "naval diplomacy" in the Indo-Pakistani cases,

> the key factor which makes a naval force preferable for the presence mission is the great degree of flexibility left to the diplomat even after the introduction of force into a crisis. A naval force is highly maneuverable; its proximity to the coast can itself be taken as a measure of one's intent. . . . Most importantly, a naval force, since it operates in its own milieu, can usually be kept out of hostilities until it chooses to participate, thereby leaving the final decision on commitment both as to time and degree to one's own diplomats.[34]

But the description of the purportedly unique capabilities of naval power does not constitute a theoretical exposition and analysis of the presence mission. Thus, prior to the mid-1970s very little systematic thought had been devoted to the problems of platform planning, tactics, or the broader relationship of the presence mission and foreign policy.[35] The rather nebulous question of naval strategy and foreign policy remains relatively unexplored, although Edward

N. Luttwak's *The Political Uses of Sea Power* and Ken Booth's *Navies and Foreign Policy* make important contributions toward closing this gap.[36] Both reemphasize the apparently unique attributes of naval power as the basis for linking it to foreign policy[37] and, as noted previously, Navy spokesmen have relied heavily on these kinds of arguments in their recent appeals for an expansion of the Navy's force structure. Admiral Holloway, for example, has reiterated the advantages accruing from free use of international waters and the ability of naval forces to engage in combat operations immediately upon arrival in a crisis situation. "Since World War II," he observes, "the United States has turned most often to the Navy when it desired to employ components of the armed forces in support of political objectives. In such cases, U.S. naval units participated in more than 80% of the total and carriers in nearly 50% of the total. Land-based forces were used in fewer cases and rarely without the simultaneous participation of naval units."[38] Moreover, Holloway implies that this joining of naval power and foreign policy has been virtually cost free and effective: "This heavy reliance on naval forces has been the case in all parts of the world. It has not been sensitive to either Soviet or Chinese participation in a particular incident, or to the political context which led to the U.S. use of force. In short, the Navy has been a primary instrument for the United States' political uses of the armed forces, at all places, and regardless of the specifics of the situation."[39]

The Limits of Naval Presence

Recent analysis of the use of armed force as a political instrument raises a number of questions concerning assertions about the efficacy of naval power. Barry Blechman and Stephen Kaplan report that, contrary to Admiral Holloway's claims, the use of naval power has been quite sensitive to a range of correlates, including the political objectives sought, the context of events, and especially the activities of the Soviet Union. Moreover, the tendency of American policy-makers to turn frequently to naval forces does not in itself provide a measure of the success associated with the use of naval power relative to other forms of armed force as political instruments.[40]

Through an examination of more than two hundred incidents in which the United States employed military force as a political instrument, Blechman and Kaplan have determined that its successful use is highly contingent upon the interaction of a range of political and situational factors. Thus, American objectives are important in that the use of military force seems most likely to be successful if the objective is the maintenance or support of a regime already in power or reinforcement of extant behavior rather than modification of behavior. The difficulty of changing behavior is evident with respect to the behavior of a third party. Furthermore, success seems more likely if the United States has been previously engaged in a particular area. Also, the likelihood of success seems to increase when the use of military force as a political instrument is directed at circumstances within rather than between countries. In addition to these political and contextual considerations, the successful use of military force, especially in the short run (six months or less), is closely related to Soviet activity:

> We did not find, as is often maintained, that the United States became less successful in the use of armed forces for political objectives as the Soviet Union closed the U.S. lead in strategic nuclear weapons. Soviet political and/or military involvement in an incident, on the other hand, was of great significance. Outcomes tended to be less favourable from the U.S. perspective when the Soviet Union was involved in an incident. Outcomes were particularly less favourable when the Soviet Union threatened to, or actually employed, her own armed forces in the incident. Interestingly, this finding pertained more to the short term (six month) success rate than to the longer term.[41]

Finally, simply increasing the size of conventional military contingents did not in itself guarantee success, although the presence of nuclear units did seem to correlate with success. The latter, Blechman and Kaplan speculate, are taken as a more earnest (if tension-heightening) symbol of commitment.

Naval presence theorists have not been insensitive to these problems. Thus we find McGruther noting:

> There are dangers in the use of naval ships for force presence. Their inherent uncertainty can also have a strongly adverse effect on nations already at war or on the brink of war, thereby actually destabilizing a crisis and possibly precipitating the very war the force was sent to deter. Another disadvantage is that the opposing superpower, misperceiving the intent of a presence force, could itself commit heavily and initiate an escalatory spiral dangerous to both. A third disadvantage is the possibility of expanding expectation on the part of the client state upon the arrival of a strong naval force belonging to its patron. . . . Finally, one cannot dismiss the possibility of an error, mistake, or miscalculation setting off a holocaust when military forces face each other in an already emotional environment. . . .[42]

Perhaps, however, these dangers and risks are more likely to be attached to what Luttwak could characterize as "active suasion," or a conscious attempt to bring about a particular reaction on the part of others.[43] "Latent suasion," on the other hand, may not automatically involve these kinds of difficulties, "for it is the perceptions of American power held by other nations, that the dominant makeweight to those perceptions is the credible mobility of U.S. power, and that the most persuasive indicator of such mobility is that manifested by the routine, day-to-day overseas presence activities of the U.S. Navy."[44] Perhaps, as McNulty has argued, it is latent suasion—the display of presence by means of routine activity—that is the most important element in the use of naval power short of war.

Thus, most presence theorists seem to be sensitive to the fact that both the advantages and risks inherent in their approach to the use of naval power hinge on the ambiguities associated with perceptions of power. Exacerbating this ambiguity, of course, is the fact that one is dealing in the peaceful presence made with the exploitation of force and military power, albeit force short of war. Goodwill tours, port calls, and the like are peaceful, to be sure. But the agent is recognized and, indeed, must be recognized as capable of inflicting damage and injury. Therefore, when one discusses naval presence, one must keep in mind that one is dealing primarily with a coercive force and not merely a cultural entity. The role is that of policeman, not diplomat or Nobel laureate. Failure to acknowledge the essentially destructive root of naval power and presence is to risk using it in a manner that will do damage to its nation's credibility and its power as a constabulary force. And finally, over-reliance on these methods detracts from more conventional forms of diplomacy.

Proponents of naval power as a political instrumentality have argued, of course, that the flexibility of naval forces constitutes their greatest asset. However, it may well be that flexibility is in fact also the source of the limits of naval power in that it heightens the ambiguities associated with its deployment. Blechman and Kaplan suggest, for example, that a key determinant of the successful use of military force as a political instrument is the extent to which the forces deployed communicate a firm and credible commitment. The inherent flexibility and heretofore "free" physical milieu in which naval forces operate allow for rapidity and ease of deployment, which undoubtedly explains the frequency with which policy-makers use them. However, these apparently unique attributes of naval power may also diminish their effectiveness in that the same characteristics which make them attractive as easily controlled political instruments may also communicate ambiguity of commitment to the "target" of the influence activity. Flexibility and ease of deployment may suggest low-cost utility to an American policy-maker, but the corollary of ease of deployment is ease of withdrawal, which may suggest uncertainty and marginal commitment to the target. Indeed, Blechman and Kaplan have found that successful outcomes are more highly correlated with the use of land-based air power precisely because it is less flexible, more difficult to withdraw, and, therefore, demonstrative of a deeper commitment.[45]

In addition, Blechman and Kaplan suggest that the effectiveness of all forms of military force as political instruments is increased if it is actually used rather than merely being "present" or "surged":

Outcomes were more often favorable when the armed forces units involved actually did something, rather than merely emphasized their potential capability to intervene, and reduced the time delay between a decision to intervene and the actual operation, by moving toward the scene of the incident or by increasing their state of alert. The involvement of the military unit in a specific operation, such as mine-laying, or mine-clearing or patrolling—and certainly when the actual exercise of firepower was involved—seems to have indicated a more serious intent on the United States' part.[46]

Thus the range of "inputs" that presence theorists such as Luttwak have suggested are primarily those of naval forces—routine presence augmented by closely calibrated incremental or rapid increases of force levels to signal concern—are not as clearly effective as theory might suggest. Indeed, effectiveness seems most closely associated with the use of forces—land-based air power or even nuclear capable units—that take the policy-maker into a realm of higher risk and uncertainty.

It may well be that the virtues associated with naval power are also the source of its limits as a political instrumentality. The American policymaker's frequent use of an inherently flexible military instrument as evidence of political will can be the source of another policymaker's confusion, for a "flexible messenger" communicates an ambiguous message.

Force Structure and Operational Implications

Admiral Turner has posed the operational problems raised by the political uses of naval power succinctly: "Are there different operating policies that would yield a greater presence capability?" And with respect to intermission tradeoffs and force structures, he has asked: "Is the presence mission becoming sufficiently important to warrant building or designing forces for that purpose?"[47] The political use of naval power, therefore, poses problems on two levels. First, there is a question of force structure design and mission interrelationships. However, the resolution of this issue is problematic unless the entire question is placed within the context of a second level of analysis: the demands and expectations of naval power rising out of American foreign policy.

Kenneth McGruther has suggested a checklist of "specifications" for a naval force that emphasize a presence or political influence mission:

—The ships should be dear, which implies to McGruther that the force should be drawn from the upper end of the force structure.

—The war-fighting capability of the force must be impressive, and it must have been proven. . . . In general, the bigger the ship the more impressive; the more guns or missiles or similar sized ships the more impressive.

—The force should also be multimission capable. That is to say that these forces should be able to deploy credibly as many as possible of the five actions with which a naval presence force could conceivably threaten another nation. As outlined by Turner these are: a) amphibious assault; b) air attack; c) bombardment; d) blockade; and e) exposure through reconnaissance.[48]

Taken together, these naval presence force parameters constitute an argument in favor of using the frequently criticized aircraft carrier task force as the basis for the presence mission. In fact, the requirements for high value, multimission capability, and significant stay-time point to a presence force not unlike that which sought to exercise "suasion" in the Bay of Bengal in the Indo-Pakistani crisis, i.e., a nuclear-powered carrier, escorts, and an amphibious-ready group.

A force structure of the sort outlined by McGruther may not, however, represent a definitive solution of the "visibility and viability" problem outlined by Luttwak: "The *perceived* balance of forces that determines the outcome of 'peacetime' confrontations can only be construed by men in terms of the predicted outcome of putative battle, and it is such predictions that determine political attitudes and, therefore, decisions." Such determinations, he suggests, will reject synthetic force-effectiveness comparisons based on elaborate, quantitative scenarios. Instead, the comparisons will begin with the salient capability data that may be available: gross tonnage levels, the number of ships by classes, aggregate gun and missile power, and so on. . . . Some equipment data of quite critical importance in actual combat may be overlooked or be altogether too intricate for considera- tion. . . . At most "dynamic" variables of sea power [seamanship, main- tenance standards, and sensor/weapon skills under stress] will be sub- sumed under presumed national characteristics.[49]

These considerations have led Luttwak to suggest that a force struc- ture designed primarily for presence and political influence should emphasize visible capabilities over such "invisible" ones as sophisti- cated sensor arrays or data processing capacity. The latter undoubt- edly provide a significant margin of capability in combat scenarios involving the Soviet Union, but, in Luttwak's view, they are simply unnecessary if one's objective is influencing the political elites of small powers.[50]

In the U.S. Navy's view, however, it seems clear that presence, if it is to have political effect, must be linked to meaningful military credibility. That is, presence is ultimately related to the threat and use of military force, and without the capacity to project violence vis-à-vis some political objective the mission of presence becomes problematical. Indeed, from the official perspective of the early 1970s, this apparently inescapable linkage of the political uses of naval force or deterrence and the capacity for projecting force from naval platforms would obviate the need to "choose" between the deterrence and war-fighting missions. Presumably those platforms which serve as war-fighting instruments are equally (indeed, essen- tially) serviceable as instrumentalities of naval presence. Finally, if, as now seems to be the case, one conceives of the strategic de- terrence mission as part of the projection function, then the inter- relationships of the functions of American naval power have been redrawn to emphasize the linkage of conventional and nuclear war.

Admiral Holloway has recently emphasized these continuities between the various points on the spectrum of potential conflict:

"Naval sources are effective across the entire spectrum of warfare, from peacetime presence through crisis management, contingency operations, limited war, major conventional war, limited nuclear war, to general nuclear conflict. Furthermore, naval forces are able to make the transition through these stages with minimum risk of escalation, due to the flexibility of forces in international waters."[51]

At the same time, however, some observers and practitioners are clearly uneasy with the notion that there is in fact no problem with respect to intermission tradeoffs within a force structure oriented toward war-fighting. Admiral Turner has gone so far as to question whether there are not force structure problems resulting from the necessity of carrying out the range of war-fighting tasks themselves. Sea control in Turner's view may require large numbers of highly capable but essentially expendable platforms, whereas projection implies larger aircraft carriers deploying large numbers of attack aircraft as well as amphibious forces:

> The . . . extreme applications of sea control and projection both call for aircraft carriers, but they need not be the same kind of aircraft carrier. In fact a much smaller, cheaper, more limited carrier would do for the sea control function (obviously, the carrier designed for projection would also do nicely for sea control, but it costs you more). . . .
>
> Still another issue that depends on relative emphasis between sea control and projection is attack aircraft. In a sea-control mode, attack aircraft are primarily directed at the enemy's surface ships, and perhaps also against his airfields, to prevent his aircraft from coming out and attacking you. But the attack aircraft would receive far less emphasis under sea control than if the stress were on the projection role. These are the kinds of debate in which we must engage, so as to weigh the balance between these two missions.[52]

The problems of designing a naval force for sea control and projection intersect the question of a presence force structure if one believes as does Turner that presence is a function of the threat of projection *but* that the sea control mission has and will continue to assume greater importance than projection. The conceptual and practical problems would seem to be compounded, of course, if one also accepts the proposition that presence or peacetime deterrence and political influence will be a task increasingly demanded of the United States Navy in the foreseeable future.

A range of alternative force structure designs is, therefore, imaginable. On the one hand, there is a fleet designed to maximize the presence mission with emphasis on "visible" capability. At the other extreme would be a force structure of more comprehensive capability designed to carry out a full range of missions beyond presence or political influence. However, our earlier discussion of the limits of the presence or political influence mission as well as attention to the foreign policy framework within which *any* mission or set of missions for the United States Navy must be conducted suggests that the narrow issue of force structure tradeoffs and mission inter-relationships can be at best inconclusive and is, in a broad policy sense, probably irrelevant.

Control over or influence on the behavior of a target state using naval power seems no more and is probably less successful than with other forms of military power, notwithstanding the frequent use of naval power as a political instrument. It is undoubtedly true, as presence and naval influence theorists such as Luttwak suggest, that the mere presence or increases in levels of naval power have about them an intangible penumbra—what Acheson once described as the "shadow of power"[53]—that serves to influence the behavior of other states in some way. Blechman and Kaplan's work suggests, however, that such influence activity is likely to be more successful when the objective is reinforcing prior behavior rather than changing the behavior of the target. Of course, an important variety of such reinforcement might include reinforcing a predisposition to inaction, i.e., deterrence of behavior not in accord with American interests. Establishing or reinforcing deterrence is an important element in many discussions of the political influence mission of the United States Navy. However, it is difficult to demonstrate that one's general naval presence or one kind of warship versus another was the causal factor in an anticipated reaction on the part of the target resulting in inaction. Indeed, even knowing that one's presence had caused such behavior could only come about *ex post facto* or in the event that deterrence subsequently failed. In any case, the development of sensitive measures of effectiveness of presence or force structure mixes would be extremely difficult at best.

Leaving aside for the moment the irresolvable, what research there is suggests that one cannot cast the shadow of power with military forces unless they constitute a credible symbol of commitment and interest. Naval power has, it has been suggested, certain inherent weaknesses in this regard. Nevertheless, when successfully employed, naval power seems more highly correlated with the actual use of military capability than with its mere presence. This suggests that any force structure contemplated for political influence must encompass a credible projection capacity. Now, if one assumes relatively weak target defenses and the lack of third party intervention or presence, then one might construct a force structure which would look somewhat different than that now employed by the United States Navy. For example, Luttwak's "visible" but perhaps cheaper force structure becomes more plausible. If, however, one accepts—and Luttwak does[54]—that target state defenses will achieve increasing capability through the deployment of point defense systems, larger air forces, or even retaliatory capability through the deployment of cruise missiles and/or fast missile boats, or that third party presence or intervention, i.e., the Soviet Union, is a real or increasing likelihood, then a rather different prospect for a credible force structure emerges. Provisions for the defense of one's platforms against the target's defenses must be available. Furthermore, if one must deal with sophisticated third party intervention of the sort that the Soviets might provide, then the credibility of one's presence becomes increasingly expensive. Indeed, one's force structure begins to assume the character of the sea control/projection forces called for by the force structure planning of the early and mid-1970s.

A forward-deployed fleet required to perform these functions on a routine basis and in a responsive manner must be composed of vessels of considerable sophistication and endurance. Technological sophistication is required in view of the demands imposed by potential threats in three dimensions: air, surface, and subsurface. Further, if naval force is to remain the subtly calibrated mixture of capability described by Holloway, the individual units that comprise the task forces, and the task forces themselves, must be closely integrated by means of sensitive and reliable networks of command and control, not only at a tactical level but also vis-à-vis national command authorities. Finally, if one further requires that these fleets "logistically [be] able to operate worldwide on the high seas without absolute dependence on forward land bases,"[55] then one must also design into one's fleet high levels of unit endurance and provide crews with a variety of amenities not required on ships whose missions do not necessitate sustained semiautonomous forward deployment.

In summary, designing a naval presence force implies the necessity of constructing and maintaining a sizable fleet of expensive vessels. Exactly how large is large enough is, of course, debatable but probably cannot be resolved as long as analysis is fixed on scenario construction and comparison. Only by working back from the demands imposed by one's foreign policy framework can questions of force structure size be approached. Similarly, the specific mix of ships required for both sea control and projection is ultimately a politically determined variable, although, as Admiral Turner has noted, as one's aspirations toward a more and more comprehensive definition of both missions increases, so also, probably, must the richness of a force structure suitable for the more inclusive notions of naval presence. Thus, for example, as one proceeds from a desire for sea control vis-à-vis one's harbors and coastal waters to an attempt to control sea lanes, broader zones of influence, and ultimately a global presence, one's force structure must be characterized by a rather full panoply of ships and aircraft. And, if one's notion of projection includes preventive and reactive presence, amphibious assault, bombardment, tactical air and nuclear strike, the range of ships and aircraft required must be even larger.[56]

Ultimately, however, the issue of force structure and force size appropriate to these tasks cannot be resolved without attention to the foreign policy demands that create the need for naval forces in the first place. Even if consensus could be reached concerning the technical requirements of a presence/political influence navy vs. a sea control/projection navy, decisions concerning which, how many, and what mix of ships to buy and how to deploy them will depend on the range of contingencies that your navy will have to confront. And these contingencies are derived from the answers to broader foreign policy questions having to do with the identification of specific regions and countries in which American interests might depend on some measure of naval power. Unless there is clarity and specification on this level of analysis—about the place, intensity, and scope of American interests—any debate concerning force structure and mission interrelationships must remain frustratingly inconclusive.

Policy Constraints, Missions, and Force Structure

Perhaps the most fundamental determinant of the Navy's conception of its objectives and missions has been the perceived necessity for the forward deployment of American military power in support of global American foreign policy objectives. For more than thirty years, this set of perceptions about the global nature of American interests has been joined with a set of geopolitical imperatives derived from the insular position of the United States to form the rationale for a preeminent Navy. Thus the official Navy eye continues to view the oceans as filled both with obstacles to our foes and opportunities for ourselves; as Admiral Holloway said recently: "It is clear that support of U.S. allies, as well as attacks against the United States, must be overseas operations. In essence, our forward strategy uses the oceans as barriers for our defense and avenues to extend our influence abroad."[57]

Reducing such generalizations to a more manageable degree of specificity has sometimes proved difficult. Events frequently lead to an important skewing of perspective with consequent major effects on priorities and derivative planning guidelines. Nearly a decade of deep military involvement in Southeast Asia resulted, for example, in the deferral of fleet modernization. Furthermore, the political consequences of Vietnam have resulted in some recalculation of the scale of American military deployment in Asia. Nevertheless, constraints imposed by American commitments in East and North Asia have not allowed for any major withdrawal of United States Navy assets in the Western Pacific. A reorientation of Marine Corps thinking is in evidence, but a continuation of an American off-shore presence of impressive magnitude has remained a fixture of naval planning.

The Mansfield Resolutions of the early 1970s and the ruminations of former Joint Chiefs Chairman General George Brown notwithstanding, the commitment of American power in support of NATO and Israel has remained the central element of force planning. The first planning guidelines of the Carter administration have underscored this point, although ambiguity concerning the Navy is now evident. Thus reports concerning five-year guidance for the military services have indicated that NATO contingencies remain most important: "Our near-term objective is to assure that NATO could not be overwhelmed in the first few weeks of a blitzkrieg war, and we will invest and spend our resources preferentially to that end. . . . When that assurance is reasonably in hand, we will turn our attention to what additional capability, if any, NATO might need to be able to fight for at least as long as the Warsaw Pact."[58]

Preoccupation with the initial days of a NATO-Warsaw Pact conflict could conceivably reduce in importance the Navy's traditional point of departure for force structure planning, i.e., that sea control in the Atlantic is the most fundamental mission of the United States Navy. Moreover, control has been conceived as involving more than control of sea lines of communication. It has also involved maintenance of the capacity to "protect the terminal ends of our essential sea lines of communication and our remote national interest."[59] In short, naval power must exercise simultaneous control of the areas required or potentially required for the transit of military power and resupply and also those areas at the end of sea lines of communication that might become the staging area for the second major cluster of missions, the projection of power. If, however, sustained combat with the Warsaw Pact countries is to be reduced to a secondary consideration, the heretofore self-evident basis for determining the role, size, and composition of the Navy must be reopened.

The other major contingency to which the military services are urged to attend by the Secretary of Defense concerns potential conflict in the Persian Gulf area: "Events in the Persian Gulf could soften the glue that binds the alliance as surely as could an imbalance of military force across the inter-German border. . . . But," he has noted, "we are as yet unsure of the utility of U.S. military power in Persian Gulf contingencies. . . ." To deal with this "half" of the overall "1½" war planning Brown has urged the organization of a quick strike force composed of a Marine division with its air wing and two augmented Army divisions;[60] the Navy's role is less evident.

The questions raised by such planning guidelines are myriad. How will such forces be moved into the crisis area? In the event of sustained combat, support seems likely to fall to the Navy, but for how long? To what extent can indigenous naval forces—e.g., the Iranians—be depended on? What are the implications of the "half war" involving U.S. forces *against* the Iranians now directed by a "radical" regime? Where should U.S. Navy assets be located if the Soviets achieve a secure naval base in the area? What are the implications for the demilitarization of the Indian Ocean so much talked about during the first year of the Carter administration? Does or should the planning area subsumed under the Persian Gulf extend to the Red and Arabian Seas and their littoral? Are the naval forces committed to these contingencies to be autonomous or "surged" from the Second, Sixth, or Seventh Fleets? If the latter, what does this imply concerning American policy in Indonesia and the Philippines?

In the face of such complexities, it is understandable that a consensus position concerning force requirements has not yet emerged. In the past, when confronted with such ambiguity, Navy planners could always assume that they must prepare to meet the demands of a globalist foreign policy requiring forward deployment around a European/Mediterranean center of gravity. Under such circumstances, force planning has tended toward meeting the worst-case war-fighting contingencies, i.e., projection and latterly sea control (war-fighting) especially with respect to a Soviet adversary in the North Atlantic. Presumably if one's force structure could deal with this set of contingencies, it could deal with those of lesser intensity including presence and political influence.

Now, however, it appears that the Carter administration will not allow the Navy the kind of resources necessary to continue planning in this manner. Indeed, reports were circulating in early 1978 that the Office of the Secretary of Defense had challenged the Navy's traditional insistence on naval "superiority" as the basis of its force posture and was insisting on a concept of "adequacy" for future planning purposes.[61] When coupled with the initial budgetary decisions taken by the Carter administration—cancellation of the CVN-71 and CSGN and deferral of the purchase of more F-14s in favor of the F-18—it would certainly appear that the framework of assumptions within which naval planning and the definition of missions that has obtained for the last decade is undergoing reexamination.

It need not follow, of course, that presence or the use of naval power as a political as distinct from a war-fighting instrument will automatically move to the top of a new hierarchy of roles and naval tasks. Pending decisions on the future of small-decked aircraft carriers, the Navy's force structure will remain, for the foreseeable future, one built around the assumptions of naval "superiority," war-fighting, sea control, protection of sea lines of communication (SLOC), and projection. Some naval theorists have nevertheless taken a difficult first step in developing a paradigm of naval power somewhat removed from the mainstream conception that has obtained since World War II. By their own account, however, much of the U.S. Navy remains skeptical if for no other reason than that advanced by McNulty that

> those same new realities which fostered the ascendancy of a conflict avoidance or deterrent national strategy have also set the stage for a basic conflict between the desires of the strategist and the values of

the warrior. It is truly difficult for men in uniform, essentially un-schooled in the nuances of diplomatic activities, to place much con-fidence in Naval Presence as an alternative to the possession of superior war-fighting capabilities which have demonstrably kept the peace since 1948. . . . the belief that "to subdue the enemy without fighting is the acme of skill," has seldom found favor in the hearts of those who conceive of themselves as warriors, charged with the military security of the state.[62]

Furthermore, in the bureaucratic struggle that is now underway, it is not likely that the "warriors" would willingly back away from their traditional values in favor of a presence argument lest they be perceived as weakening and therefore be pressed even harder by advocates of a no-growth navy.[63]

In the final analysis, however, the presence or political influence emphasis might well prove inappropriate to what some students of world politics envision for the future. That is, the articulation and refinement of the naval presence mission may be but another ex-ample of military planning more suitable for an era—the simple, bipolar, "rationalized" conjoining of force and diplomacy of the Cold War—that is closing, rather than for a new era that may soon be upon us. For a theory of presence suited to an age of limited threats and limited war may find itself contending with an evolving political and technological environment which may confound the meaningful execution of the presence mission.[64] For example, it used to be true that a task force could be inserted into coastal waters unopposed and present the leadership of the militarily inferior state with an obvious excuse of pleading *force majeure*. Now, however, a minor state could have the capacity to injure severely very expen-sive ships with a relatively cheap volley of precision-guided weap-ons. At a minimum, technological change and proliferation of mili-tary capability complicate the projection of power and thereby undermine credibility as a political threat. Further, the time may soon be at hand when the once free movement of a task force will be inhibited by the closure of the ocean through the extension of coastal state sovereignty under new legal regimes for the oceans.

And, finally, the contemporary reality of an expanded Soviet naval counterpresence complicates the American exercise of naval force short of war. We will examine these problems—problems complicating *any* paradigm of naval power and its use—in the next chapter.

CHAPTER FOUR

An Uncertain International Future

OUR SURVEY of United States Navy missions suggests that the successful application of naval power, whether for sea control, projection, or presence, rests on a number of assumptions concerning the naval environment. Three assumptions seem most significant:

(1) An abundance of United States naval assets;
(2) A relative predominance of United States naval power understood as the capacity of the United States to maintain and/or project significant naval units virtually any place on the globe; and
(3) A relatively benign or, at worst, neutral global order and/or ocean legal regime which provides for and facilitates relatively unencumbered movement and manipulation of one's naval assets.

Such an environment allows the relatively easy movement of variable levels of naval force in and out of areas in which active presence, sea control, or projection is or may be desired. At the same time, routine or latent presence could be maintained. Thus, the psychological prerequisites of keeping international order—the perception of a potentially actualized naval power—are husbanded in contemporary contemplation of the future of the Navy. But only so long as the ocean environment remains neutral and/or American power is predominant are the apparently unique attributes of naval power manifest. In other words, the unique attractiveness of naval power as a means for maintaining a regulated international environment favorable to American interests is in large measure a function of the structure of world and domestic politics and world balance of naval power that has obtained for the last twenty-five years. Recently, however, intimations of a very different environment have emerged. Moreover, all of the preconditions for the successful application of sea power as noted above are brought into varying degrees of question by these changes.

The Bear and the Eagle at Sea

Any assessment of the likelihood that the United States Navy can maintain the necessary margin of superiority to exercise effective presence or its other missions must address the constraints imposed by the major potential adversary of the United States—the Soviet Union. Debate as to the size, capability, and missions of the Soviet Navy now occupies a major segment of the literature on modern sea power and its use.[1] Opinion concerning the threat posed by Soviet naval forces includes claims that "today, the Soviet Union can boast the world largest and most modern surface navy; the largest and most modern ocean research and fishing fleets; a potent naval air arm; and one of the most advanced shipbuilding industries in existence."[2] Norman Polmar has concluded that this capability qualifies the Soviet Navy as a "supernavy in every sense of the term; quantity, quality of forces, and operations. . . . Thus, a Soviet Navy rebuilt in the 1950s and again in the 1960s, probably with the purpose of fighting the United States and NATO, has provided the USSR with a fleet-in-being that can be employed directly in support of political and economic goals without having to fire a shot. The Soviets have learned that a ship built to sink another has [many other] uses, while still retaining a potent combat capability."[3] Admiral Worth Bagley, (USN, Ret.) and former Vice-Chief of United States Naval Operations, has offered the following gloomy comparison of the Soviet and American navies:

> In the past fifteen years, the Soviet Union has built its 1,000 ship navy; since 1969 the United States has reduced its 960 ships to 477. Numerical balance is not the only measure of relative strength, but the Soviets have achieved greater flexibility. There are three nuclear-powered cruise missile submarines for every American carrier; one cruise missile and two torpedo diesel submarines for every two American missile ships; an advantage of at least 20 percent in number of American attack submarines and, if each side positions for the anti-SSBN option, two-thirds of the Soviet attack force would be unopposed by other submarines; and land-based naval bomber aircraft have a 25 percent numerical advantage over American carrier interceptors.[4]

Finally, a recent Chief of Naval Operations emphasizes that "In assessing the maritime balance, it is more important to focus on trends than raw statistics." Predictably, he does not find the "trends" favorable to the United States:

> Three points deserve emphasis. First, over the past decade, Soviet naval construction has progressed at a rate four times that of the United States. Second, the growing Soviet Fleet increasingly has been making its presence felt in areas more distant from the Soviet Union. Third, the dependence of the United States and its allies on the sea lines of communication will continue to be more crucial than that of the Soviet Union and its allies. Our dependence upon these sea lines of communication is especially significant when one considers that a sea denial capability requires a much smaller investment than the sea control capability required to defend against it.
> . . . Today, we retain a slim margin of superiority with respect to the Soviet threat in those scenarios involving our most vital national interests. The concern is for the future, because the trend line in United States Navy capability has been on a downward slope.[5]

On the other hand, some observers, most notably perhaps Michael MccGwire and his associates,[6] have suggested that although the Soviet Navy has been required by Soviet political leadership to assume a greater "foreign policy" role, its capacity to do so while simultaneously carrying out its war-related missions is severely strained. In contrast to Polmar's and Bagley's image of the Soviet Union as the dominant sea power today, MccGwire and his group take note of constrained shipyard capacity, limited blue water support ability, marginal air cover, consequent heavy dependence upon politically uncertain overseas basing, and the prospect that significant Soviet fleet expansion is uncertain in the future.[7] Indeed, Weinland and MccGwire suggest that Admiral Gorshkov's series of articles, "Navies in War and Peace,"[8] rather than heralding a new prominence for Soviet sea power in the Soviet Union's arsenal of politicomilitary instrumentalities, was in fact an only partially successful plea to defend the limited gains made by Soviet sea power advocates over the course of the 1960s. MccGwire concludes:

> There are no indications that the Navy's relative standing within the political leadership has improved, and if membership of the Central Committee is any guide, Ground Force domination of the military leadership has increased progressively since 1961. Therefore, one suspects that Gorshkov's strictures will fall on deaf ears and that the political leadership will not choose to increase the Navy's relative share of resources.[9]

Recently disclosed Department of Defense comparisons of the United States and Soviet fleets support MccGwire's conclusions and reveal that even during the period of escalating Soviet fleet size, the United States was outbuilding the Soviets in those classes of ships larger than 3,600 tons, and will probably continue to do so for the foreseeable future (see Figure 1).[10] Similarly, while Bagley's analysis of the current balance of submarine strengths is not inaccurate, it obscures the fact that the great bulk of Soviet submarines are nonnuclear, a type of attack submarine that the United States Navy does not even build. Moreover, since the mid-1960s, United States nuclear attack submarine construction has outstripped that of the Soviet Union and will continue to do so throughout the 1970s (see Figure 2).

NUMBER OF SHIPS

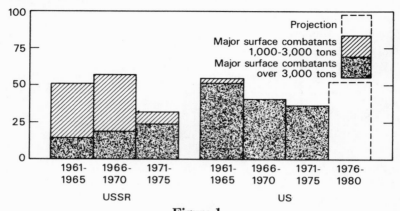

Figure 1.

Production of Major Surface Combatants

Source: "The Trend in the Naval Balance," A Fact Sheet by Representative Les Aspin (Washington, D.C., July 1976), p. 12.

NUMBER OF SUBMARINES

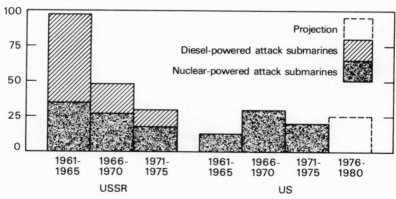

Figure 2.

Production of Attack Submarines, 1961–1975

Source: "The Trend in the Naval Balance," p. 11.

Recent projections concerning Soviet shipyard capacity and construction rates suggest that with the exception of submarines, the Soviets will do well to maintain replacement rates for a navy that now confronts block obsolescence problems as severe as those confronted by the United States Navy in the late 1960s and early 1970s.[11] Indeed, by 1974 the relative modernity of the two fleets had begun to shift in the direction of the United States Navy (see Table 2).

Table 2

Ages of the U.S. and Soviet Active Fleets*

Category	1968		1974	
	U.S.	Sov.	U.S.	Sov.
Submarines	12.6	10.1	9.9	9.5
Large Surface Combatants	18.0	10.4	11.9	13.1
Small Combatants (patrol and minewarfare included)	13.5	7.7	11.2	11.0
Amphibious	18.7	5.7	7.6	7.4
	16.4	8.4	10.8	10.4

*Excludes aircraft carriers.

Source: U.S., Congress, Senate, Hearings before the Armed Service Committee, *Fiscal Year 1976 and July–September 1976 Transition Period Authorization for Military Procurement, Research and Development, and Active Duty, Selected Reserve and Civilian Personnel Strengths, Part 2—Authorizatons,* 94th Congress, 1st Session, 1975, p. 798.

Even more striking, however, are the trends in retirements for both navies projected for the 1980s. In the case of both major surface combatants and attack submarines, the Soviet Navy is on the verge of block obsolescence.[12]

Finally, the United States Navy's superiority in naval aircraft remains significant and seems likely to remain so with the prospects that the new F-18 and F-14 will be unchallenged by anything the Soviet Navy could conceivably mount on its helicopter-V/STOL carriers (see Figure 3). Furthermore, the deployment of the *Harpoon* missile in the late 1970s and early 1980s could well result in American superiority in an area of naval armament previously dominated by the Soviets—anti-surface ship missiles.

NUMBER OF PLANES

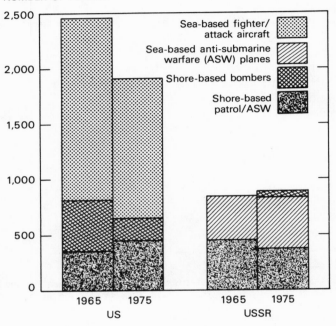

Figure 3.

Naval Aircraft

Source: "The Trend in the Naval Balance," p. 13.

Official Department of Defense views on the relationship of the two fleets are predictably cautious. However, former Secretary Schlesinger in his last posture statement took note of the mission asymmetry of the two fleets—"the United States and its allies emphasize sea control and projection of power ashore. . . . The Soviet

Union, at least for now, stresses defense against United States power projection efforts and interdiction of United States and allied military and economic support shipping on the open oceans."[13] Schlesinger was obviously cognizant of the fundamental differences between the Soviet and American naval force structures: "Once one removes the mission asymmetry and measures the balance, it becomes clear that the naval forces of the Soviet Union and its allies are not generally superior to those of the United States and its allies, and that this should be perceived by well-informed observers."[14] Nevertheless, he was particularly concerned about Soviet antiship capability and the strong Soviet potential for attacks on United States and allied shipping. But even here he concluded that, notwithstanding significant shipping losses resulting from a Soviet antishipping campaign, "the net effect on the U.S. and allied war effort would not be crippling."[15]

More recently, Admiral Holloway has suggested that the U.S. carrier force will be the primary target of Soviet forces in most conceivable war-fighting scenarios. Significantly, the primary source of that threat is not seen as the Soviet surface navy: "The most serious individual threat to our forces would be the submarine. It is, by its nature, difficult to deal with. Next in priority, and logically I think, is the aircraft. The combined subsurface-air threat is especially challenging. The surface force, again by its nature, is easier to handle. But, again, probably none of these individual threats will be encountered in isolation."[16] While recognizing the development of "naval support of foreign policy" as a "new and evolving role for the Soviet Navy," Admiral Holloway has concluded that the primary missions of the Soviet Navy remain oriented toward "defending the shores of the USSR in depth." The "main thrust" of the Soviet Navy is therefore ranked as to:

a. deploy naval forces in an attempt to counter the U.S. sea-based strategic nuclear deterrent,

b. encircle the flanks of her potential continental adversaries in order to deny them reinforcement and resupply from the United States, and

c. use naval forces to extend her political influence, especially in the Third World.[17]

Thus the official assessment of the Soviet naval threat is not far removed from the summary provided by Barry Blechman, formerly of the Brookings Institution:

> Generally, and with the exception of strategic submarines, the Soviet Navy does not appear to be designed to project the Soviet Union's power into distant oceans but to defend the security and interests of the USSR—by preventing attacks on its homeland and by limiting the role of the United States and other Western powers in regions close to Soviet shores, notably the Middle East. The Soviet Navy's past building programs, its exercises, its peacetime deployments, and Soviet military doctrine all support the assessment that the primary emphasis in Soviet naval evolution has been and is likely to remain oriented to the accomplishment of these missions.[18]

How this assessment coincides with the maintenance of a viable presence mission is open to question. However, there has been no change in the situation described by former Secretary of Defense Schlesinger: "As far as peacetime naval presence is concerned, aggregate Soviet activity increased sharply in the late 1960's but now appears to have stabilized somewhat below the overall U.S. level. . . . U.S. forces tend to have a greater surge capability to most theaters of primary interest to the United States and its allies."[19]

Before concluding, however, that on balance the Soviet Navy does not constitute a decisive constraint on the exercise of U.S. naval missions, one should take careful note of Blechman and Kaplan's general findings on the use of military force as a political instrument as well as the specific caveat entered by most observers—that of the Middle East. Blechman has underscored the special position of the Eastern Mediterranean in Soviet and U.S. naval deployments.[20] Thus, while the more extreme statements of alarm concerning the development and capability of the Soviet Navy are probably overdrawn, the Soviet Union's ability to move naval forces into crisis areas[21] does not augur well for the unfettered exercise of naval suasion. In addition, the apparent severe limitations on Soviet missile reload capacity noted by most observers, including Department of Defense analysts,[22] further confounds the necessarily close calculations associated with the exercise of sea control, projection, or presence in a competitive environment. The structure and dynamics of naval deterrence in the presence of escalating naval forces are, at best, complicated. The probability that the Soviets are limited in their war-fighting options, i.e., to striking first, imparts a dangerous fragility to the exercise. Nor, for that matter, can one take much comfort from the fact that the Soviet Union has shown a capacity for escalating its naval presence in a part of the world characterized by a large and potent U.S. naval presence and a surfeit of opportunities for volatile and escalating crisis. Of course, none of this has precluded the exercise of naval presence in the area in the past. But with the advent of significant Soviet naval capability and will to use it in the region, the mission has become increasingly difficult to fulfill. One suspects that it will be no less so in the future.

In conclusion, whereas Admiral Holloway may be correct in contending that the United States Navy's capability was once on a downward slope, it seems questionable whether this is any longer the case. Indeed, both navies may well have reached something of a plateau, departure from which will be difficult to effect. Nevertheless, the Soviet navy is now and will continue to be a constraint on the exercise of United States naval power although the nature and magnitude of the constraint will undoubtedly be less clear cut than many recent comparisons of the fleets and their futures have led us to believe.

The Strategic Relationship at Sea

There are still other complex considerations which bear on the future uses of the Soviet-American strategic relationship at sea and the evolution of international society. The nuclear deterrent relationship between the Soviet Union and the United States has shaped a large part of the structure of international society. Nonetheless, recent improvements in antisubmarine warfare technology such as the Moored Surveillance System (MSS) and the large surveillance array systems (SAS) have begun to elicit concern with respect to the stability of the mutual deterrent relationship at sea. The Navy's spending on antisubmarine warfare has risen significantly in the last few years.[23] One public study completed by Frost and Sullivan, a market analysis firm, has placed the growth in Navy ASW spending at about $2 billion per year in 1975 over what was being spent in 1972. Much of this spending has been directed at improving the tactical antisubmarine warfare capability of the Navy. Recent analysis by Kosta Tsipis for the Stockholm International Peace Research Institute[24] reached the conclusion that the use of existing area-defense ASW capability might well, under some circumstances, contribute to a destabilization of the mutual deterrent relationship:

> The U.S. area-defense ASW tactics which can support a damage-limiting counter-SLBM strike, and the attempted trailing of Polaris submarines by Soviet SSNs, contain a germinal capability for ASSW [anti-strategic] submarine which may not only raise doubts in the minds of strategic analysts and politicians about the survivability of the SLBM forces, but also has already created the operational capability in both nations to support a damage-limiting attack against the SSBN fleet of the other. Since a first-strike attack as a credible threat to the integrity of the sea-based deterrent of the two countries is not supported by existing or even envisioned technologies, the interaction (both political and technical) of area-defense tactical ASW with damage-limiting ASSW emerges as the major threat to the strategic stability inherent in the posture of mutual deterrence.[25]

Neither Tsipis nor any other observer feels that this capability has profoundly affected the deterrent relationship. Nonetheless, the potentiality for problems is now on the distant horizon and this has raised, in turn, the question of whether there should not be some attempt to anticipate possible threats to mutual deterrence. Two courses of action are generally proposed. First, there is the simple expedient now being pursued by the Soviet Union and United States of developing longer-range submarine-launched ballistic missiles, such as the C-4 and the Soviets' SS-N-8, and deploying them on better strategic submarines such as Trident or the Soviets' *Delta*-class submarine. This response allows for close-to-home deployment with no loss of targeting ability. Indeed, the Soviets seem already to have taken this step in that few of their *Delta*-class boats are reported deployed outside the Barents Sea.[26]

A second recourse involves some measure of international agreement to constrain the tactical and strategic ASW capability now available or under development. Tsipis summarizes some of the steps which might be taken:

> (a) restricting the appertures (for passive) and frequencies and power levels (for active) ocean-surveillance arrays so that their capability is restricted to coastal monitoring, for example about 1000 km. (b) prohibiting the implantation of large ocean surveillance arrays in mid-oceanic regions: (c) prohibiting the development and deployment of surface ships or aircraft capable of tracking submarines uninterruptedly for long periods of time; and (d) setting an upper limit to the ration of the number of SSNs of one country to the number of SSBNs of the other.[27]

Tsipis has few illusions concerning the asymmetric effect of such arrangements on the United States. They would require removal of area defense systems already deployed by the United States. In addition, it should be noted that to the extent that these tactical capabilities are linked to the preoccupation of the United States Navy with sea control vis-à-vis sea lines of communication to support a European and/or Mediterranean presence-force projection contingency, such constraints on ASW might well be impossible to accept short of a fundamental shift in American policy in Europe and the Mediterranean. Similarly, constraints on surface ship and aircraft deployment will undoubtedly prove difficult to agree on, given the thrust of the Navy's current shipbuilding program.

SSN-SSBN deployment ratios could be a useful point of departure. Even more than with the SALT negotiations, however, the establishment of such ratios will involve complex, perhaps prohibitive, definitional questions. In the case of SALT, the negotiations concerning systems "common to both sides" were facilitated by the fact that ICBMs and SLBMs were generally perceived by both sides as existing for a singular reason—retaliation in the event of nuclear war. Attack submarines (SSN), on the other hand, can and do serve functions other than SSBN. For a major dimension of the SSN's mission profile involves anti-surface ship missions. Thus negotiating SSN-SSBN ratios is analogous to the extremely difficult issue of Forward Based Systems (FBS) in SALT—an issue not yet satisfactorily resolved and probably unresolvable within the context of negotiations confined to "strategic" weapons and weapons platforms.

Unlike the case of surface naval force, technological change—though it raises disquieting distant prospects—has not yet radically affected the strategic role of naval force. Nevertheless, the objective of a secure and stable deterrent relationship seems attainable, paradoxically, only by continuing the potentially destabilizing process of further weapons development and deployment. As Kosta Tsipis has noted: "While it would be desirable to insure the stability for all the SLBM forces by . . . a series of arms-limitation agreements, it appears that the only realistic way to achieve this highly desirable result is, ironically, to introduce a new weapon, the 7,000–10,000 km submarine ballistic missile."[28]

On the other hand, related technological change such as tactical cruise missiles and other precision-guided antiship weapons might well encourage escalation and instability in any contemplated future Soviet-American antagonism. For a logical use of such weapons would be as nuclear-tipped, relatively low-yield delivery systems, targeted against ships with particularly sophisticated electronic defenses or heavily compartmentalized hull designs. Land targets may also become logical targets for small nuclear strikes. As John P. Craven writes in a recent *Adelphi Paper*,[29] "Logistic choke points will make inviting targets, their characteristics being their invulnerability to conventional and vulnerability to nuclear weapons, and their existence being crucial to the outcome of the conflict." In addition, Soviet surface ships seem designed with little reload capacity—as Admiral Gorshkov puts it, for the "battle for the first salvo."[30] These operational features of Soviet ship design combined with defensive Soviet naval doctrine and the confined basing of the

Soviet fleet encourage the Soviets to plan for a quick "surge" through selected "choke points" before U.S. naval forces can close them. This need for quick egress, speedy dispersion, and the necessity of striking first may, in part, encourage a Soviet plan for a preemptive strike.

Naval Parity and the Future

The Soviet-American relationship at sea has reached an especially uncertain and dangerous point. Whereas the strategic relationship has been viewed for some time as the basis of a stable mutual deterrence, technological change threatens dangerous instability by the end of the century. Moreover, the apparently irreversible desire for war-fighting or intrawar deterrent capacity for strategic arsenals seems likely to hasten the search for antisubmarine technologies especially if the SSBN and/or SSN become platforms for hard target killing ballistic or cruise missiles. In the absence of naval arms control agreements designed to anticipate the current thrust of strategic naval research and development, the 1970s may well be viewed in the future as a "golden age" of stable deterrence.

The interaction of the Soviet and American surface fleets seems no less a source of concern for the future. Leaving aside the heated but often inconclusive debate about who is "ahead," it is clear that the Soviet Navy has now achieved a kind of situational parity with the United States Navy. That is, although it probably cannot claim equality with the U.S. Navy on a global basis (the Soviets seem unable to forward-deploy and sustain several blue water fleets simultaneously), it clearly does have the capacity to maintain or "surge" roughly equivalent fleets on a regional basis, especially in the Mediterranean and perhaps in the North Atlantic as well.

It is difficult to foresee exactly how these fleets would engage one another in either of these areas for any length of time at a subnuclear level. The U.S. Navy's recent preoccupation with war-fighting capability on a ship-to-ship basis implies a belief that such conflict could be confined to the sea and to conventional or at most "tactical" nuclear weaponry. However, the lack of air cover for the Soviet fleet suggests that the Soviets would be forced to use their land-based naval air capability (e.g., the "Backfire") fairly early on in such conflict. Under such circumstances one wonders whether American commanders would forego retaliatory or even preemptive attacks on the land bases of such aircraft notwithstanding the escalatory implications of such a response.

In sum, the "tactical" or "limited war" engagements of the two fleets are hard to visualize outside a strategic or general war framework. The Soviet Union has achieved, in short, the capacity to take hostile contacts with the United States Navy over the threshold of nuclear war. Indeed, the present configuration and limitations of their naval capability make such escalation increasingly likely. In some measure, therefore, the *political* utility of U.S. naval power is constrained when compelled to interact with Soviet naval power in part, ironically, because of Russia's limitations in her war-fighting alternatives. Thus, the mere presence of Soviet naval power complicates and indirectly constrains American initiative and options. And to the extent that the Soviet Union has now developed a presence navy, the flexibility, visibility, and universality of American naval power, both with respect to the Soviet Union and to other powers, have been diminished.

Finally, it is not self-evident how the political and military leverage once available through American sea power can be resurrected. The Navy's proposal for a 600-ship fleet seems unlikely to become a reality. According to a recent report by the bipartisan Members of Congress for Peace through Law, even if the most optimistic assumptions concerning congressional appropriations, current procurement schedules, shipyard availability, and retirement levels were granted (these were U.S. Navy projections), the Navy could expect no more than 550 ships by 1985.[31] Moreover, even if one assumes procurement budgets allowing the authorization of 45 new ships a year, constraints imposed by shipyard availability and manpower shortages resulting in delivery delays would conspire against a Navy of much more than 514 ships by 1985. Finally, the report concluded with an assessment that "would take into account the multitude of pressures that hold the Navy's shipbuilding budget in check." These constraints are summarized from the report as follows:

These pressures come from the Office of the Secretary of Defense, from the Office of Management and Budget, and from the Congress. The Navy's 35-ships-per-year target for FY78 to FY80 could cost $8–9 billion per year in constant fiscal year 1976 dollars, which would be about twice the size of the congressionally approved FY76 shipbuilding budget (about $4 billion). This $8–9 billion figure would also be well above Navy shipbuilding budgets of the previous 5 years which have averaged about $4 billion (FY76 dollars). If experience is any guide, the Navy's budget requests will be substantially trimmed. A more likely occurrence is that shipbuilding authorizations will probably stabilize at about the present level of $4 billion (i.e., about 23 ships per year).[32]

In sum, this "constrained budget" projection would envision the fleet size of the U.S. Navy stabilizing over the next decade at or even slightly below its projected 1976 level of about 500 ships. Table 3 summarizes the Members of Congress for Peace through Law Projections based on: (1) Navy assumptions in 1975; (2) unlimited budgets with shipyard production constraints; (3) a constrained budget/constrained production projection; and (4) a "pessimistic" projection incorporating both budgetary and nonbudgetary constraints with the higher retirement rate (25–30 ships noted by former Secretary of the Navy Middendorf). The initial rescission and budget decisions along with the reported force structure planning guidelines of the Carter administration make it likely that the MCPL's constrained budget/production projections will be a somewhat closer representation of the Navy's future force levels than the Navy's 600-ship dream fleet. Moreover, with a fleet of around 500 ships the basic mission recently ascribed to the 600-ship Navy—"to assure our simultaneous control of all ocean areas adjoining the Eurasian Continent,"[33]—will have to be scaled down.

In conclusion, the United States in its naval relationship with the Soviet Union now finds itself in a situation not unlike that which developed at the strategic level in the 1960s. In the case of strategic weapons and now naval power, the Soviet Union achieved a measure of rough parity. In retrospect, it is not clear how, given the nature of the Soviet-American interaction during the 1950s and 1960s and the scope of American commitments and domestic constraints during this period, such a situation could have been

Table 3
MCPL Aggregate Fleet Projections FY75-FY85

Categories		Projections		
	USN	Unlimited Budget/ Constrained Production	Constrained Budget/ Constrained Production	Pessimistic Projection*
Fleet Size End FY75	496	496	496	496
Ships Added FY76-FY80	87	65	65	65
Ships Retired FY76-FY80	93	93	93	125
Fleet Size End FY80	490	468	468	436
Ships Added FY81-FY85	157**	138**	114**	114**
Ships Retired FY81-FY85	92	92	92	125
Fleet Size End FY85	555	514	490	425

*Constrained budget, constrained production, high retirement (25-30 ships/ year).

**With 6-year lag between authorizat:n and delivery and constraints notes, this is sum FY75-FY79 authorizations.

Source: Members of Congress for Peace through Law, "The Feasibility of a 600-ship Fleet" (prepared by Congressman Les Aspin), *Congressional Record-House*, vol. 21, no. 147 (October 2, 1975), pp. H9450-H9453, 94th Congress, 1st Session.

avoided. It is even less clear how a continuation of the present situation can be escaped. "So far, the super-powers have not engaged in the kind of tightly-locked naval race into which Wilhelmian Germany and Great Britain were driven before World War I," observes Johan Holst.[34] However, a return to a potentially crushing American lead in naval power would be unacceptable to the Soviets and would likely fuel an attempt by them to match the effort of the United States.

This prospect of competitive and ultimately inconclusive fleet expansions suggests the necessity of beginning immediately the search for alternative futures. Precisely such a search was initiated with respect to strategic weapons when a similar future seemed likely. Unfortunately, it is likely, given the pronounced mission, fleet, and technological asymmetries which characterize the Soviet and American navies that naval arms control agreements will be even more difficult to achieve than the present fragile strategic arms regime. Nevertheless, such a course seems no less promising than a continuation of the present interaction, which seems to point toward an even more dangerous and constrained mutual relationship and a diminished capacity to deal creatively with the broader changes at work in the international system.

The New International Order and the Future of U.S. Naval Power

Academic, "official," and journalistic writings are now preoccupied with the problem of defining and understanding an elusive set of "new forces" in world politics, variously characterized as "interdependence" or "transnationalism." Many would concur with Seyom Brown's judgment that:

> The weakening of [the old international system] gives other bases of political community—ethnicity, religion, social class, economic function, generation—more opportunity to assert themselves and to vie for the loyalty of individuals. . . . The resulting incoherence in the world's political structure is likely to be profoundly inadequate to the tasks

of global management required to assure the healthy survival of the human species.[35]

The varieties of this "incoherence" are numerous, but include the probability of changes in the international legal regime for the oceans, the emergence of terrorism as an instrumentality of "the other bases of political community" in the new international system, significant technological change, and the possibility that the defensive capability of even small coastal states will increase. In addition to the Soviet presence, the United States Navy must chart its future course somewhere within these interactive changes.

The Enclosure of the Great Commons?

If there has been a structural element that has seemed in the past quite constant and predictable—indeed, the very foundation of the claims made for the uniqueness of naval power—it has been the notion that the oceans were "international," that they were "free." Admiral Holloway, for example, like so many other commentators on the use of naval power, has linked the unique quality of naval power with "freedom of the seas":

> There are special advantages and broad options inherent in the employment of naval forces that make them uniquely valuable to the national command authorities. Naval forces have the organic capability to respond to contingencies or crisis situations worldwide with the precise type and magnitude of force necessary to achieve a given objective, from the classic show of force, through landing of troops, to strategic nuclear attack.
> Freedom of the sea has long been a principle highly valued by seafaring nations, and one almost universally recognized and accepted. Because of the international character of the sea, several benefits accrue to naval forces. . . .[36]

But, as Elizabeth Young has argued recently,[37] we may be moving away from the traditional doctrines of *mare liberum* toward an incrementally established system of *mare clausum* based on twelve-mile territorial seas that close important straits and two-hundred-mile Exclusive Economic Zones within which some measure of sovereignty is enforced. This process of closing Mahan's "great commons" may come with decisive suddenness through a United Nations Law of the Sea Conference; or, as seems more likely, more slowly and less orderly as coastal states gradually develop technological and economic bases (through, for example, association with multinational corporations) for exploiting the oceans and seabeds. In any event it is now conceivable that:

> The great navies will find their traditional roaming of the open seas, "showing the flag" in their interest, constrained, psychologically where not physically, by the multitude of new jurisdictional boundaries. The rights of foreign naval vessels within boundaries of quite unfamiliar texture . . . will need establishing not only by theoretical definition, in terms of international convention, but also by subjection to all the normative pressures of practice and experience.[38]

The openness of the "great common" is of course the basis of the purported uniqueness of naval power—its flexibility and universality—which is in turn one of the necessary conditions for conceiving and undertaking most naval missions. If, however, a naval force is no longer "highly maneuverable" or does *not* operate in an "international" medium and *does* need to be very concerned "with violating sovereign territory," has not one of the key features that make the naval force *most* appropriate to the conditions of contemporary world politics been removed?

Avoidance of the closure of the seas and oceans to the free movement of naval vessels and aircraft has been a primary objective of U.S. negotiators at the Law of the Sea Conferences. Indeed, the United States had succeeded by the end of the Ford administration in expanding the prevailing, somewhat constrained concept of "innocent passage" to a much broader and less restrictive notion of "unimpeded transit" which would allow the free transit of warships and would not require permission for overflight and the surfacing of submarines.[39] The United States clearly has a great deal at stake in an outcome of the Law of the Sea Conference that would result in an orderly—though permissive—legal regime. Thus John Norton Moore, former Chairman of the NSC Interagency Task Force on the Law of the Sea, has observed, "Law, not anarchy, will best serve man's future in the oceans. The real problems of nations that make this negotiation difficult will not disappear if we do not succeed; they will become worse."[40] However, by the end of 1977 conflict between the Group of 77 and the industrialized states on the question of resource control and exploitation had deadlocked the Law of the Sea Conference, with many in the United States urging unilateral action to insure U.S. advantages in exploiting the seabeds.[41] Indeed, some were prepared to forego a comprehensive agreement altogether in favor of "mini-treaties,"[42] notwithstanding the fears that "bilateral negotiation or forced transit by the powerful maritime nations until a right of transit is assured would be extremely costly, if not impossible, because of the number and location of the areas through which the maritime countries would want to assure military and commercial transit."[43] Hence, the future of the legal regime of the oceans as it affects American naval power remains unclear. While not necessarily portending a future of "smash and grab" or radical constraining of U.S. strategic interests,[44] the heretofore predictable and benign ocean legal environment seems headed for a future of "unfamiliar texture."

The possibility that the legal regime of the oceans will change significantly in the next few decades is a reflection of deeper changes in the structure and dynamics of international political and economic affairs. Among the potentially unpleasant manifestations of the emergence of what some have referred to as a "new world order" are those recently outlined by Robert W. Tucker.[45] In Tucker's view, lower level and regionally focused conflict will likely increase as Third World countries, in control of raw materials essential to the developed world, militantly try to exploit whatever advantages they possess. Tucker feels that the situation is exacerbated because of ambivalence toward the use of force on the part of the developed nations, which fear the costs of force, as well as the risk of escalation. In sum, "interdependence" may well come to represent a kind of fractious and conflictual international immobility. As Tucker despairingly concludes: "Even if one accepts the view of an over-riding interdependence occurring at the expense of the state, the prospect of a growing disjunction between power and order is not thereby excluded."[46]

Tucker's projection of the systemic decoupling of military power and international order seems counterintuitive in view of the present military hierarchy of the international system. Moreover, in the realm of naval power the ordering potential of the military hierarchy seems even more potent with the United States standing as the only power capable of mounting the vast complex of technology necessary to maintain the global forward deployment of naval power. Notwithstanding political and economic fragmentation and changes in the legal and economic regime affecting the oceans, the concentration of global naval power in the hands of, at most, two powers would seem to argue decisively against the anxieties of a Tucker. However, changes in the current and future proliferation of military technology (both conventional and nuclear) could transform this situation and thereby compromise the use of naval force both in and short of war. More specifically, the availability of precision-guided munitions—a process already well underway in no small part as the result of aggressive arms sales policies in the West—seems likely to exacerbate and confuse the traditional relationship between power and order by seriously complicating the presence and power projection function of even the largest navies. The future of this question is murky. However, the handful of observers who have examined this issue in a preliminary fashion are not entirely sanguine. Lawrence Martin, for example, has recently predicted an increase in military conflict at sea as jurisdictional claims and conflicts proliferate and as coastal states increase their capacity to enforce their claims to this newest dimension of their sovereignty[47] through the acquisition of precision-guided munitions.

Much, perhaps most, of this conflict will be regionally contained, directed by coastal states at each other, and confined to the level of conventional military technology. Nevertheless, the major naval powers will probably not be able to escape the implications of this situation, especially the effects of the acquisition of missiles, missile boats, land-based aircraft (and air defense systems), and even small submarines by many coastal states should they choose to intervene. "During the next decade," the International Institute for Strategic Studies projects, "when 200 miles of sea is likely to be added to the effective jurisdiction of coastal states, smaller states will be in a position to support their claims to extended sovereignty by the ability to police and defend large areas of ocean from intrusion by outside power. Outside military intervention would be much more costly."[48]

Precision-Guided Munitions

In the introduction to his recent *Adelphi Paper*, "Precision-Guided Weapons," James Digby notes: "Ever since men began shooting things at enemies, most shots have missed or been ineffective. The remarkable thing that has happened over the past few years is that new weapons have been developed which can hit with most of their shots, usually effectively. . . ."[49] Digby cautions that thinking concerning the use, effects, and implications of precision-guided munitions (PGMs) is only tentative, but there is consensus that the 1973 Arab-Israeli War demonstrated their potentially revolutionary effects on warfare. Though much analysis and speculation on the effect of PGMs have concentrated on land warfare, the potential proliferation of precision-guided weapons in the hands of lesser powers does not seem to favor the expressive use of naval power, especially if that power presupposes the classic, vastly asymmetric circumstances of gunboat diplomacy wherein a powerful state attempts to coerce a state with a relatively primitive military establishment.

Lieutenant Linton Wells II (USN), has summarized these developments and some of their implications at the recent Conference on Conflict and Order in Ocean Relations:

> The advent of surface-to-surface missiles has given the coastal states the ability to inflict serious damage on destroyer or cruiser-size ships within twenty miles or so of the coast. Moreover, later versions of these weapons, such as Exocet, Harpoon, or Gabriel are essentially pre-

packaged rounds. Their performance is minimally dependent on the skill of local mechanics and not much more so on that of local commanders. To be sure, these probably can be countered by an alert crew, but the warning times are so short (less than two minutes in the usual figure), that even a brief lapse in readiness on the part of the target could be fatal. The likely proliferation of laser-designated, electro-optical and other guided aircraft ordnance will provide additional complications for the distant water navy.[50]

Most analysts have little doubt that precision-guided weapons will become more widely developed, accessible, and economical. For instance, India, according to Onkar Marwah, a research fellow at the Harvard Program for Science and International Affairs, has already tested an indigenously-made, remotely-piloted vehicle of a type that could readily be converted into a cruise missile. India is also testing on-board inertial guidance systems and super alloys. The cost of *each* of these nuclear capable cruise weapons, Marwah estimates, is only $200,000 to $300,000.

The volume of recent exports of late model patrol boats, hovercraft, frigates, fast patrol boats, destroyer escorts, destroyers, aircraft such as the F-14 and F-15, and surface-to-air missiles such as Gabriel, Exocet and Sea Killer, surface-to-air and air-to-air missiles (Rapier, Seacat, Hawk, Sidewinder, and Sparrow), and even antisubmarine aircraft to the Persian Gulf, for example, is astounding. Since the start of the decade these countries have ordered more than 1,800 aircraft, 15,000 missiles, and 100 ships.[51] Present leadership in most of these countries is now pro-American—but there are no guarantees for the future. Moreover, this kind of arms buildup is not likely to go unnoticed among other coastal states of the Gulf or other regions. Further:

The net effect of these arms exports will be to increase coastal state freedom of action at the expense of the maritime powers. This latitude vanishes, of course, should the latter choose to employ all the means at their disposal, but at lower levels of conflict and new equipment can reduce some of the Western navy advantages. On the other hand, the simple knowledge of their possession may lead to an overrating of the developing country's power and thus dissuade attempts to test it.[52]

This acquisition by coastal states of a new generation of precision-guided weapons is noteworthy for it strikes at one of the key elements of the presence mission. As described by McGruther and others: "Most important, a naval force, since it operates in its own milieu, can usually be kept out of hostilities until it chooses to participate, thereby leaving the final decision of commitment both as to tone and degree to one's own diplomats."[53] Yet, if observers emphasizing the transforming effects of new technologies are correct about the capacity of coastal states to inflict damage at some distance, the decision to commit will of necessity be of a very different sort than that foreseen by the theorists of naval presence. In the emerging naval environment one cannot be sure that a presence force can avoid hostilities until or as it chooses to participate, or to control the tempo of engagement once committed. Finally, if active suasion now becomes fraught with peril, even the activities associated with latent suasion must be undertaken with a degree of preparation and care that cannot be counted as "routine."

It is essential in trying to come to grips with the possible ramifications of precision-guided munitions for the political uses of naval power to draw certain conceptual and practical distinctions. It will be recalled that Admirals Holloway and Turner as well as the research of Blechman and Kaplan have emphasized that the *political* use of naval power assumes credibility primarily within the context of calculations concerning the magnitude and quality of the *military threat* posed by naval presence. That is to say, naval presence is meaningful politically only if the object of the presence exercise believes in the capability and willingness to use the naval power displayed. In short, the political uses of naval power entail a complex joining of "hard" military capability assessments and "softer" and less predictable psychological elements.

It seems likely that PGMs will affect these sets of elements differently. There seems little reason to believe that coastal states possessing such weapons will be able to attack with a high probability of success, the major platforms comprising a defensively alerted task force. The air defense systems of the task force are presumably capable of dealing with a modest PGM attack. Absolute success is more problematic, of course, and would depend on a rather broad range of factors including the sophistication of the over-the-horizon targeting capacity of the coastal state, the penetrability of the PGMs, and, of course, the readiness levels of the targeted platforms. Detached units could prove more vulnerable without the more comprehensive defense envelope provided by the integrated defenses of the task force. But if the platforms "showing the flag" are relatively immune from direct and effective attack, can the same be said of the units of military power they must project in order to actualize their military potential? That is to say, PGMs and attendant coastal defenses may become such as to make projecting power ashore either by means of air strikes or amphibious assault quite costly. And, as U.S. Navy spokesmen stress, in the absence of a credible threat of projection, how meaningful can mere presence be?

Beyond simple shows of force, successful "opposed" projections of power may soon face serious obstacles. The critical element of surprise necessary for a successful landing is unlikely to be attained. For one thing, the offending state would know that it had committed an obnoxious act. And the time required to assemble a landing force sufficiently powerful to overcome local resistance would allow the offending state to place its forces on a full readiness alert. If, on the other hand, the attack was not expected, then an air strike or amphibious landing would represent not only a failure of diplomatic communication but also the absence of an effective wedding of diplomacy and force.

The American experience in Vietnam may be instructive. Few would contend that North Vietnam was a military power of great significance. In addition, the Russians withheld "state-of-the-art" defensive and offensive weapons. Nevertheless, in Vietnam, fighter bomber aircraft were forced toward the limits of their capability in order to have a reasonable chance of survival. In the future, air support for surface operations may become less practical.

Not only has providing air cover become much harder, but amphibious assault itself also appears increasingly difficult to achieve except at prohibitive cost. "Vertical envelopment"[54] provides only a marginal advance, for helicopters seem no less vulnerable to the new weaponry than fighter bombers. Notwithstanding the ad hoc character of much of the *Mayaguez* operation, Brookings analysts Binkin and Record point out, "Of the eleven helicopters employed in the initial assault on Tang Island (in the Mayaguez Crisis) five were quickly destroyed or disabled by small arms and machine-gun fire. Moreover, evacuation of the Marines from Tang was delayed as the defenders, estimated about 150 men, drove off helicopters trying to land on the island. Withdrawal only became feasible after two U.S. navy destroyers and two attack aircraft laid a heavy suppressive fire."[55]

Nor is skepticism confined to the nongovernmental defense community. Dr. Schlesinger also expressed doubts about the future of amphibious capabilities and a competent sea lift capacity in "times of rapid mobilization, deployment and attack." He answered these ostensibly "rhetorical" reservations with the seemingly uninspired response that obtaining a credible sea lift capacity eliminates the necessity of putting all "our mobility eggs" into the single airlift "basket,"[56] and, moreover, that the Russians would be emboldened if they saw our sea lift capacity reduced. Such a reduction, he stated, was "unthinkable." Although Schlesinger also asserted that amphibious forces and surface ships are useful in those areas not defended by sophisticated defense systems, the U.S. Navy and Marine Corps, the Defense Secretary conceded, has not "seen anything more demanding than essentially unopposed landings for twenty years"; and would have "grave difficulty" in a "high threat environment. . . ." Schlesinger concluded his last official statement—made before Tang Island—on this matter with the not altogether convincing statement that "there is a certain salutary value in having reinfused marine battalions aboard their assault ships in sensitive parts of the world."[57] One wonders, of course, how "salutary" these forces are if they are not competent to perform their mission at an acceptable cost, as recent studies from Brookings indicate.

The problem, therefore, is far more complicated than assuring the protection of major naval platforms against a coastal state's

PGMs. If the political uses of naval power in what may prove to be an increasingly fragmented, nationalistic, and belligerent non-Western world require the projection of military power against more effective coastal defensive systems, then the necessary conjoining of presence and projection may become increasingly attenuated. In sum, the crux of the problem posed by PGMs for the political use of naval power is not that they threaten superior U.S. Navy combat capability; rather, the advent of PGM proliferation may work to increase the military costs associated with the actualization of that superior capability to a level that is thought to be politically unacceptable by political decision-makers.

"The direction of change," the IISS has observed, suggests that the ultimate beneficiaries of the new developments may well be smaller coastal states—both because small navies will be able to acquire an unparalleled capability for detecting, tracking and attacking potential targets and because the existing equipment and doctrine of larger navies may be unsuited to the emerging era of naval warfare."[58] If this proves to be the case, then Tucker's vision of the "new international order" where force is at a discount may well be realized. However, the "disjunction of force and order" will come about not merely because of a collapse of will on the part of the industrialized world but in part because of its own technological excrescence.

Some Other Problems

PGMs seem likely to confuse a number of other missions and political-military relationships. For example, the relationship of allies and clients with great powers—especially the United States—against "local" aggression could be affected. Thus, alliances may become more explicitly supply arrangements and less territorial guarantees. To this extent, at least, the erosion of the impermeable boundaries of nation-states—one of the more widely touted signs of their imminent demise—may be halted as nations become better able to defend their territory. Supply arrangements will, however, become critical unless middle-range nations acquire their own competence in the production of precision-guided weapons. Middle-range powers can further lessen their reliance on superpowers by gaining the capability to manufacture arms—as the Israelis have attempted to do. But since the consumption of military stocks in an era of PGMs is said to increase by a factor of 10,[59] it is probable that no drastic disassociation of lesser states from the major arms suppliers will be feasible in the immediate future.

PGM-induced changes in the military environment might also vitiate another centerpiece of American naval strategy—sea control as the basis of secure SLOCs—which is viewed as the corollary of naval presence. Sea control is "the fundamental function of the U.S. Navy and is a prerequisite in one degree and form or another for all naval operations" for an effective sea control capability, for it "provides for secure projections of power . . . embraces survivability for the strategic deterrent . . . protects commercial shipping and . . . is . . . a prerequisite to the conduct of sustained operations by the U.S. Army and Air Force. . . ."[60]

However, cargo ships and their escorts may be vulnerable to PGMs as well as being too slow, perhaps, to affect the battle situation. (The other side of this coin, however, is that cargo vessels could be armed with PGMs of their own.) But, if surface vessels and escorts prove vulnerable to PGMs, how can effective sea control and commerce be maintained? One answer, at least with respect to enemy surface platforms, may be to give up some of the "expressive" function of surface craft in favor of submersible patrol craft. The potential destruction or capture of ships at sea might be deterred at less risk and with more chance of success by using "marshals riding shotgun" via relatively simple but fast and lethal submarines. As Captain S. W. Roskill, the official historian of the Royal Navy, has written: "The scope for employment of submarines on duties either to be performed by surface ships or aircraft [is] limited only by the cost of submarine production. Indeed, the command of the surface sea whereby a maritime power seeks to secure the uninterrupted passage of mercantile or military cargoes, seem[s] likely to increasingly depend on control of the waters beneath."[61]

And, in a similar vein, Vice Admiral George P. Steel wrote in May of 1976: "Today, and for many years to come, the really battle-worthy capital ship is the nuclear powered submarine. It has the unique ability to get close enough to destroy the enemy surface ship, using missiles or torpedoes without great risk, regardless of how much airpower is ranged against it. The only adversary that it really need fear is another and better submarine . . . using the same advantages of mobility and stealth."[62]

Alternately, as Admiral Zumwalt has suggested, emphasis might be put on large numbers of conventionally powered "work-horse" escort vessels, e.g., the FFG-7 class of ship. These ships could not, of course, cost much or "bristle" for show, but knowledge of the presence of the undersea and/or surface lawmen could be reassuring to Western commerce against one of the most probable kinds of sea threats of the future. The problem of air power directed at the SLOCs remains, however, and is not likely to diminish.

On the other hand, if the increasingly common prognostication of a short war in Europe holds, then the sea control and supply function of carriers and other surface weapons platforms becomes superfluous. One might speculate, of course, that since the rate of fire of PGMs tends to be very rapid and entails high ordnance consumption levels there might well be an increased need for resupply. The future importance of surface cargo vessels and thus support ships not only remains, in this view, but it increases. However, the compression of combat time envisaged in much speculation concerning PGM-based warfare—even if it remains below the nuclear threshold—may obviate the need for even the most speedy cargo ships especially in the absence of port facilities.[63]

With long-range in-flight refueling now available for fighter planes, the need for carriers to supply tactical air cover in either brush-fire wars or other engagements might well diminish. On the other hand, the limits of physical endurance for fighter pilots and their craft would constrain the projection of tactical air power over long ocean distances. In any event, concern about the vulnerability of carriers and their cost will most likely increase, thereby intensifying doubts about the future role of carriers and much of the rest of the fleet designed to protect them. Secretary Schlesinger was known to be less than enthusiastic about maintaining a large super-carrier program through the 1990s, but was opposed by Secretary Kissinger, who was said to be much taken with the "expressive" potential of carriers.[64] Indeed, Secretary Schlesinger, in his last posture statement, anticipated the current skepticism concerning the future of the large surface ships. One element of this judgment is the observation that the cost of congressionally mandated nuclear surface ships may force the Navy to procure more versatile, although admittedly less awe-inspiring, surface vessels to perform sea control missions. Yet, even small patrol craft may not be as efficient as submersible patrol boats. As Dr. Schlesinger explained: "Our shipbuilding program has already suffered severely from the impact of inflation. . . . [As] nuclear power . . . becomes the main source of propulsion for the Navy in the future, we must also consider the versatility of nuclear attack submarines on the ASW mission and against enemy surface ships. Indeed, despite their high cost, we may well want to regard them as competitive with surface escorts. . . ."[65] In addition, there are now reports of a Defense Department analysis of the potentialities for a large land-based multipurpose naval aircraft (LMNA) which might undertake virtually all sea control functions and thereby supplement or even replace some of the surface navy's primary platform, the aircraft carrier.[66]

Finally, these technological changes could presage an extension of the capability for more unconventional violence to the world's seas and oceans. It is not inconceivable that a small state or states might initiate and then deny responsibility for a future *Maine*-type incident. The benefits to be derived from such unconventional or quasi-terroristic acts might not be calculable in terms of conventional military payoffs. If, however, superpowers were thereby made less willing to forward deploy naval power and/or "show the flag" because of the risk of purportedly "random" violence, then small states might regard their latitude as having increased.

A refinement of the above could involve quasi-official sponsorship of terrorist groups who might bring unconventional violence to bear on vulnerable seaborne commerce. This would obviously alter the maritime and naval environment as well as the conditions for the use of purely "expressive" naval force on the part of a great power, and might be an incentive for powers great and small to search for unofficial agents. Of course, the rules of confrontation in such an environment would initially be ambiguous and would evolve only through repeated engagements, much as the rules of deterrence were learned and manipulated in the Cold War. The emergence of such unconventional war at sea in international society would not necessarily portend an increase in the volume of violence. Indeed, if the great nations use transnational agents, as weaker states have recently begun to do, then the tendency may be to dampen the potential for great power conflict. If the U.S., for instance, were to sponsor a kind of resuscitated IRGUN while the Soviets forthrightly backed the P.L.O., it might well have the serendipitous effect of widening the interval between conventional and nuclear war.

Ultimately, of course, pure terrorism—i.e., terrorism other than that manipulated by states—could move to sea. The seaborne commerce of states or their efforts to exploit their new economic zones could well become the target of terrorism rooted in subnational or ethnic identifications. As David Fromkin pointed out recently, the strategy of terrorism is unlike anything that modern naval power or any other form of state power has ever had to confront before:

> The uniqueness of the strategy lies in this: that it achieves its goal not through its acts but through the response to its acts. In any other such strategy, the violence is the beginning and its consequences are the end of it. For terrorism, however, the consequences of the violence are themselves merely a first step and form a stepping stone toward objectives that are more remote. Whereas military and revolutionary actions aim at a physical result, terrorist actions aim at a psychological result.
>
> But even that psychological result is not the final goal. Terrorism is violence used in order to create fear; but it is aimed at creating fear in

order that the fear, in turn, will lead somebody else—not the terrorist—to embark on some quite different program of action that will accomplish whatever it is that the terrorist really desires.[67]

The three logical responses to terrorism are:
1) to focus on the protection of people and property;
2) to focus on the retrieval of people or property;
3) to wreak havoc on the perpetrators of terrorism on the seas so that they will be deterred from doing it again.

The last prospect, reprisal, has never been particularly effective and can have unintended consequences (as the French discovered in Algeria, as the U.S. found out in Vietnam, and as the Israelis have had occasion to discover on the West Bank and in Lebanon). The second course may be neither technologically feasible nor particularly cost-effective. As in the skyjacking phenomenon, therefore, the answer may be more in the prevention than the cure. Yet as Fromkin and others have suggested, no technological defense is perfect—which suggests in turn that the maritime environment might well become increasingly less secure even as, ironically, the capability of the superpowers and many coastal states increases.

Summary and Conclusion

In this chapter we have surveyed a number of conditions in the international system that seem on balance to constrain most of the attributes of naval power that have purportedly made it a uniquely applicable instrumentality in contemporary world politics. The flexibility and universality of a naval force operating in an international medium are qualities not easily matched by land or air power. Moreover, post-World War II American naval power has served as a politically unfettered base from which to launch both air and land operations. Furthermore, the technological changes associated with nuclear propulsion would seem to extend further the range and ubiquity of American naval power. However, other technological changes such as relatively cheap but lethal precision-guided weaponry, the onset of proliferation of such technology, and the emergence of a Soviet naval presence suggest that earlier assumptions concerning the efficacy of naval power require reexamination. The complexity of the present situation is heightened by the possibility that the strategic relationship at sea—in the past the foundation of a stable mutual deterrent relationship—may be headed toward a period of increasing instability. Finally, analysis and calculations of the effects of these conditions must be carried out with reference to considerable systemic change in world politics, i.e., the deterioration of the structural and dynamic simplicity of post-World War II bipolarism.

Technologically, precision-guided munitions seem likely to have considerable effect on the "ordering" potential of naval power in that they severely erode the potential for gunboat diplomacy. On land, PGMs may place a premium on dispersion and concealment. But on the sea, dispersion and concealment are the very antithesis of the traditional presence and show of force. The ships that loom so awesome and impressive in their traditional role may find it more difficult to operate in a PGM environment. The advent and proliferation of PGMs make unopposed landings less plausible and therefore less credible as a deterrent. PGMs could also escalate the level and intensity of combat activity. The result, therefore, may be a blurring of the distinction between low- and high-intensity operations.[68] The advent of PGMs may, in short, force another rupture in the theoretical and practical attempt to marry force and diplomacy.[69]

Michael Klare has argued that much of the current preoccupation on the part of U.S. Navy and DOD spokesmen with the growth of the Soviet Navy is rooted in the fear that the Soviets will be able to neutralize or circumscribe the political uses of U.S. naval power, especially in the Third World.[70] The present analysis suggests that a combination of developments, but especially the confluence of Third World militancy and the advent of new naval weapons technologies, will tend to complicate further the use of naval power by a superpower even if it possesses a measure of superiority with respect to the other superpower. It seems likely, in short, that the naval environment will be characterized by a general increase in the destructive capability of small naval forces operating in coastal waters or shore-based coastal defense systems. At the same time, superpower rivalry at sea may well have reached an approximation of parity such that Soviet presence can be situationally augmented to a level that makes American sea control problematical, thereby dangerously complicating, if not actually neutralizing, the credibility of the projection threat and, hence, the exercise of presence and political influence.

It may be that these changing circumstances will dictate a different set of missions on the United States Navy. If one sees future global interdependence as a volatile mix of mutual economic need and uneven but significant proliferation of military (including naval) capability and even, in some instances, area or regional military self-sufficiency, then something approaching Elizabeth Young's "constabulary" missions looms as a possibility:

> The likelihood is that whenever economic interests on or in the seabed or in the superjacent waters are internationally recognized as exclusive to the coastal state, the continued existence of the traditional high seas regime (whatever the hopes or intentions of the maritime powers) will progressively be degraded into mere legal superstition. In all the heavily used seas—and those of the North Atlantic are the most heavily used—there is no foreseeable alternative to the steady erosion of the old freedoms and the substitution of civil (or military) occupation, nationally or regionally organized. As on land, the symbol of such occupation will be the constable on the beat and the presence of legitimately deployed force: a concept totally at variance with that of the freedom of the seas.[71]

Perhaps Ms. Young overstates the case,[72] but if hydrospace does become subdivided, the task of national naval forces may well become primarily that of policing regional coastal economic claims either as distinct national units or as contributors to some form of internationalized constabulary.

In any event, even if one rejects the idea of an alternative future for the U.S. Navy based on the constabulary mission (a rather dif-

ferent conception of presence than that discussed above), the seemingly irreversible proliferation of sophisticated military technology
alone raises questions concerning the profile of missions employed
by the U.S. Navy today. Indeed, the volume of arms transfers
raises serious questions about the entire regulatory image of world
politics within which the current debate over U.S. naval missions is
being carried out. Both the regulatory concept and the idea of using
naval power short of war imply a purposeful control of the exploitation of force so as to maximize American power and interests or,
more abstractly, "international order." If, however, some approximation of the fractured, conflictual, but interdependent world foreseen
by Robert Tucker[73] comes to pass, we may be compelled to look at
international relations in terms of systems of multidimensional stale-
mate.[74]

PART II

American Naval Power
and the Domestic Environment

CHAPTER FIVE

Congress and the Future
of American Sea Power

AMONG THOSE aspects of the American domestic scene that have attracted much recent attention has been the purported transformation of the United States Congress from a supportive, sometimes cheerleading, accomplice in the establishment and maintenance of the "imperial presidency" into a more autonomous, even adversial, factor in the policy-making process. One of the most conspicuous characteristics of the "new" Congress has been considerable rhetoric concerning the need for a more skeptical look at military spending. In this chapter we will be concerned with how this rhetoric has translated into action during the 1970s especially as it relates to recent Navy budget requests and what this might portend for the future.

In approaching this question, we will focus on the executive-legislative relationship as reflected in defense budgets in general and the Navy's budgetary requests in particular. Implicit in this approach, of course, is acceptance of the notion that the budgetary process and its outcomes are perhaps the most important policy dynamics of the United States government.[1] Our analysis of the executive-legislative interaction will involve two levels of analysis. First, we will establish the broad framework of congressional behavior with respect to the Nixon-Ford administration's defense requests.[2] Second, we will examine the Navy's budget requests with special attention to new shipbuilding procurement requests during the early 1970s. Given the prominence of the shipbuilding procurement account in the Navy's annual requests, the category seems to warrant close attention.

Congress and the Defense Budget

Prior to the 1970s an assessment of the domestic factors affecting the future of the Navy and its missions might have stopped with the outcome of the executive branch decision-making process. The passivity and acquiescent posture of Congress regarding executive branch initiative in the realm of national security policy were the empirically demonstrable essence of the congressional role in the making of American foreign and national security policy. With few exceptions, the outcome of the inter- and intrabureaucratic struggles within the executive branch *was* policy. But, as American foreign policy floundered in Vietnam and the domestic, foreign, and defense policy consensus of the Cold War decades began to disintegrate, a number of observers discerned a fundamental change in the role of Congress. For example, Alton Frye noted recently:

> One may characterize the recent transformation of the congressional role in national security policy by noting shifts along several continua. Congress has moved—and forced the entire government to move—from a relatively closed to a relatively open process in addressing these issues. Congress has shifted from a relatively prodefense attitude to a relatively negative and skeptical posture; nourished by competing demands for resources, the impulse for thrift has begun to reassert itself after a long period of open handedness on defense budgets. And Congress has turned from a relatively deferential stance toward executive leadership in national security to a determined effort to get into the act itself, grasping for handles that work effectively in steering executive conduct of defense programs.[3]

This perception of Congress was not always held by political scientists. Lewis Dexter was not untypical of those who summarized the role of Congress in the 1950s and the subsequent decade:

Members of Congress share the views which they generally attribute to their constituents: they hesitate to question the *basic* proposals of the military: that is, they regard the military as *experts*, not only on matters of organization and command, but on types of war plans, etc. Said one member of a relevant committee, better prepared by previous experience than most committee members, "The whole problem is that we are not military experts, and we have to rely upon what military people tell us." He repeated several times in the course of our talks the rhetorical question: "Who are we to say 'no' to the military people?"[4]

A significant dissent to this position, however, has been entered by Samuel Huntington, who argues that during the late 1940s and 1950s "Congress [gave] considered and effective attention to the major issues of military policy involved in the budget."[5] Huntington has placed great stress on an elaborate, but essentially informal, process of bargaining. To Huntington, negotiations in foreign and defense policy are important within the executive branch and between the executive and Congress, especially on the part of those few senior members responsible for the major committees such as the Armed Services and Appropriations Committees and the Senate Foreign Relations Committee.[6] And Alton Frye alludes to the same process at work throughout the 1960s: "Until the late nineteen-sixties, national security was the virtual monopoly of an almost hermetically sealed community in Congress, no less than in the executive. To be sure, there was often quite sophisticated interplay among the small number of players in the closed game of legislating for defense in the key committees."[7] But Frye concedes, in other sectors of Congress and the public, "it is exceedingly difficult even now to judge how well the Armed Services and Defense Appropriations subcommittees were performing in previous years."[8]

The 1960s

One way to resolve the problem of measuring performance is to look at congressional action on the budget requests of the Department of Defense. Arnold Kanter, who has analyzed congressional behavior with respect to the defense budget between 1960 and 1970, has concluded:

The dollar magnitude of Congressional changes in level of *total* defense spending obscures variations which occur within the budget. . . . Congress almost always has made larger changes in Procurement and RDT & E (Research, Development, Test and Evaluation) than in the other budget areas. As a result, computation of budget changes based on the total defense budget consistently understates the size of the change in the former two appropriations titles and exaggerates the changes in Personnel and O & M (Operations and Maintenance). While the dollar magnitude of Congressional changes has been small, it has been somewhat greater for those budget categories which contain funds for development and production of weapons systems.[9]

Support for this conclusion lies in two measures of congressional behavior with respect to presidential national security requests between 1960 and 1970. First, Kanter has identified the concentration of "no change" decisions made by Congress in the president's budget. These "no change" decisions were highly concentrated in the Personnel and Operations and Maintenance (O & M) titles of the annual appropriations bills; conversely, "change" actions were concentrated in Procurement and RDT & E. Inasmuch as the Personnel and O & M titles accounted for about 57% of the total appropriations requests during the years studied, the concentration of "no change" actions in these titles obscured in the' *total* budget figure the magnitude of congressional action on Procurement and RDT & E—those two titles of the appropriations bill usually deemed most important to the national security policy-making process.[10]

Whereas identification of concentrations of "no change" behavior raises questions about the use of aggregate budget figures as a basis for evaluating congressional behavior, the identification of the locus of small or infrequent changes would provide an even more complete picture of congressional activity. Kanter derived such a measure[11] by comparing percentage changes between the request of the president and the actual amounts appropriated by Congress for each major budget title (see Table 4).

These results underscore Kanter's central conclusion. Whereas Personnel and O & M were undergoing slightly more than 1% changes on average throughout the decade of the 1960s, Procure-

Table 4

Congressional Percentage Changes In President's Budget
Requests 1960–1970, Mean Annual Absolute Difference

	Personnel	*O & M*	*Procurement*	*RDT & E*	*DOD*
Mean Absolute Difference	1.069	1.246	4.401	4.547	2.308

Source: Kanter, "Congress and the Defense Budget: 1960–1970," Table 5, p. 134.

ment and RDT & E experienced changes of 4.4% and 4.5% respectively. Because of the larger magnitude of the cumulative Personnel and O & M budgets, however, the greater changes in the other two titles tended to be washed out for the budget as a whole, thereby yielding a 2.3% change in the total Defense Department budget for the eleven-year period. Moreover, Kanter found no significant correlation between the size of year-to-year changes in presidential requests and the size of congressional changes in line items.[12] That is to say, the empirical evidence does not clearly support the argument that Congress merely reacts in an incremental and nonprogrammatic fashion to the president's initiative.[13]

The 1970s

It is now commonplace to view the Vietnam War and especially the period after the Tet Offensive of February 1968 as a turning point in American foreign policy. The change has extended not only to the substance of American policy but also to the institutional arrangements whereby policy is made. The executive-legislative relationship is no exception, for after 1968 a major turnover of congressional membership and institutional change ensued. Usually changes in congressional processes have been described primarily in terms of institutional reform, specific restrictions on presidential power, or as a function of the evident increase in tension between Congress and president. The latter has been exacerbated, of course, by the presence of Democratic majorities in Congress and Republican control of the White House from 1969–1976. However, a synthesis of the data on congressional budgetary behavior for the 1971–1977 period, when added to the data developed by Kanter for the 1960–1968 period, can provide an additional indicator of the changed executive-legislative relationship.[14]

The contrast in congressional budgetary activism in the two periods is marked. Between 1960–1968, for example, Kanter reports only three examples of budget request changes in the Procurement and RDT & E titles of more than 5%. In the 1969–1977 period, however, there are seventeen changes out of eighteen opportunities to make such changes (sixteen if transfer authority is included).[15] Indeed, in the latter period, seven of the changes are more than 10%, one other is more than 9.5%, and two more are at the 8% level. (When transfer authority is included the changes are six, none, and three respectively.) Furthermore, if budget *reductions* are taken as an even stronger indication of congressional activism, then only one of the changes in the "supportive" period was a reduction of more than 5%, whereas all seventeen of the significant changes in the 1969–1977 span were reductions.

A summary of the two periods is available through a comparison of the percentage changes by title for the two periods (see Table 5). The changes for the 1960–1968 period clearly show the incremental budgetary behavior traditionally associated with Congress's role in foreign and national security policy-making. Furthermore, these marginal adjustments to the defense budget are in evidence not only with respect to Personnel and O & M, but across the board. The percentage changes for 1969–1977 are indicative of incremental behavior with respect to Personnel and perhaps O & M. But in contrast, if 5–10% reductions are regarded as significant, nonincremental behavior for Procurement and RDT & E occurred in 1969–1977. Moreover, the reductions in the case of Procurement and RDT & E for 1969–1977 are sufficiently large that the total change for the Department of Defense budget as a whole is pushed almost to 6% (5.186% if transfer authority is included). That is to say, congressional activism with respect to the president's request for DOD "investment authority" has been sufficiently great since 1969 to offset somewhat the normally obscuring effects of incrementalism regarding the 60% of the national security budget consumed by personnel costs and operations and maintenance.

Table 5

Congressional Percentage Changes in President's Budget Requests
1960–1968 and 1969–1977, Mean Annual Absolute Differences*

	Personnel	O & M	Procure-ment	RDT & E	DOD
1960–1968	0.726	0.549	2.196	3.774	1.239
1969–1977	1.672	3.436	11.972	6.848	5.713
W/T.A.		(3.326)	(10.265)	(6.624)	(5.186)

*MAAD with transfer authority included in parentheses.
Source: Kanter, p. 132 and Appendix D and E.

Undoubtedly many observers and students of American national security policy would regard reductions in the 5–10% range or even the occasional 14% or 15% cut in evidence in the 1969–1977 period as marginal, token, or, in any event, long overdue. Nevertheless, it seems fairly clear that this period represents a change in congressional behavior from the almost unquestioning support of the 1960s. The early 1970s have been different. A literally as well as figuratively new Congress has undertaken more than marginal institutional reform of itself and become more aggressive in its budgetary behavior. In sum, the early 1970s would appear to have been a decidedly stormy sea upon which to launch the reconstruction and modernization of the United States Navy. And yet this is precisely what the Navy undertook after the drastic reductions in fleet size between 1968 and 1970–1971. The above analysis would suggest that such an enterprise might not have fared well, nor would it suggest a very benign prospect for the construction of a fleet composed in large part of extremely expensive vessels. Let us turn, therefore, to the Navy's relationship with the "new" Congress of the early 1970s, for how the Navy's requests fared during this recent past may suggest something of its future as well.

Congress and the Navy in the 1970s

Perhaps the simplest and most direct measure of the Navy's success in Congress is a comparison of the relative aggregate shares of new obligational authority (NOA)—i.e., the new spending authority granted in a given year—for the four services. In general, such a comparison for the Nixon-Ford years confirms the trends identified by Lawrence Korb in his analysis of the relative position of the Navy in the executive branch budgetary process.[16] Thus, whereas the four services increase the absolute size of their shares of the new obligational authority by the end of the period, their *percentage* of total NOA at the end of the period is significantly different. Only the Navy shows a positive percentage increase; the Marine Corps holds even; the Air Force holds almost even; but, as was the case with the executive process, the Army's percentage share has dropped.

A similar picture emerges when we examine the relative shares of the "investment authority" titles—Procurement and RDT & E.[17] In the area of procurement, the Navy emerges from the congressional process as the dominant service throughout the Nixon-Ford years. Congressional action on the first Nixon request for new obligational authority for procurement left the Navy with over 43% of total new procurement authority, the Air Force with almost 37%, and the Army with slightly over 18%. By mid-decade the relative standing remained the same. And, in some years, the Navy's share of new procurement authority approached and slightly exceeded one-half the total. By the end of 1977 the Army's cut of procurement authority stood at slightly more than 15% which was itself a recovery from a low point of 13% in fiscal 1974; the Air Force share remained relatively unchanged at slightly more than 36%.

Although Congress does not provide the Navy with the largest share of the RDT & E authority appropriated during the period, the Navy's percentage share is the only increase during the seven years. As is the case in the development of executive budget requests, the Navy's growth and the Air Force's relative stability throughout the period come at the expense of the Army, which took no more of the total RDT & E new obligational authority appropriated in fiscal year 1977 than in fiscal 1971.

It would certainly appear, therefore, that at an aggregate budget level the congressional judgment parallels that of the executive: the Navy and the instrumentalities and missions that it represents have become the major claimants of defense resources not only within the executive branch but within the congressional budgetary process as well. Incrementalist explanations of executive-legislative relations in the national security and foreign policy issue areas would of course predict such an outcome. But as Kanter's research demonstrates, congressional behavior is a good deal more complex than is revealed through the analysis of aggregate budget totals.

Congressional Oversight and United States Navy Resources

Although Congress has allowed the Navy large shares of the new obligational authority appropriated to the Department of Defense during the early 1970s, congressional activism with respect to the Navy's requests has not been lacking. In four of the seven Nixon-Ford budgets, for example, the Navy's requests have been subjected to the largest percentage reductions.[18] Similarly, the percentage difference between presidential requests and congressional appropriations suggests high levels of congressional activism with respect to the Navy's requests. Indeed, Table 6 underscores the fact that even as Congress was allowing the Navy sizable shares of total NOA and "investment authority" in the defense budget, it was simultaneously inflicting reductions on the Navy's budget requests greater than for the Army and Air Force.

Despite such activism, by mid-decade the Navy had emerged as the major claimant of congressionally appropriated NOA, for, as Korb has found, it has been permitted by the Defense Department to request greater budget increases than the other services. The net result has been an increasingly high rate of growth for the Navy's budget base.

Table 6

Congressional Percentage Changes In Service Budget Requests
1971–1977, Mean Annual Absolute Difference

	Army	Navy	Air Force	DOD
Mean Annual Absolute Difference	5.322	5.35	5.006	5.312
MAAD with Transfer Authority	4.473	5.246	4.359	4.652

Source: Appendix H

However, it is necessary to keep in mind when evaluating the apparent jump in recent Navy investment authority that much of the appropriated "new" authority for procurement is to cover cost growth on previously authorized ship construction, e.g., 25% for fiscal 1976. Congress has chosen thus far to cover such growth in the shipbuilding accounts, obliging the Navy even when its requests reached dramatic proportions, as between 1974 and 1975,[19] without reducing the total number of units authorized (as has been the case with the other major weapons systems such as the C-5 or, for that matter, the Navy's F-14). However, the budgetary committees have shown no enthusiasm for the Navy's desire for large future-year cost escalation appropriations or its "multi-year ship authorization concept."[20] Moreover, Navy attempts to renegotiate contract claims with the major shipbuilding companies in the wake of the 1976 appropriation have proved extremely difficult, with some Navy spokesmen charging a "rip-off" on the part of the companies, others arguing the necessity of the adjustment; and the companies threatening to stop work on a number of ships including nuclear submarines, nuclear aircraft carriers, nuclear cruisers, and helicopter carriers (LHA).[21]

On balance, the picture of the budgetary relationship between the Navy and Congress provided by these indicators of aggregate budget change and the trends in NOA and investment is not an especially grim one. This is not to say that Congress has not undertaken significant changes in the budgetary requests asked by the Navy. In fact, the pattern of congressional activism vis-à-vis the DOD budget's appropriation titles is, as one would expect, repeated in the services' requests. This of course means significant reductions in Procurement requests. Insofar as this title is of peculiar salience to the Navy's technology intensive force structure, a survey of congressional action *within* the Procurement title is essential to a truly comprehensive understanding of the Navy's success and the future of sea power in the congressional environment of the 1970s.

Congress and Naval Force Structure

Almost 40% of the Navy's annual request for new obligational authority is for procurement, and throughout the 1970s ship construction (SCN) has accounted for more than a third of the total procurement request. From 1974 through 1977, SCN has been the single largest item in the Procurement title. Clearly, therefore, what the Congress does to this particular line item will have a significant effect on the Navy's future.

Apart from the sheer quantitative size of the SCN portion of the Navy's request, SCN is central for important substantive reasons as well. Throughout the 1970s the rationale for the Navy's entire request has been built around an official perception of the dramatically escalating Soviet threat to U.S. naval supremacy on and below the ocean's surface. To deal with what has been proclaimed to be a rapidly deteriorating naval balance, the Navy placed before Congress in the early and mid-1970s a program for new ship construction that encompassed eight new types of ships, including strategic and attack submarines, a new class of cruiser, guided missile frigates, destroyers, a "sea control ship," patrol frigates, and the patrol hydrofoil. In his appearance before the House Armed Services Committee's Seapower Subcommittee, Admiral Zumwalt framed the new ship construction program for fiscal 1975 in terms of distinct mission-related areas: Strategic, Sea Control, Support, and Miscellaneous.[22] Within the "Strategic" mission the only new ship construction centered on the Trident ballistic missile submarine. "Sea Control" during the 1970s has included the most new construction and has been subdivided into Hi- and Lo-Mix vessels. In the former group of high-cost and high-capability vessels have been the SSN-688 attack submarine, a new class of nuclear-powered guided missile frigate (DLGN, reclassified CGN in 1975) and the new *Spruance* class of destroyer (DD-963). At the lower end of the Sea Control mix were the proposed Sea Control Ship (SCS), a new class of patrol frigate ("PF" originally, but as of FY 1977, FFG-7), and the patrol hydrofoil (PHM). In addition to these classes of combatants the Navy requested a patrol gunboat (PGM) and the helicopter carrier approved in fiscal 1969 (LHA). The "Support" component of the program required the construction of a number of new tenders (ASs and ADs), oilers (AOs and AORs), tugs (ATSs and T-ATFs), and research vessels (AGORs). Miscellaneous craft included service craft, barges, landing craft, floating drydocks, and pollution abatement craft.

Throughout the early 1970s, therefore, Congress was given the opportunity by means of its authorization, appropriations, and oversight powers to significantly influence the future of the Navy's force structure. Thus, congressional behavior with respect to the Navy's new ship construction requests is a useful indicator of the Navy-congressional relationship. For in acting on the Navy's budgetary requests for new obligational authority to build and commit funds for the procurement of new ships, the Congress influences not only the size of the Navy but also the structure and character of the Navy's force structure for literally decades to come.

Table 7 provides an overview of Navy requests for new obligational authority for new ship construction and the congressional response to these requests during the Nixon-Ford years. Navy priorities are apparent in the sequence in which new classes of ships are requested and the percentage of the new ship construction budget devoted to the various mission areas and the Hi-Lo Mix within these mission areas. Throughout the period and beginning in the transitional year of 1970, the attack submarine (SSN-668) has been a high-priority item in the Navy's requests. Similarly, the DD-963 has been a major component of SCN requests during the 1970s with the Navy asking for seven new ships of this class each year between 1972 and 1975. Six DD-963 were requested in 1971 and five during the transitional year. Another major Hi-Mix request was a nuclear aircraft carrier. Finally, in four of the seven years (and in the transitional year as well) the Navy has requested funds for one CGN.

The general effect of this pattern of requests has been the dominance throughout the early 1970s of the Sea Control mission and Hi-Mix ships appropriate to that mission. Only after the initiation of the "1-2-1 . . ." sequence of Trident buys in 1974 does the Sea Control/Hi-Mix portion of the new SCN drop below 70% of the SCN budget request. The onset of procurement requests for Sea Control/ Lo-Mix ships in fiscal 1975 in conjunction with the continuing Trident program and the authorization of the last of the DD-963s had reduced the Hi-Mix claim on new ship construction to less than a third by mid-decade.

The core of the "Sea Control/Lo-Mix" request is the Patrol or Guided Missile Frigate (FFG-7). The FFG-7 class is to protect "underway replenishment groups, amphibious forces, and convoys which proceed at relatively slow speed and are generally expected to operate in areas of less intense air threat,"[23] whereas the Hi-Mix ships are to "operate in areas of severe enemy air and submarine threat, and to conduct sustained independent operations." Advance procurement and lead ship requests appear in the Navy's request early in the period, but only in fiscal 1975 do they become a major procurement item. Supplementing this Lo-Mix construction program were requests for a small number of Patrol Combatants (PGN) and the lead ship in a new Sea Control Ship class. "Support" ships and "Miscellaneous" craft have constituted a minor element in the Navy's requests of about 10% per year throughout the

Table 7

Congressional Action on New Ship Construction Requests, 1971–1977 (in millions of dollars)

	1971 DOD No.	Amnt.[1]	1971 Congress No.	Amnt.[1]	(%NSCN)	1972 DOD No.	Amnt.[1]	1972 Congress No.	Amnt.[1]	(%NSCN)	1973 DOD No.	Amnt.[1]	1973 Congress No.	Amnt.[1]	(%NSCN)
Strategic															
Trident												361.0		311.0	
Total												361.0		311.0	
Sea Control															
Hi-Mix															
CVN		152.0		0								299.0		299.0	
SSN688	3	475.5	4	664.0		5	881.0	5	903.5		6	1039.0	6	1175.0	
CSGN															
DLGN[2]	1	221.3	6	221.3		1	209.2	1	194.6						
DD-963	6	459.5	6	459.5		7	599.2	7	599.2		7	610.0	0	247.0	
DDG-47															
Total Hi-Mix	10	1308.3	11	1344.8	(79.5)	13	1689.4	13	1697.3	(82.1)	13	1948.0	6	1721.0	(69.9)
Lo-Mix															
FFG-7							51.6		0		1	191.5	1	191.5	
PHM							5.1		5.1		2	60.4	0	0	
PGM												10.0		0	
SCS														0	

LHA	2	313.5	2	313.5								
Total Lo-Mix	2	313.5 (19.1)	2	313.5		56.7		5.1 (2.8)	3	261.9	1	191.5 (9.4)
Total SC	12	1621.8 (98.6)	13	1658.3	13	1746.7	13	1702.4 (84.8)	16	2209.9	7	1912.5 (79.2)
Total Combt.	12	1621.8 (98.6)	13	1658.3	13	1746.7	13	1702.4 (84.8)	16	2470.9	7	2223.5 (92.2)
Support												
AS					2	214.0	1	108.0	1	64.9	1	64.9
AD									1	86.9	1	86.9
AO												
AOR												
ATS					1	56.5	1	56.5				
T-ATF					1	30.4	1	30.4				
AGOR	2	7.3	2	7.3					2	53.1	1	31.0
Total Support	2	7.3	2	7.3	4	300.9	3	194.9	4	204.9	3	182.8
Miscl.		15.6		15.6		11.9		11.9		13.0		13.0
Total Non-combt.	2	22.9	2	22.9 (1.4)	4	312.8	3	206.8 (15.2)	4	217.9	3	195.8 (7.8)
GRAND TOTAL	14	1644.7	15	1681.2	17	2058.9	16	1909.2	20	2788.8	10	2419.3

[1]Includes Advance Procurement

[2]"CGN" as of July, 1975

Table 7 (cont.)

	1974				1975			
	DOD		Congress		DOD		Congress	
	No.	Amnt.[1]	No.	Amnt.[1] (%NSCN)	No.	Amnt.[1]	No.	Amnt.[1] (%NSCN)
Strategic								
Trident	1	867.8	1	627.8	2	1166.8	2	1166.8
Total	1	867.8	1	627.8 (28.1)	2	1166.8	2	1166.8 (19.0)
Sea Control								
Hi-Mix								
CVN	1	657.0	1	657.0				
SSN688	5	913.2	5	913.2	3	502.5	3	502.5
CSGN								
DLGN[2]					1	244.3	1	244.3
DD-963	7	585.8	7	585.8	7	457.1	7	457.1
DDG-47								
Total Hi-Mix	13	2156.0	13	2156.0	11	1203.9	11	1203.9 (36.4)
Lo-Mix								
FFG-7		6.8		0	7	436.5	3	186.0
PHM		3.9		3.9	4	92.3	4	92.3
PGM					2	14.3	0	0
SCS		29.3		29.3	1	142.9	0	0

	Col 1 No.	Col 1 $	Col 2 No.	Col 2 $	Col 3 No.	Col 3 $	Col 4 No.	Col 4 $
LHA								
Total Lo-Mix	13	40.0	13	33.2 (1.3)	14	686.0	7	278.3 (20.1)
Total SC	14	2196.0	14	2189.2 (71.2)	25	1889.9	18	1482.2 (57.1)
Total Combt.	14	3063.8	14	2817.0 (99.3)	27	3056.7	20	2649.0 (92.4)
Support								
AS								
AD					1	116.7	1	116.7
AO					1	81.4	0	0
AOR								
ATS								
T-ATF					1	10.8	1	10.8
AGOR								
Total Support					3	208.9	2	127.5
Miscl.		19.4		10.4		41.6		32.4
Total Non-combt.		19.4		10.4	3	250.5	2	159.9
GRAND TOTAL	14	1644.7	15	1681.2	17	2058.9	16	1909.2

[1] Includes Advance Procurement

[2] "CGN" as of July, 1975

Table 7 (cont.)

	1976 DOD No.	1976 DOD Amnt.[1]	1976 Congress No.	1976 Congress Amnt.[1]	1976 (%NSCN)	1977 DOD No.	1977 DOD Amnt.[1]	1977 Congress No.	1977 Congress Amnt.[1]	1977 (%NSCN)
Strategic										
Trident	1	602.6	1	641.3		1	833.0	1	833.0	
Total	1	602.8	1	641.3	(19.0)	1	833.0	1	833.0	(16.9)
Sea Control										
Hi-Mix										
CVN							350.0		350.0	
SSN688	2	541.0	2	541.0		3	925.6	3	925.6	
CSGN		60.0	0	0			170.0[3]		170.0[3]	
DLGN[2]	1	257.0	0	0						
DD-963										
DDG-47						1	858.5	1	858.5	
Total Hi-Mix	3	858.0	2	541.0	(27.0)	4	2304.1	4	2304.1	(46.8)
Lo-Mix										
FFG-7	10	955.5	9	802.5		8	1179.5	8	1147.1	
PHM	2	83.4	0	39.0						
PCM										

LHA

Total Lo-Mix	12	1038.9	9	841.5	(32.7)	8	1179.5	8	1147.1	(23.3)
Total SC	15	1896.9	11	1382.5	(59.7)	12	3483.6	8	3451.2	(70.1)
Total Combt.	16	2499.5	12	2023.8	(78.6)	13	4316.6	13	4284.2	(87.1)
Support										
AS	2	393.2	1	201.9		1	260.9	1	260.9	
AD	2	231.8	2	239.4		1	260.4	1	260.4	
AO						2	205.3	1	102.3	
AOR										
ATS										
T-ATF	3	41.4	3	41.4						
AGOR										
Total Support	7	666.4	6	482.7	(21.4)	4	726.6	3	623.6	
Misc.		12.9		12.9			13.5		13.5	
Total Non-combt.	7	679.3	6	495.6	(21.4)	4	740.1	3	637.1	(12.9)
GRAND TOTAL	23	3178.8	18	2519.4		17	5056.1	16	4921.3	

[1] Included Advance Procurement

[2] "CGN" as of July, 1975

[3] Subsequently replaced by a modified DLGN-42

period. Much of this almost residual appearance is due, no doubt, to the lower unit costs of these vessels. Thus for this 10% of its request budget the Navy could purchase more than twenty auxiliary vessels; the remaining 90% of the SCN budget during the 1971–1977 period was to purchase more than 100 vessels.

The decision to procure Hi-Mix vessels first is perhaps an indicator of the Navy's greatest fears about the Soviet Navy: its concerns have not been with the number of Soviet ships, but rather with their increased unit capability. Hi-Mix vessels—CVNs, CGNs, DD-963s—would be those most appropriate to countering this perceived deterioration in the qualitative naval balance, whereas FFG-7 size ships would be a priority buy if numbers were a real concern. In a broader foreign policy context, Hi-Mix ships would also be of immediate importance to a foreign policy that was increasingly ambivalent concerning direct military intervention but that required high levels of symbolic presence to maintain its "credibility." Indeed, some observers have concluded that recent anxiety over the Soviet Navy is not rooted in any great fear that Soviet war-fighting propensities or capability have increased significantly vis-à-vis the American Navy. Rather, the concern in the White House, State Department, and Department of Defense is that even marginally expanded Soviet naval presence could give the impression of neutralizing the primary military instrumentality of an American foreign policy now dependent upon posturing and threat rather than sustained, intense conventional military intervention.[24]

Congressional Action on SCN Budgets and Force Levels

In any event, congressional action on the new SCN portion of the Navy's budget requests conformed to the general pattern of behavior discussed above. During most of the Nixon-Ford years there was some evidence of "significant" congressional activism. In the final analysis, however, this activism occurred within a programmatic framework set by the executive, and throughout most of the period it did not decisively change the thrust of these priorities concerning naval force structure.

The evidence of congressional activism lies in the magnitude of congressional changes in the president's aggregate requests for new ship construction. Table 8 arrays the percentage changes effected by Congress on the president's new SCN budget requests for the period fiscal 1971 through fiscal 1977. The percentage changes have not been computed on individual ship requests but rather on the aggregate of vessels grouped into the mission-related areas noted by former CNO Zumwalt and displayed in Table 7. In addition, differences in the presidential budget requests and final congressional action have been computed and are displayed in the last column.

These percentage changes are certainly suggestive of high congressional activity. Thus, for example, the aggregate new SCN budget was changed more than 9% and the difference in the presidential and congressional requests for Sea Control/Lo-Mix ships is a dramatic 30%. Similarly, changes in the Support class requests is in excess of 20%. It would seem, therefore, that our summary indicator confirms considerable congressional activity in the form of nontrivial adjustments of the president's new SCN program. Closer attention to the range of percentage changes, the mission area/ship class concentration of the smaller changes, and the force size indicators in Table 7 suggests a much more ambiguous picture, however.

First, let us note that the lower percentage changes fall on those classes of vessels which have been the higher priority elements of the executive request throughout most of the Nixon-Ford years. Thus, Sea Control/Hi-Mix ships have averaged more than 60% of the new SCN request throughout the 1970s and they have been subject to the lowest percentage changes. Moreover, in two of these years the congressional changes were in the form of *increases* in the administration's request. And in three other years, Congress made *no* change in the Hi-Mix request. The next lowest percentage change in the executive's request concerns the Strategic mission area, the Trident. Furthermore, the Trident program has been second only to the Sea Control/Hi-Mix ships in the portion of the new SCN request it has commanded—almost 24% since fiscal 1973.

Table 8

Congressional Percentage Reductions in President's New SCN Budget Request, 1971–1977, Mean Annual Absolute Differences

	1971	1972	1973	1974	1975	1976	1977	MAAD
Strategic			−13.850	−27.656	0.000	+6.035	0.000	9.508
Sea Control								
(1) Hi-Mix	+2.790	+0.468	−11.653	0.000	0.000	−36.946	0.000	8.643
(2) Lo-Mix	0.000	−91.005	−26.880	−17.000	−59.431	−19.001	−0.027	30.478
Subtotal	+2.251	−2.537	−13.458	−0.310	−21.573	−27.118	−0.009	9.608
Combatants	+2.251	−2.537	−13.513	−8.055	−13.338	−19.032	−0.008	8.391
Noncombatants	0.000	−33.887	−10.142	−48.454	−36.168	−27.043	−0.139	22.262
Grand Total	+2.219	−7.271	−13.249	−8.297	−15.067	−20.744	−0.027	9.553

Source: Table 7

Here again, more than half of the congressional changes have been either program increases or no-change decisions. In contrast, Sea Control and Support ships which through most of the period consumed the smaller portions of the SCN request have been subject to the highest percentage changes. And with only minor exceptions, these congressional changes have been reductions in the administration's request.

A second indication of consonance in outlook between executive priorities and congressional behavior can be found in the combatant/noncombatant mix. Thus combatant vessels are subjected to a congressional percentage change of less than 9% while accounting for about 90% of the average presidential request. At the same time, noncombatants as a class were receiving changes of more than 20% while accounting for about 10% of the presidential request. Moreover, the Sea Control group of warships which has constituted the center of gravity for the Navy's SCN request during the 1970s— even with the larger changes in the Lo-Mix component—also receives somewhat gentler treatment from Congress than, for example, Trident and the noncombatant class of ships.

A possible explanation of this favorable treatment of SCN requests for Hi-Mix ships is that the Congress, its purported defense skepticism notwithstanding, wants even more than does the executive a Navy composed of larger ships with considerable offensive capability (the corollary being, of course, higher prices as well). Smaller vessels with lesser or no significant strike capacity are seen as desirable but of a lower priority, hence subjected to higher budget changes generally in the form of reductions. Indeed, congressional action with respect to the Defense Department's request for the PHM, Sea Control Ship, and the initial procurement of the FFG-7 class of guided missile frigate suggests that its penchant for Hi-Mix platforms may even run against DOD desires upon occasion. Thus, even after DOD procurement priorities had begun to shift to the Lo-Mix end of the spectrum in fiscal 1975, Congress cut the Lo-Mix request severely—59% including termination of the SCS program—in contrast to no change in the Hi-Mix request.

Similarly, congressional changes in executive force-level requests tend to concentrate[25] at the Lo-Mix end of the force structure mix. Conversely, congressional "no-change" decisions concerning force levels cluster around Trident and Sea Control/Hi-Mix requests. If we accept the idea that "no-change" outcomes reflect agreement with executive decisions, then these findings lend support to the notion that Congress looks most favorably on DOD requests for high-capability ships.

In summary, during the early Nixon-Ford years Congress seldom changed significantly the Department of Defense's new SCN requests. Only in three instances did it depart from a pattern of broad acceptance of the executive's priorities: (1) a denial of all DD-963 requests in fiscal 1973, (2) the DLGN (CGN) program initiated during the transitional year of fiscal 1970, and (3) the rather high level of budgetary antipathy it displayed throughout the period toward DOD requests for Lo-Mix Sea Control ships. In the first case, the congressional rationale was not the product of any rejection of the concept of the ships in question. The DD-963 reduction of fiscal 1973 seems to have been entirely the result of a congressional decision simply to stretch out the purchase of the ships in view of production slippages that had developed at the Litton shipyards where the *Spruance*-class destroyers were being constructed.[26] Even though the force-level request was denied in this case, Congress appropriated almost a quarter of a billion dollars for advanced procurement to protect the Navy's contract options on the same seven DD-963s being "rejected." Thus, in the case of the DD-963 program changes, congressional action was not the result of any programmatic policy disagreement with the Navy or DOD. In the case of the DLGN-38, the congressional action was related to a perceived inadequacy in the weapons complement for the ship.[27]

The third instance in which Congress has balked at executive priorities—the entire group of Lo-Mix ships—is by far the most important and revealing of a congressional propensity for larger, high-capability ships. Though most recent congressional antipathy for smaller combatants has focused on the FFG-7 program, resistance to the Lo-Mix group has been evident throughout the authorization phase of the Navy's modernization program.

One of the lower-capability SCN programs that has encountered congressional resistance but not outright rejection is the Patrol Hydrofoil Boat (PHM). Four PHM have been approved, but in fiscal 1976 Congress rejected the DOD request for two additional craft, noting that test results were ambiguous and cost escalation significant. At the same time, however, it did not reject the concept of the PHM. Indeed, the Senate Armed Services Committee (the point at which the program reduction was initiated) was explicit that its action was related to program management and not the PHM concept. In fact, the committee urged the Navy to pay close attention to the use of such craft by other navies.[28]

Two other Lo-Mix programs have not been handled with such gentleness. In the most important case, the FFG-7, there are strong echoes of concern for the management of the development and procurement of the ship. In fiscal 1972, for example, a congressional committee voiced its sympathy for the program but felt that advanced procurements were premature.[29] Again in fiscal 1973 skepticism was expressed concerning the practice of procuring the lead class of a ship as a prototype vessel, although the procurement funds were allowed.[30] By fiscal 1975, this skepticism fixed on development problems for the ship's fire control system as the basis for denying procurement authority for four of the requested seven ships.[31] In addition, however, there does seem to be a congressional undercurrent of doubt concerning the capability of the ship. Perhaps in anticipation of such sentiment, Secretary of Defense Rumsfeld pointedly noted in his fiscal 1977 presentation on the FFG-7 that the frigates "will carry the Harpoon missile, which, together with their other weapon systems, will make them as heavily armed as any ships of their size in the world."[32] In addition Rumsfeld responded to previously expressed congressional concerns about the unit cost of the ship, its limited offensive capability, and reported sea-keeping problems.[33]

A preoccupation with the capability of Lo-Mix ships has not been confined to the FFG-7. Earlier, Congress proved unwilling to buy the Sea Control Ship which was envisaged by the Navy as performing a role related to that which the FFG-7 is to fill. In this case, however, the SCS was to carry a complement of aircraft, but of limited offensive strike capacity. Congress supported the SCS while it remained in the research and development stages but refused a request for procurement funds in fiscal 1973. Advanced procurement money was granted in fiscal 1974, but House Appropriations added an ominous caveat: "It would appear that a mini-aircraft carrier, if you will, with arresting gear and catapults could provide the Navy with far more flexibility than the Sea Control Ship concept."[34] This reasoning was a harbinger of the fiscal 1975 decision to terminate the program because of the SCS's limited offensive and defensive capability. Congress made it known that it preferred greater offensive capability for Lo-Mix ships by authorizing the use of previously appropriated SCS funds for the study of a mini-aircraft carrier which, though performing Lo-Mix missions, would nevertheless employ existing attack and defensive aircraft.[35]

Congressional behavior with respect to Lo-Mix requests does reflect, therefore, programmatic concerns in that Congress seems to seek the most potent and highly visible offensive force structure possible. Indeed, some elements in Congress apparently have doubts about the entire Lo-Mix concept. Congressional budgetary and force level scrutiny has been concentrated on the Navy's Lo-Mix items and has proved far more likely to cut these requests than any other element of the SCN requests. Moreover, when changing Navy requests in the Hi-Mix sector, Congress has proved as likely to *increase* the Navy's request as reduce it. None of the Lo-Mix changes have been of this nature. Additional evidence of this skepticism lies in the House Armed Services Committee's unsuccessful attempt to replace four of the FFG-7's requested by the Ford administration in fiscal 1977 with four DD-963s—a Hi-Mix (though nonnuclear) ship.

Other Sources of Congressional Behavior

The end of the Ford administration and the early months of the Carter administration revealed an additional form of congressional activism with respect to executive requests. In those instances when the executive demonstrates internal disagreement as to its priorities, the Congress is not likely to approve executive budget requests involving new programs. The transition of administrations frequently involves such uncertainty, especially if a change in parties results from a presidential election. The fiscal year 1978 request was of course subject to all of the disjunctions of the American electoral and budgetary calendars. But the uncertainties implicit in a situation in which an outgoing president prepares and submits a budget immediately subject to amendment and rescission by his successor were compounded in 1976–1977 by divisions within the executive against a backdrop of prior legislation. An underlying issue in this case was the requirement under Title VIII of the 1975 DOD Appropriation Act that all new major combatants be nuclear powered unless the president can satisfy Congress that a conventionally-powered combatant is in the national interest. President Ford and the Secretary of Defense attempted in 1975 and 1976 to minimize the force planning and budgetary constraints implied in Title VIII by gaining congressional acceptance for the continued use of conventional power on major combatants. The focus of the effort was the new Aegis system with President Ford requesting in fiscal 1977 that the first new Aegis platform be a conventionally-powered adaptation of the DD-963 to be reclassified DDG-47. At the same time, the Ford administration renewed a requested new class of nuclear-powered strike cruisers (CSGN) with Aegis to become the basis of CNO James Holloway's greatly augmented Hi-Mix Sea Control fleet. Congress had rejected the CSGN in fiscal 1976, perhaps anticipating that the CSGN request involved a division within the executive branch as well as the fact that it was a last-minute insertion into the FY 1976 request.

The fight over the Aegis platform in 1976 and, by implication, the future of Title VIII also revealed some differences within the Congress. The House Armed Services Committee—long a stronghold of nuclear navy sentiment—denied the DDG-47, approved advanced procurement for three CSGN, and authorized funds for the conversion and modernization of the *Long Beach* as an Aegis/CSGN. The Senate, perhaps reflecting the skepticism of its Chairman concerning some recent Navy requests,[36] approved the DDG-47 and denied the CSGN request as well as the *Long Beach* conversion funds. A compromise was subsequently worked out between the Armed Services Committees as both the DDG-47 and the new CSGN were denied but with the conferees on the Authorization bill agreeing to consider requests for supplemental funds.[37] At the same time the conferees agreed with the House decision to allow funds for the conversion of the *Long Beach* into a nuclear-powered Aegis platform.

In effect, the fiscal 1976 decisions were not rejections of Navy programs so much as deferrals of issues that had not yet been resolved within the executive in a presidential election year. The willingness to consider supplemental requests can be viewed as an open invitation to return to Congress with a request for the new class or classes of ships once the executive was able to place its house in order. Congress seems to have said in the fiscal 1976 decisions that it would not resolve internal disagreements for the executive or ignore such disagreement by giving both sides of the argument what they wanted. The fiscal 1976 decisions may also have represented congressional insistence upon a nuclear navy as mandated by Title VIII. Some congressional dissatisfaction with Title VIII is evident in the Senate Armed Services Committee's attempt in 1976 to repeal the nuclear navy requirement of Title VIII and in the Senate Committee's support for the president's DDG-47 Aegis platform.[38] However, the Senate lost on both counts.

Summary and Conclusions

In this chapter we have surveyed the congressional perception of and behavior concerning the United States Navy and its force structure. The apparent renaissance of sea power, the salience of the Navy and the instrumentalities it represents in the American defense posture, and hence the Navy's relative success in the inextricably linked bureaucratic and budgetary arenas of the executive branch are fairly well documented. However, considerable speculation about the emergence of a "new Congress" more hostile to reliance upon military intervention in support of a globalist foreign policy has raised doubts about its receptivity toward the Navy's desire to reconstruct and modernize a naval force structure sufficient to maintain superiority vis-à-vis America's most likely naval adversary, the Soviet Union.

Congressional budgetary activism in the 1970s has indeed been significant. Thus the differences between presidential requests and congressional appropriations for new obligational authority for the total DOD budget as well as for its major appropriations titles suggest even higher levels of congressional activism than during the 1960s. The Navy has not escaped this activism inasmuch as the congressionally inflicted percentage changes in the Navy's aggregate budget requests have been at least as significant as for the other services. Nonetheless, larger annual increases in the Navy's requests for NOA have resulted in higher levels of Navy budgetary growth than for the other services. Thus, by the mid-1970s the Navy's share of congressionally allowed NOA was the largest of the three services and its rate of growth, congressional activism notwithstanding, was greater than Army, Air Force, and aggregate DOD budgetary growth during the 1970s.

A more intensive analysis of the programmatic heart of the Navy's budget requests—new SCN procurement—suggests, however, that despite the appearance of high levels of congressional activism the Navy's program priorities were not severely transformed by Congress during the early and mid-1970s. A combination of relatively smaller percentage reductions and higher than expected concentrations of "no-change" decisions on the Navy's higher-priority SCN procurement requests has meant that the Navy's priorities, though affected, remained more or less intact. More specifically, the Navy throughout the early 1970s placed emphasis on the development and procurement of high-capability and high-cost surface and submarine combatants so as to offset perceived Soviet naval expansion. With minor exceptions, Congress prior to fiscal 1976 gave the Navy what it wanted of these classes of ships when it wanted them. In fact, in the case of the attack submarines, Congress occasionally increased the rate of procurement. The only exceptions to this trend emerged at the end of the Ford administration with respect to the DOD's request for a new class of "strike cruiser" and an adaptation of the DD-963 as a conventionally powered platform for the Navy's new fleet defense system, Aegis. Both requests were denied but congressional action seemed a function of congressional hesitancy in the face of continuing debate within the executive branch, between the executive and Congress, and within Congress itself concerning Title VIII's mandate for a nuclear navy. In addition, perhaps, Congress was reluctant to accept new program departures with a presidential election pending. With the election over, it accepted a request for the first DDG-47.

More recently, however, congressional activism with respect to the Navy's lower capability and lower cost SCN requests may have crimped Navy priorities somewhat. By fiscal 1975 the Navy's top priority new SCN procurement program was the Lo-Mix guided missile frigate, the FFG-7, yet congressional scrutiny of this program had become especially intense in fiscal 1975, 1976, and 1977. Previous negative congressional action on lower capability ships such as the Sea Control Ship and the Patrol Hydrofoil boat has been predicated upon concern about the combination of lower offensive capacity and escalating unit costs that have been characteristic of this class of ships. Also, we might speculate that congressional concern that Title VIII be controlling in the future of the Navy is of importance in understanding its past hostility toward

Lo-Mix ships. Although they do not fall within the definition of a "major" combatant, the predominance of FFGs in the Navy's Five-Year Shipbuilding Programs might well be viewed by congressional nuclear Navy advocates as subterfuge on the part of Navy officials who have proved something less than enthusiastic about the budgetary and force structure/level implications of Title VIII. In any event, congressional hostility toward the Navy's lower capability ships is not revealing of hostility toward the use of sea power. Rather, many in Congress seem to be more willing than the Navy to support a "big ship fleet" in the sense of large, high capability, and nuclear-powered ships.

During his campaign, Jimmy Carter promised reductions in the defense budget but at the same time suggested that he would support "an aggressive shipbuilding program with concentration on quality and mobility," and perhaps an expansion of the U.S. naval presence in the Mediterranean coupled with a reduction of American naval assets in the Pacific.[39] Among his first acts as president, however, was the elimination of the strike cruiser within an overall reduction of the Ford administration's last ship construction requests. Other Carter rescissions included one attack submarine (Ford had requested two) and two FFGs (Ford had requested eleven).[40] Even more portentous was the affirmation by the Carter administration of the outgoing Ford administration's last-minute rescission of a fifth nuclear aircraft carrier and the conversion funds for the *Long Beach* to a nuclear-powered Aegis platform.

Despite a closely divided House Appropriations Committee (the rescission of the aircraft carrier carried by a 24–23 vote), Congress supported Carter's decision on the *Long Beach* and nuclear carrier.[41] Furthermore, in action on the FY 1978 SCN authorization, the House accepted the Carter administration's decision that the first Aegis platform would be a conventionally powered DDG-47. Nevertheless, the House Committee, while accepting the administration's decision on the nuclear carrier, blasted Carter's overall shipbuilding program as "grossly inadequate" and pointed toward a continuation of the "trend toward fewer and less capable ships which, in view of the Soviet naval buildup, can result in a navy 'second to one.' "[42] The idea of smaller carriers deploying V/STOL aircraft was greeted with the same skepticism that led to the rejection of the SCS earlier in the decade.

The initial congressional reaction was therefore tolerant of the Carter administration's desire to mark time on new program departures until it could write its own defense budget.[43] But when that first wholly Carter administration budget was forthcoming in 1978, absent a fourth *Nimitz*-class aircraft carrier, it seemed a confirmation of the reported reduction in the Navy's role and led to the mobilization of congressional sentiment favoring a highly visible surface Navy centered on the large-decked nuclear-powered aircraft carrier. In a series of actions on the FY 1979 procurement budget Congress first authorized and then appropriated more than $2 billion for the construction of the fifth nuclear carrier while moving cautiously on research and development of the Navy's V/STOL capability.[44] In response, President Carter vetoed the congressional action and when his veto was not overridden compelled Congress to delete the carrier.

In summary, this first major test of congressional constraints by the Carter administration suggests that where the administration's Navy budget priorities run counter to the pattern of congressional behavior and preferences during the early and mid-1970s, the executive can expect a vigorous congressional response. Indeed, the persistence of nuclear navy sentiment within the Navy and Congress would appear to be such that should the Carter administration persist on the course set during the first two years of its tenure,[45] it might be confronted with the reemergence of the kind of fissures that appeared in the early 1960s as Robert McNamara assumed a position against rapid expansion of nuclear power in any other than submarine forces. On the other hand, the Navy's proposed "balanced" approximation of a 600-ship force structure would seem to have been precluded by a combination of budgetary and shipyard constraints, notwithstanding apparent congressional support for a large and visible surface Navy.

Of course, congressional constraints on the use of the naval instrumentality may manifest themselves in nonbudgetary ways.

Congress may try, and indeed has tried in recent years, to limit, influence, or otherwise constrain the actual use of military power by the executive branch. Here, however, the post-Vietnam indicators are quite ambiguous and provide little basis for confident prediction. The Warpowers Act seemed to many to have been a decisive circumscription of presidential power; the *Mayaguez* incident seems on the other hand to confirm the worst fears of the skeptics. Similarly, the expansion of an American presence on Diego Garcia can be paired with the congressional refusal to support Secretary of State Kissinger's posturing with respect to Angola as contradictory precedents for congressional behavior.

But insofar as the budgetary process and its outcome are indicative of congressional behavior and priorities, there seems to have been some tendency during the 1970s to favor the instrumentality of sea power over others. Implicit in this is the assumption that sea power has unique demonstrative capacity with few or relatively low political costs and risks—the ideal instrumentality, in short, for an era in which the executive insists and Congress concurs that there is a continued necessity for "demonstrating will" while simultaneously the public displays ambivalence toward foreign commitments involving significant and/or intense conventional conflict. Herein, perhaps, lies the basis of much of the Navy's recent success in both the bureaucratic and congressional arenas: the apparent capacity of sea power for extending U.S. influence at relatively low cost, at least in a political sense. As long as this perception remains unshaken one would expect continued success for the Navy in the executive-legislative interaction, a change in administrations and a "new" Congress notwithstanding. Thus, the "new" Congress is at most an ambivalent constraint on American security policy in general and the Navy in particular. Ambivalence is, of course, a different posture from that of the 1950s and 1960s.

CHAPTER SIX

Public Opinion and Naval Power:
An Ambiguous Relationship

PUBLIC OPINION, as V. O. Key once put it, sets "general limits within which government may act."[1] This function of setting the boundaries of permissible behavior for policy has also been described by Harold Laski as being like the extended jaws of a shark: within this cavity, policy-makers must operate carefully. Thus, the public may be seen as having, at a minimum, an "osmotic" effect on policy-makers.[2] As Professor Bernard C. Cohen suggests, "the climate of opinion [becomes] part of the environment and cultural milieu that help to shape the policy-maker's own thinking [and] may consciously affect his own official behavior. . . ."[3] For much of the period after World War II, American foreign and defense policy-makers have been able to assume that the limits of public permissibility were rather broad, set by a public whose attitude was trusting and supportive. The public opinion data of the last decade, however, suggests a decidedly less permissive set of limits.[4]

In this chapter we will outline the nature and implications of this change in the climate of public opinion for the exercise of U.S. military power in the future. The task of relating these attitudes to the use of naval power is especially difficult. Public opinion polling does not ask questions at such a level of specificity. Moreover, it seems to be the case that the constraints imposed by public opinion will

164

be, as in the past, indirect. That is, the effect of public opinion on the use of naval and other forces of military power will likely be filtered through layers of political leadership, both executive and legislative, that seek to employ the instrumentalities of military force in international politics. Finally, there is now evidence that the policy community and elites are divided concerning the efficacy of military force.[5] Thus, unlike military technological change or the presence of the Soviet fleet, the effects of American public opinion are diffuse and nearly intangible at the level of employment of naval power. The effects on American foreign and defense policy-makers have been and will be no less real, however; and insofar as the United States Navy will be asked to respond to policies derived from a milieu conditioned by the public's and policy elite's expectations, fears, and demands, they can be regarded as no less important by the executors of naval power.

As a first step we will sketch some of the dimensions of the "new mood" of American public opinion. Second, we will identify some of the broad policy implications of these changes; and, finally, we will offer some speculation as to how this combination of conditions might affect thinking about and use of American naval power.

The Contemporary Public Mood: A New Reality

Throughout most of the period after World War II, the attitudes, opinions, or moods of the American public concerning foreign policy have been characterized by most analysts as swinging, sometimes unpredictably, between polar extremes: pessimism and optimism, pacifism and belligerency, or idealism and realism.[6] Retrospective analysis of the early Cold War and the apparent changes in the structure of American public opinion during the Vietnam War has given rise to some reinterpretation of this earlier view.[7] The dynamics of public opinion and belief system change are now regarded by some observers as more complex than a simple mood theory would suggest, and the overall pattern of public perceptions and opinions on foreign affairs is believed to be somewhat more stable than previously thought. Greater sensitivity to the problem of question and interview schedule construction has led some to ask whether much of the apparent swing in public mood is not a product of the instruments used in measuring it.[8] Furthermore, there is some evidence that the view of an unpredictable and potentially "dangerous" public held by many policy-makers may be a product of the mood changes of the opinion leaders most closely read by the policy elite itself. Thus one comparison of change in public opinion and shifts of position by leading columnists such as Lippmann, Alsop, and Reston during the depths of the Cold War concluded that the columnists were, if anything, more likely to display shifts in mood and attitude as the transient fortunes of the Cold War changed than was the public.[9] It is worth noting that insofar as these columnists and commentators rely on inside information, their shifts in mood are reflections of similar shifts within the government. It may be, therefore, that the conventional wisdom concerning the structure and dynamics of opinion change has been in some measure misdirected.

But we do not mean to argue that the public mood does not change. Rather, changes in public perceptions of the world must be understood as proceeding within a broad and relatively stable framework of self-interest and pragmatism. The dimensions of this framework cannot meaningfully be determined by surveys directed at using the specificity and quality of public information as indicators of attitudes. Thus questions which reveal popular ignorance of world geography or inability to spell "Dag Hammarskjöld" are of questionable utility in indicating anything beyond, perhaps, the pollsters' preconceptions concerning public opinion.[10] It is our contention that there has developed over the last decade a likely long-term change in the public temper that extends to the most fundamental dimensions and determinants of popular attitudes. Further, the structure of emerging public attitudes about government in general and foreign policy in particular will probably constrain a highly secretive, manipulative, or unconsciously interventionist foreign policy. And the new public mood may well curtail any policy which seems to have as its price continued social and economic dislocations. Most importantly, a policy which risks and fails will likely be in deep trouble; for public opinion now shows decreasing deference toward a public officialdom at odds with itself concerning the "lessons" of the last decade.[11] This closing of the limits of permissibility is not, it would seem, a temporary or transient phenomenon.

Among the important elements of this overall change has been the frequently noted decline in public confidence in the institutions and individuals responsible for the conduct of American foreign policy. Apart from the periodic personal approval ratings of particular presidents—which have shown a tendency for increasingly abbreviated postelection honeymoons—public confidence in the executive branch of government has plunged dramatically in the last decade. Even at the relative high point of 1966, those expressing "a great deal of confidence" in the people who run the executive branch stood at only 41%. Moreover, even *before* the Watergate trauma, similar expressions of confidence had declined in 1972 to 27%. By 1975, however, only 13% of the American people were willing to express a great deal of confidence in the executive branch. Similarly, the ratings of Congress have dropped from 42% in 1966 to 13% by the spring of 1975. Interestingly, only the military could command a significant majority of Americans willing to grant a great deal of confidence—62%—in 1966, but by 1975 that percentage had dropped to just over a third.[12] Polls conducted by the private sector have detected the same trend as well as an even deeper sense of alienation. Thus James B. Lindheim of the Yankelovich, Skelly and White polling company summarized the findings of recent polling conducted for the DuPont Corporation:

> [There] is a widespread sense of loss of autonomy, a loss of control over one's own life in a complex society that increasingly appears to be dominated by institutions, both public and private. That diminished confidence fosters a feeling of dependency, demonstrated by such recent issue concerns as health care and old-age security.
>
> An increasingly self-centered individual with a greater emphasis on self-interest, self-discovery and an insistence on freedom to decide

whether many of the traditional rules of personal conduct are proper or necessary. At the same time, people are much more strict in the standards they want to impose on institutions.

Lindheim suggests that there is nothing less than "a fundamental change in the social contract between individuals and institutions."[13]

Perhaps no less important is the evidence that the American people have a reasonably accurate sense of where the major institutions have stood with respect to one another in the making of American foreign policy in the recent past. And further, their conception of what the relationship of those institutions *ought* to be is rather different from their perceptions of the reality. Louis Harris recently described findings of his organization concerning the public's perceptions of the relative standing of major institutions and people as well as their preferences concerning these institutions and people:

> way ahead of the list of very important was the Secretary of State, 73 percent, the President only 49 percent, and then came American business 42, Congress 39, State Department 38, military 36, CIA 28, U.N. 28, labor unions 24, and down at the bottom of the list, public opinion 19.
>
> We then said which should be more important. At the head of the list came public opinion 59 percent, which is a big difference from how important people think it is, followed by Congress. People wanted Congress (48 percent) to have a more important voice, and then the President (45 percent) but still not substantial, and only 30 percent wanted the Secretary of State to have a more important voice, with a bit of slipoff on military's role. People don't want the military nor the CIA to have a more important role.[14]

Harris's findings have been confirmed by the Mervin Field California Poll where the President's position vis-à-vis the Congress was even weaker,[15] and by the findings of the Yankelovich organization, whose director has concluded:

> We have found some erosion in the virtually automatic public support for presidential initiatives in foreign policy. . . . In the past, large majorities of the public swung behind the President whenever he committed the country in a foreign policy action—whether or not people

agreed with the action. . . . This automatic support is far from dead; many people will still back presidential foreign policy initiatives irrespective of their own reservations. But uncritical trust in the President's judgement is gone. The assumption that in matters of foreign policy the President surely knows what he is doing and is surely pursuing the national interest has been deeply shaken. In the future, patterns of public support on foreign policy are more likely to resemble those on domestic policy where the majority does not always assume superior presidential knowledge, wisdom, and pursuit of the national interest.[16]

Recent analysis of the "rallying around the flag" phenomenon lends support to Yankelovich's point as well as the observation by Louis Harris that beginning with the mid-sixties, "As each crisis receded, national unity diminished. . . ."[17] An analysis of short-term foreign policy events by Professor Jong R. Lee concludes that "the events that tend to have relatively lasting impacts on presidential popularity are wars and military crises, with the average duration of five months. Policy initiatives tend to be associated with the greatest average change in popularity, while their duration is slightly shorter than that of military crises. Summit conferences tend to have a relatively low impact with extremely short duration."[18] If we examine chronologically Lee's data on popularity change and duration of the change for military crises and wars after World War II, the general erosion of automatic support for presidential initiative is evident (see Table 9).

After the peak in Cold War tension of the early 1960s (with the Berlin and Cuban Missile Crises), the duration of the expected change in presidential popularity is not especially impressive. The exceptions are the invasion of Laos in 1971 and the *Mayaguez* incident in 1975. The two exceptions are quite different, however, in that the Laos invasion resulted in a sustained negative shift in popular perceptions of the president, whereas the *Mayaguez* incident resulted in a more significant shift in popularity for a shorter period of time. Whether the *Mayaguez* case should be taken as an indicator of a new trend is not clear. As will be discussed below, it may be that the *Mayaguez* incident is indicative of elements in public opinion other than any incipient reversal of the last decade's erosion of public rallying around the flag. In any event, Lee concludes: "A President can count on increased popularity after a salient international event, but he cannot expect it to last very long. Nor can he expect the public to approve indiscriminately of his performance after the major crisis or event."[19]

Table 9
"Rallying around the Flag, 1948–1975"

Year	Event	% change in popularity	Duration in months
1948	Berlin Blockade	+3	1
1950	Invasion of South Korea	+9	5
1958	Troops to Lebanon	+6	3
1961	Berlin Crisis	+8	12
1962	Cuban Missile Crisis	+12	8
1965	Bombing of North Vietnam	+1	1
1965	Troops to Dominican Republic	+6	3
1966	Extension of Bombing, Hanoi	+8	2
1967	Mid-East War	+8	1
1970	Invasion of Cambodia	+3	2
1971	Invasion of Laos	−7	14
1975	*Mayaguez* Incident	+11	8

Source: Jong R. Lee, "Rallying Around the Flag: Foreign Policy Events and Presidential Popularity," *Presidential Studies Quarterly*, Vol. 7, no. 4 (Fall 1977), Table 1, p. 254.

In summary, what appeared in the 1950s and early 1960s to be substantial, basic trust of American institutions and leadership has vanished in the wake of Vietnam and Watergate. Marginal shifts in "optimism" concerning the private lives of individuals cannot erase the implications of the deeper changes that have occurred since the early 1960s. At that time 85% of the American people regarded their government and political system as the elements of their country of which they were proudest;[20] by the mid-1970s Harris found that 75% of the American people believed that their government lied to them in some degree.[21] A Department of State-commissioned survey recently found that a majority of Americans believe that "This country's leaders really don't want to know what people like me think about foreign policy."[22] It is little wonder, therefore, that Henry Kissinger fretted upon leaving office that "the fundamental necessity of American foreign policy . . . is to restore our national consensus on our broader purposes in the world."[23] But there is little evidence that the reconstruction of that consensus will occur rapidly or easily.

A New Isolationism?

In the late 1960s and throughout the 1970s, public opinion analysis detected a trend in American attitudes toward foreign involvement that parallels the general decline in support for those institutions most intimately associated with foreign and defense policy. The once significant support for American global involvement has eroded among mass publics and perhaps most significantly within those attentive or elite publics that were most predictably "internationalist" throughout the post-World War II period prior to Vietnam. It is less clear, however, that these developments can be characterized as the reassertion of the "isolationism" long feared by Cold War foreign policy elites as the latent "normal" American attitude toward the world and American involvement in it. A decade of Vietnam and post-Vietnam polling suggests an increase in attitudes that are "isolationist," especially among the young, but the picture now emerging is much more complex, suggesting instead a public that is skeptical but not unalterably opposed to humane, cautious, and pragmatically conducted foreign involvement.

The Decline of "Internationalism"

Beginning about 1968, periodic public opinion surveys of foreign policy attitudes have chronicled a decline in the unquestioning and unequivocal "internationalist" segment of the public, culminating in the late 1970s in an "American public . . . that continues—in principle—to support activist ideals in foreign policy, despite the bitter experience of Vietnam. At the same time, opinion on specific policy issues appears to be governed by a more pragmatic, cautious, and skeptical orientation than prevailed before Vietnam."[24] Between 1968 and 1974, for example, Harris found that the percentage of clearly "isolationist" Americans increased from less than 10% to about 21%. At the same time, 60% of the American public who were "internationalist" in 1968 declined to 41% by 1974. During the same period, those regarded by the Harris organization as "completely internationalists" dropped to just under 20% from about 30% in the mid-sixties.[25]

Poll data from the 1975–1976 period shows some, but not major, change in these trends apart from some diminution in the rate of growth of what some pollsters regard as "isolationist" sentiment. Nevertheless, such sentiment after a modest decline in 1975 had grown to 23% by 1976, and "internationalist" sentiment had dropped to 44% in 1976 after temporarily climbing to 45% in 1975.[26] Watts and Free note that one of the most significant characteristics of public attitudes is the emergence of a substantial portion of the populace—about one-third—who do not fall neatly into either category and now must be characterized as "mixed" in their attitudes towards American involvement abroad.[27] At the same time, the *direction* in which popular attitudes have moved and, to a certain extent, continues to move is quite clear. Moreover, if, as Watts and Free have contended, "isolationist" sentiment has peaked at mid-decade, the new structure of belief systems concerning American foreign policy is hardly supportive of the kind of activism that has marked the last several decades.

The new mood is therefore one of considerable skepticism concerning the prospects for the future and the responsiveness of the international system to American values and objectives.[28] Earlier, during the decade 1965–1975, there was indeed evidence that this skepticism would manifest itself in isolationism. The Vietnam War, for example, was believed by 65% of the public to have been "immoral." Louis Harris wrote that when he asked what troubled people most about the war, easily the dominant reply at any point from 1965 on was "all the killing."[29] By mid-1969, the Harris organization found that there was no country among the network of allies comprising the American post-World War II global security system which a majority of Americans was willing to use force to defend.[30] Fewer than 20% were prepared to use American troops in defense of Israel, 27% in the case of West Berlin, and as recently as 1974, fewer than half were prepared to use military force in the defense of either Japan or Western Europe.[31] More generally, 50% of Americans in 1972 could not agree with the proposition, "The United States should maintain its dominant position as the world's most powerful nation at all costs, even going to the very brink of war if necessary": 56% had agreed with that sentiment in 1964. On the other hand, 77% agreed in 1974 that "We shouldn't think so much in international terms but concentrate more on our own national problems and building up our strength and prosperity here at home."[32]

By the late 1970s, there was evidence that, as the Vietnam War receded somewhat in time, there might be some moderating of these sentiments. Analysis is complicated by the fact that results on comparable questions are not yet available; nevertheless, a poll released by the Kettering Foundation in early 1978 found that: 54% of the public was prepared to keep U.S. troops in Japan; 56% favored leaving American troops in Korea; and almost 62% supported their presence in Europe. At the same time, however, the percentages favoring withdrawal of American troops were 37%, 36%, and 30% respectively.[33] Supporting the presence of American troops is, of course, quite different than actually using those forces in combat. Questions to this point were not asked by the Kettering researchers; however, in their summary of findings concerning a number of other questions designed to determine support of foreign military activity by the United States, they conclude:

> If anything, the public is even less enthusiastic about foreign military activities than about the pursuit of democracy. Fewer than 25% support increased military spending. In addition, "stopping wars between small countries" and "protecting weaker countries against ag-

gression" were rated at the bottom of the list of ten foreign policy goals given to respondents, drawing ratings of "very important" from only 29% and 28% of the sample respectively. Even less support was evident for conducting secret interventionist activities in other countries: only 19% supported the use of covert methods to overthrow unfriendly governments. Support increased, but still to less than 30% for U.S. secret help to groups in other countries attempting to overthrow communist governments. About the same percentage felt the U.S. should help fight communist-backed groups in a non-communist country.[34]

Paralleling these findings are those which measure the public's attitudes concerning defense expenditures. Once again there is a shift in popular attitudes after 1968. Professor Bruce Russett's analysis of the evolution of popular attitudes toward defense spending from 1937 to the early 1970s found that before the early to mid-1960s no more than 20% of Americans wanted to cut defense spending. By the early 1970s, however, the figure had risen to a majority of the public as a whole and in none of the standard survey categories (sex, race, education, occupation, age, politics, etc.) did it drop below 40%. Moreover, the greatest sentiment for reducing defense spending, 60%, was found among the college educated.[35]

The Kettering data for the late 1970s show some reversal of this trend. From January 1976 to December of 1977, sentiment was found to shift away from reduction of defense spending although most of the change in opinion was not necessarily in favor of increasing defense spending. By late 1977, therefore, 30% of the public seemed to favor an increase in defense spending, 15% a reduction, and 47% maintaining defense spending at current levels.[36] Here again the problem of question comparability enters into any analysis of a trend. Unlike the data employed by Russett, the Kettering interview schedules linked the question of defense spending with questions asking the respondents to compare American military strength with the Soviet Union. Even so, it is interesting to note that only 48% of these polled were prepared to advocate that the United States must "spend whatever is necessary to keep ahead of Russia";

42% were prepared to accept keeping "even" and 8% accepted the proposition that "it is all right if the U.S. gets slightly behind Russia."[37]

Skepticism and the Future

As the United States moves into the 1980s, therefore, it seems that whatever disaffection there was in the late 1960s and early 1970s has not coalesced into a mindless desire for withdrawal from world politics. The foreign policy priorities of the American people are by no means inconsistent with internationalism, although it is equally clear that they do not view the international system as requiring, nor are they supportive of, the policy instrumentalities of the last twenty-five years. Domestic concerns are now accorded highest priority, but the public continues to view the Soviet Union and the People's Republic of China as hostile powers requiring a strong American defense posture.[38] However, the public no longer believes it necessary that international relations be characterized by tension and the fear of war. Indeed, the latter fear has declined in the view of most Americans and with it a growing sense of the need for international cooperation, especially with America's traditional allies, is evident.[39]

Harsh ideological confrontation is no longer seen as necessary or desirable and there seems to be a fairly broad acceptance of a more complexly textured international order. For example, Louis Harris reports:

> No more than 28 percent of the public gives a top priority to helping bring a democratic form of government to other nations. . . . We are by no means convinced that other peoples and other countries have to be a mirror of American democracy in order to find their ultimate salvation. This finding is important, for it means that as a people we are prepared to live with a kind of pluralism in the world.
> . . . By 60 to 25 percent, a majority endorse the idea of trading with Communist nations.
> By 58 to 20 percent, a substantial majority support the policy of "backing socialist governments that respect the basic rights of their people."

By a narrower margin, a plurality of 41 to 32 percent feel our country is justified "to recognize democratic left-wing governments when they come to power."

And by a close 45 to 42 percent, a plurality also supports our "backing governments which believe in free enterprise but not in democracy."[40]

President Carter's emphasis on human rights will, in view of Harris's findings, be well received. However, while Carter's campaign has thus far been directed primarily at the Russians, public sentiment runs to rejection of almost all forms of totalitarianism including those extending benefits to the United States. Thus, almost three-fourths of the people interviewed by Harris in 1975 subscribed to the proposition that it was "morally wrong for the United States to back military dictatorships that strip their people of their basic rights, even if that dictatorship will allow us to set up military bases in that country."[41] Moreover, the apparent rejection of American activism built around military instruments does not translate into a simple-minded rejection of all activism. Harris has found a majority of the American people favoring economic assistance if the people of the recipient countries benefit, more than two-thirds willing to cut the nonessential use of fertilizer if it would mean a rise in world food availability, and more than 75% agreeable to one meatless day a week to help out with food shortages globally.[42]

In sum, the American people, as virtually all public opinion analysts have found, feel that the position of the United States in the world has declined and that something ought to be done to restore that position. But it is apparently inaccurate to infer from that finding that Americans have turned inward to a surly "go-it-alone" nationalism.[43] Thus Harris, among others, has found that Americans believe that this decline can be traced to "Watergate, our role in Vietnam, our interference in the internal affairs of other nations, and our lack of compassion for humanitarian objectives."[44] There is a clear consensus that the United States should "avoid commitments, and potentially bloody involvements, where security interests are not clear."[45] But more positively, the implicit notion of the public as "beast" that runs throughout much Cold War rumination by American policy elites[46] seems clearly wide of the mark. Daniel Yankelovich notes concerning Vietnam:

> Their response to defeat in Vietnam can only be described as mature and sensible. There is no hysteria, no stab-in-the-back psychology but simply a desire to put that unfortunate chapter of our history behind us so that we can get on with the job of making our country a better place to work and live and of finding a new moral direction worthy of the United States. Overall, the American people are in a sane, mature, and stable if troubled state of mind. They are prepared to support any reasonable foreign policy initiatives that reflect an enlightened view of American self interest.[47]

The concern about and desire for an enlightened and moral policy are underscored by Harris:

> The American people are prepared to take giant strides toward international participation, well beyond what their leaders have asked. In foreign policy, as on most domestic issues, the problem is not one of a leadership trying to get a reluctant flock of followers to consent to necessary foreign policy measures, but rather one of a people deeply traumatized by the Vietnam experience, who have become far more selective and articulate about what they are willing to see their Government stand for. . . .
>
> Leadership which has the courage to ask the public here in this country to make sacrifices to help the lot of people around the world, which believes that a sense of genuine morality should guide our foreign policy, which goes beyond simple balance of power considerations in choosing our allies will find a responsive public out there.[48]

Other observers are less confident. In early 1978, the *New York Times*, for example, could be found editorializing about an "inward-looking nation" characterized by "indifference," "dispiriting modesty," and "a deeper trend that finds Americans turning their backs on public affairs altogether."[49] A week earlier in a commentary on the decade following the collapse of American policy and "The Consensus That Died at Tet," the *Times* editorialist summarized a decade of poll findings:

It is a peculiarity of the present time that American concerns about the world are in transition. The once overriding commitment to resist Communism everywhere is seen as having been profligate. The defense of the nation's economy—and even liberty—is seen as requiring a distinction between the Soviet exertions that threaten us and those that merely annoy. But there is no handy measure for such selectivity. There is no consensus either about how to rank rival objectives abroad —promoting the economic strength of the industrial democracies or containing such dangers as the poverty of over-populated societies and the proliferation of nuclear know-how.[50]

"What is lacking," the *Times* suggests, "is not a sense of the world, or of its problems, only confidence."[51] Presumably, as Harris has posited and the *Times* implies, leadership can instill that confidence. However, the *Times* as an instrument of elite communication reflects the substantial evidence that the traditional policy elites which have provided that leadership throughout the Cold War are no less disoriented than the people they would lead.

The Lessons of a Bad Decade

The capacity of American leaders to mobilize public opinion is dependent in large measure on their own reactions to the last decade. Somewhat less attention has been devoted to the analysis of "attentive publics," opinion leaders, or the leadership elite itself concerning the Vietnam War and its implications for American policy. Nevertheless, the public statements of President Carter's Secretaries of Defense and State concerning the "lessons" they had drawn from the country's and their own involvement in Vietnam as well as some preliminary attempts to measure elite attitudes suggest a picture not unlike that described above for the public in general. Indeed, in some respects American elites are more polarized and uncertain than mass publics.

Economic and Military Elites

Russett's research, for example, indicated much support among the "attentive public" for the so-called new isolationism. These atten-

tive publics have been and remain the source of most internationalist sentiment: the only majorities expressing internationalist sentiments are those with college educations (58%), incomes of $20,000
or more (53%), and professional and business people (54%).[52] At the
same time, however, American elites display an increasingly quali-
fied acceptance of some elements of "internationalism," especially
U.S. military intervention. Thus a recent survey of corporate executives found that a majority believe that the commitment of U.S.
ground troops in Vietnam was wrong—bad for the economy and bad
for American social and political institutions. Future U.S. intervention in the event of an armed attack by Communist forces was supported by a majority only with respect to West Germany and Mexico and there was no majority in favor of U.S. military intervention against indigenously controlled Communist insurgencies anywhere.[53]

Russett found that middle-level military officers were only slightly
more interventionist. When the same questions asked of the business community were put to some six hundred military officers of
colonel and lieutenant colonel rank, a majority would add only
Brazil, Japan, and Thailand to those countries in which the U.S.
should respond in the event of an invasion. Furthermore, a majority would intervene against an indigenously controlled insurgency
only in Mexico. "The apparent reluctance to be drawn into an overseas war is striking," Russett concludes. "All these results, but especially those for the business executives, seem very strange com-
ing from a formerly 'internationalist' elite."[54]

Finally, among the corporate respondents there was majority acceptance of significant reduction in American defense expenditures
and although a bare majority (52%) felt that a reduction of as much
as 25% would adversely affect U.S. security, only a third felt that
such a reduction would hurt the American economy.[55] Moreover,
business elites saw no self-evident negative relationship between a
retrenchment of American foreign commitments and the foreign
economy of the U.S., especially the foreign economic expansion of
the U.S. Predictably, there was near-unanimity (98%) that American

trade with the Soviet Union and China would expand and that "trade, technical cooperation, and economic interdependence" were considered (by 65%) "the most important approach to world peace." U.S. military superiority and/or a balance of power were named by only 19.5%.[56]

The 1976 Kettering data for the elite portion of their sample is generally supportive of Russett and Hanson's earlier findings. Detailed follow-up analysis of what was regarded as a "conservative" Pittsburgh elite was conducted by the Kettering researchers. Concerning this group, they concluded:

> Generally speaking, the elite took an even more activist orientation toward world affairs than the public generally. . . . This activism was particularly dramatic for Soviet trade, third world aid and interventionism. The elite were also more active supporters of aid to and alliances with non-democracies. At the same time they were less interested in simply pursuing narrow national economic interests and in stopping the spread of communism or dictatorships. Instead, elite activism seemed directed toward developing an expanded world economy, a goal in which their self-interest more clearly resides.[57]

Within this group there was overwhelming support for keeping U.S. troops in Europe (91%), spying on other countries (100%), and engaging in covert operations (54%). However, against these interventionist indicators, the Kettering study notes: only 29% feeling that the U.S. must remain "well ahead" of the Soviet Union militarily; 62% wanting to trade with the Soviets "on credit"; 92% committed to helping the less developed countries including 60% willing to reduce their standard of living if necessary; but only 29% feeling that "stopping the spread of communism" was a "very important" goal of American foreign policy.[58]

When extended to the elites of major cities in all regions of the United States, the Kettering researchers conclude: "The better-educated and more affluent are less ideologically opposed to the Soviet Union and more ideologically supportive of human rights, trade, and aid to Third World countries. In each city surveyed, the better educated showed less concern for protecting American jobs, defense activities, and alleged 'waste' in foreign aid."[59] Economic elite opinion seems, therefore, no less marked by cross currents than the public in general concerning the tradeoffs between global activism and the painful experiences of the last decade. The differences within the elite as a whole are nowhere more apparent than with respect to that most painful of experiences—Vietnam—and the "lessons" to be drawn from it.

The "Lessons" of Vietnam

In a 1976 study[60] Professors James Rosenau and Ole Holsti found that, skepticism notwithstanding, military officers, business executives and, to a somewhat lesser degree, lawyers feel that "the war should have resulted in victory, and it could have except for self-imposed restraints."[61] Moreover, the "lessons" drawn are extensions of the above perception: "Emphasis on the bipolar structure of the international system, credibility, and the domino theory; doubts about the permanent fragmentation of the communist block; and skepticism about the value of detente characterize some of the more important aspects of world politics—lessons—that respondents in these groups perceive as confirmed by the Vietnam experience."[62]

Other elements of the American "attentive public" or policy elite, such as educators, the leadership of the various media, and to a certain extent foreign service officers, tend, however, to draw a rather different set of conclusions. The reasons for American failure are traced by this group to "unrealistic goals; to lack of knowledge and understanding, especially of Third World nationalism, the history and culture of the region, and the motivations of the adversary; and to the short-comings of the regime in Saigon."[63] Consistent with their different analysis of the causes of American failure, the "lessons" drawn by these elite elements are mirror images of those drawn by military and economic elites. Only foreign service officers demur from the more generally held view of these groups that the United States should reduce its international activism significantly.[64]

In sum, elite belief systems appear to fall into more or less distinct groups, one tending toward "internationalism," the other toward the "isolationist" pole. Both groups, however, would seem much more cautious in their approach to all involvement in international affairs. Perhaps because the research of Holsti and Rosenau was focused on the Vietnam experience, the polarization of viewpoints seems more dramatic than it in fact is. Elites were, after all, more bitterly divided on the war than perhaps any other segment of American society and the residue of that bitterness will likely remain for some time.[65] Russett's research, on the other hand, does suggest that among economic elites at least there is skepticism concerning American globalist involvement and intervention. At the same time, however, commitment to and expectation of expanding economic interaction and even interdependence is equally marked. On the other hand, political and military commitment as the measure of internationalism has clearly declined.

In the longer run, the tendency of educational and media elites to move toward the pole of less or significantly transformed American involvement in international politics may prove most significant. To the extent that these elites will have a major impact on the socialization of subsequent generations, their predispositions would seem to be congruent with and therefore likely to reinforce the view of the young where the decline in internationalist sentiment is clearly apparent.

National surveys during the early 1970s found that internationalism declined most sharply in those under thirty years of age—down to 42% by 1974.[66] The "new generation of isolationists" feels that time and events have rendered obsolete the traditional concept of collective security.[67] Graham Allison's summary of his survey of "elite" young Americans at schools such as Harvard in the late 1960s and early 1970s confirms this picture. The world view of young adults aged 25 to 34,[68] Allison discovered, held that a bipolarized world of immutable hostility between the United States and the Soviet Union is no longer relevant as the basis of American foreign policy. Revolutions based on nationalism in the Third World are expected, accepted, and young people see no obvious relationship between developments virtually anywhere on the globe and the security or vital interests of the United States.

Moreover, it is held with especial certitude that American military force is inapplicable to the achievement of any worthwhile objective. And finally, no current foreign policy issue or problem has self-evident priority over any domestic issue or problem. Poll data from sixteen universities in four regions of the nation lend weight to the earlier assessment of Allison:

> Our basic . . . hypothesis is that the Vietnam conflict as a general experience is producing a generation which is opposed to the use of military force except as a last resort (in self-defense). The events which have occurred can be conjectured to have had a dramatic socializing effect upon an entire generation of future leaders. Indeed, it seems possible that Vietnam will be identified as the "Munich Analogy" of the future.
>
> In effect, we believe that Vietnam is producing a group which is more pacifist than its predecessor.[69]

The essence of the new "Vietnam Analogy" in contrast to the Munich Analogy is, Roger Handberg declares, "an aversion to the use of force in international politics at any level, for any reason other than perhaps self-defense."[70] The recently released Kettering data is even more clear cut in its findings:

> Age seems to be an even more important dividing line in the public than education. . . . In each instance, younger people are much less "hard line" than older people; they are less anti-Soviet, more sympathetic toward the third world, less interventionist, less isolationist, and less pragmatic. The progression, moreover, tends to be steadily accumulating; that is, people under 25 are even less hard line than those 25-34, i.e. that group which during the 1960s was under the important boundary age of 30. . . .[71]

In a talk before a college audience in 1973, William Bundy, former Assistant Secretary of State for Asian Affairs in the Johnson administration and now editor of *Foreign Affairs,* recalled the impact of World War II on his generation:

The makers of American policy from 1950 right through the present time were members of a generation of Americans—men ranging from their mid-eighties to their fifties—who had lived through a period of extreme rejection of force. . . . And those policies of rejecting force and rejecting American involvement in the world seemed to contribute . . . to . . . the most ghastly human phenomena . . . of history. To the men who made the Vietnam decisions . . . all the men . . . Kennedy, Johnson, Rusk, my brother, myself, McNamara—all of us had participated . . . in the greatest debate over American entry in World War II on the side of intervention. We were interventionists at a time when you could assemble an interventionist meeting . . . and get 25 people . . . and in the end, after the intervention came and succeeded, it had universal support. . . . The interventionist point of view was vindicated. . . . It could prevent vast evil and open the way to progress. . . . War was viewed . . . not as "Catch 22" or "Mash" or even "Patton" . . . but as the only way to deal with world order.[72]

An at least plausible interpretation of the findings surveyed in this chapter would be that the situation described by Bundy has been reversed. That is, it is now noninterventionism that has been vindicated by a series of events nearly as traumatic as those visited on Bundy's generation.

Uncertainty and Its Implications

In some respects, naval doctrine and force planning might find it easier to respond to an unequivocally isolationist America than to the situation described above. Thus, if it was indeed the case that public opinion as well as the foreign and defense policy-making community had now swung to a position of stable neo-isolationism, then one might surmise that such a domestic climate would not support a naval force structure predicated on forward positioning and significant projective capacity. Strategic deterrence and something more than marginal sea control capacity might follow, but those political uses of sea power normally associated with presence could well be circumscribed. In sum, a navy certainly not much larger than the present force structure and perhaps in time somewhat smaller, as those forces designed primarily for projection of power ashore and the maintenance of a large sea control/presence mission in forward areas such as the Eastern Mediterranean were allowed to decline by attrition or accelerated retirement.

But another interpretation of the possible implications for foreign policies involving the use of force growing out of the public mood outlined here suggests that while Americans are now much more cautious about foreign involvements, they are by no means predisposed to be passive in the face of a complex and unresponsive international system. Watts and Free argue, for example, that perhaps the best characterization of the public mood is one of renewed nationalism which carries with it an undertone of latent interventionism if the American life style is threatened by overseas developments:

> A majority of Americans, while tempered in their internationalism, remain deeply concerned about America's standing in the world. Following a number of reverses in the world arena, and perhaps prodded a bit by a measure of introspection in this bicentennial year, Americans seem infused with a certain sense of nationalism that dominated American outlook during most of our earlier history. Such nationalism is by no means logically incompatible with the aspects of unilateralism that also hold widespread appeal. We want to be number one once more, but we want to attain that goal with a measure of caution, and without the excess of commitment that resulted in Vietnam.[73]

In support of this conclusion, Watts and Free point to their finding that for the first time since 1968, a majority of the American people now feel that the United States should go "to the very brink of war if necessary" in order to "maintain its dominant position as the world's most powerful nation at all costs. . . ."[74]

Such a position is certainly not without support among policy elites and attentive publics. As noted, Rosenau and Holsti's research reveals that especially among military professionals and business executives the conviction that military force remains a useful tool of diplomacy remains quite strong. Moreover, these same respondents regard one of the most important lessons of the Vietnam experience to be that the use of military force should not be restrained by po-

litical considerations once the decision is taken to employ such instrumentalities. Finally, these elements of the attentive public and
policy community hold that the level of violence employed should
be higher than that envisioned under the doctrines of controlled
escalation and the political uses of military instruments current over
the last decade.[75]

Such a mix of general public and elite opinion would seem supportive of the kind of navy planned during the early 1970s: significant capacity for the projection of power and sea control comple-
menting the strategic deterrence mission. Moreover, forward positioning of these forces would not be severely questioned by a public
desiring the image of the United States as "Number One." But such
a public frame of mind would be a mixed blessing, for although it
might prove more permissive concerning the size of the Navy and
force structure oriented toward significant strike capacity, it might
well prove less supportive of the actual *use* of such power if echoes
of Vietnam became too loud. Furthermore, though the apparent desire of some military professionals supported by elements in the
attentive public to move away from controlled escalation may strike
a responsive chord with many in the public who desire a refur-
bished image of American power, the proponents of such a policy
had best be right and quickly, for the same studies pointing toward
a "new nationalism" also underscore considerable skepticism concerning the responsiveness of the international system to any American instrumentalities as well as little public tolerance for policies
that lead to lengthy Vietnamlike involvements. On the latter point,
the most recent findings concerning the attitudes of the young toward interventionist involvement are especially important. The Kettering researchers note that "It is particularly on the scales dealing
with international conflict, . . . that the younger people differ so
widely from their parents."[76] From this they conclude:

> Such age differences are pronounced enough that some future inter-
> national developments could generate a more serious generational split
> in this country than appeared during the Vietnam period. To the ex-
> tent that this event involves U.S.-Soviet attitudes or interventionist

activities, the split could be very critical, since it is the young who are usually called on to bear the brunt of our international conflicts. Those who favor a more active military role for the U.S. in world affairs should be aware that such a policy could well entail severe recruitment and morale problems on the part of the age segment most needed in the trenches.[77]

Finally, while military professionals and business executives are relatively free of public sanctions directed at their professional lives, presidents and members of Congress are not. It is not unlikely, therefore, that political decision-makers will remain mindful of the ambivalence revealed in virtually all recent analyses of American public opinion. Here again the implications for the size of the United States Navy may not be all negative. As our review of congressional decision-making suggests, congressional support for a big ship navy is not unrelated to the desire to preserve the image of American power and interventionary capacity. At the same time, however, it seems unlikely that a Congress that has undergone significant membership turnover in the last decade will be insensitive to a public that supported an end to the Vietnam War long before American leaders could bring themselves to a similar position and that remains deeply skeptical of such involvements. Similarly, Mr. Carter's narrow victory against a backdrop of massive nonparticipation (turnout continued its pattern of decline for the fourth consecutive presidential election) would seem to preclude a dramatic return to the kind of activism in the use of military power that brought his predecessors so much grief.

In sum, notwithstanding the apparent adjustments in popular consciousness concerning foreign policy, it seems unlikely that the foreseeable future holds any dramatic crystallization of popular constraints on naval power per se. The design of force structures will remain the province of the professional—though within more stringent budgetary limits than those assumed when a 600-ship navy built around a dozen or more large-decked aircraft carriers was planned. Moreover, the effects of public opinion on the commander of a war ship or task force are likely to remain quite indirect except perhaps for the attitudes of the men who serve under him. Nevertheless, the skepticism of the American public and the polarization of American elites concerning the actual use of military power seem likely to frustrate the professional's desire for clear direction and definition of his mission. In this respect, the absence of any real consensus within the policy community concerning the scope of American military involvement and the instrumentalities appropriate to its use suggest that the Navy's future is likely to remain very cloudy, especially as it relates to the *use* of naval power. Under such circumstances, political leadership is not likely to be more decisive than its understandably conservative perception of an ambivalent public. The tendency may well be, therefore, to continue cautiously and somewhat indecisively with consequences not unlike those which have characterized the transition from the Ford to Carter administrations. The problem, of course, is whether this is sufficient given the very significant legal, technological, and political-economic changes emerging in the international system.

CHAPTER SEVEN

The Future of the
United States Navy

MODERN NAVAL power would seem, at first, very appropriate to an American foreign policy that now finds itself at mid-passage in an international system that no longer corresponds to the once familiar rigidities of the Cold War, but is not yet approaching even an approximation of world order. Yet the use of naval power is not without its limitations. Some of these are inherent in naval power itself. Thus the much applauded flexibility and universality of American naval power may also act as limits if routine presence is taken for granted or if flexibility comes to be seen as evidence of American ambivalence rather than resolve. No less important limitations are those growing out of the ambiguous opportunities and difficulties inherent in the domestic and international environment of post-Cold War world politics.

In this concluding chapter we summarize the major observations made in the preceding survey of the often paradoxical circumstances that seem likely to shape the future of American naval power. We close with an assessment of the more important implications of these conditions for the role of naval power in American foreign policy.

American Naval Power Today

Naval power has come to be viewed as having more advantages than any other military instrument. For one thing, the geopolitical context in which naval power operates has always seemed unambiguous; for another, there has been a presumption of control surrounding the deployment of naval force. This apparent susceptibility to management simply does not always pertain to other military instruments. As Army Colonel Zeb Bradford recently conceded, one "lesson" of Vietnam inevitably drawn is that ground power can be "quite inflexible once committed. . . . ships can often reverse course and make a clean break, [but] ground forces rarely can do so once engaged."[1]

The traditional naval presence mission, in contrast to land operations, may be as explicit or as subtle as policy-makers desire. For example, when reports appeared in the Western press in January, 1976, that Soviet warships were moving off Angola, the flotilla was publicly discounted by the Kremlin. Nevertheless, the mere fact that these ships were maneuvering in South-Atlantic waters, far from the usual Soviet shipping lanes, served as a pointed and impressive indication of Soviet concern on the eve of an important all-African conference which was to meet to discuss the Angolan civil war. This naval display was managed with great delicacy. It did not violate norms of sovereignty. Nor did it provoke much more than verbal protest. Yet, it made a pointed declaration of interest and, in this case, accurately presaged Soviet intentions about the future political determination of the target area on shore.

The choreography of force available to navies—interdiction, blockade, warning shots—contains, in the abstract at least, options which can plausibly be taken in isolation one from the other. In theory, these measures need not provoke the kind of expansion of force that might result if similar undertakings were attempted on land. "Expressive" and "coercive" naval exercises can take place without a shot being fired. If a government decides in the cool light of another day to minimize a situation, a task force can simply be withdrawn. Sufficient time in which to make decisions can usually be obtained by comparatively easy engagement and disengage-· ment. Targets of influence can be chosen that are proportional in value to policy and goals. Hence, navies have seemed peculiarly well adapted to a closely calibrated mixture of force and negotiation. Indeed, the case has been made that "reliance on naval force . . . is itself a contribution to moderation in international society."[2]

The inherent advantages of naval force have coincided with an American policy environment which has been especially hospitable to sea power in the early 1970s. One senses that during the early 1970s, the Navy came to view the Nixon doctrine and the Kissinger style as a mandate for preeminence in the American defense community. The Nixon doctrine placed great emphasis on strategic stability and the maintenance of a global array of commitments while avoiding some of the previous domestic and international costs associated with having to honor these obligations. Moreover, Mr. Kissinger's tactic of resourceful, dextrous juggling seemed to buttress the possibilities of a further renaissance of naval power.

Although the domestic political sentiment had changed dramatically since 1968, throughout the mid-1970s the Navy still remained confident that shifts in public opinion and augmented congressional interest in the defense budget would leave it as the preeminent service. Inasmuch as the Navy seemed an arm of coercion, which promised both the least domestic visibility and the fewest casualties, it would seem relatively favored as an instrument of policy. Moreover, Congress, although it has been more actively involved in examining Navy procurement requests than in the past, tended to reduce the Navy's requests for smaller, less potent ships and support craft, while encouraging its requests for larger, nuclear-powered vessels which would be most appropriate to operations in a high-risk environment. Congress had not taken any real initiatives regarding the Navy's future. When there was any reluctance to fund Navy requests (e.g., for the nuclear strike cruiser with an Aegis air defense system), it was only because there had been obvious inconsistencies in the intensity of desire for these systems between the Office of the Secretary of Defense on the one hand and the Department of the Navy on the other. In the absence of opposition from the Secretary of Defense or the White House, Congress had been strongly influenced by the commanding presence of Admiral Rickover. Rickover's unstinting and powerful advocacy of a large nuclear Navy usually carried the day in Congress. And the Navy, generally, prospered as a result, even though there arose within its ranks increasing opposition to a wholly nuclear Navy on the grounds, if nothing else, of cost.

The arrival of the Carter administration did not seem to portend any immediate change in the confidence the Navy might hold for its future. After all, Carter campaigned for office as a "Navy man" whose career was profoundly influenced by Rickover. During his campaign, Mr. Carter was heard to call, on the one hand, for a reduction in overall defense spending, indicating, most probably, a scrapping of the B-1, and, on the other, for a larger ship construction program. Upon assuming office, Carter quickly recalled Rickover to yet another tour of duty—the Admiral's eighth since he passed mandatory retirement in 1964.

During the first year and a half of the Carter administration, there were still felicitous continuities from the previous eight years. Mr. Carter, in a ringing declaration at Wake Forest University, declared that it is a "myth" that "our defense budget is too burdensome." It is another "myth" that "this country somehow is pulling back from protecting our interests and its friends around the world." The problem of American security has been compounded, Mr. Carter said, by "the Soviets, who traditionally were not a significant naval power, but now rank number two in the world in naval forces." To counter the increase in Soviet activism, Mr. Carter concluded, "the Secretary of Defense . . . is improving and will maintain quickly deployable forces—air, land and sea—to defend our interests throughout the world."[3] In addition to vowing to husband the whole panoply of commitments that Carter had inherited from previous administrations, the President seemed to be willing to bestow special emphasis to the Navy's role as part of the deterrent triad. Indeed, Carter's first move toward the Soviets was to offer them an arms control agreement which would encourage the Kremlin and ourselves to augment our submarine based missiles systems in exchange for a lower ceiling on other systems.

Yet, that which might be construed as auspicious for the Navy soon was overshadowed by Carter's first budgetary initiatives and alterations in strategic formulations. In the wake of a 1977 interagency study that found "serious deficiencies" in the North Atlantic Alliance, Carter quickly moved to enhance the European contingency in force planning. The *Draft Consolidated Guidance for Fiscal 1980* stated, "Our near term objective is to assure that NATO could not be overrun in the first few weeks of a blitzkrieg war, and we will invest and spend our resources to that end."[4] The phrasing of the mission of the Navy seemed, in the light of this kind of emphasis, almost residual: It should "concentrate on localized contingencies outside Europe."[5]

Mr. Carter shelved the fourth 94,000-ton *Nimitz*-class nuclear carrier in favor of a smaller, oil-fired 60,000-ton platform. The year before, the Navy had agreed that they might accept the loss of a large-decked carrier if they could have two smaller ones instead. Now, it seemed, they were only being offered one. In addition, promising new naval technologies were hit hard by Mr. Carter's proposals. Vertical takeoff aircraft programs were cut in half. There were no requests for hydrofoils. And the nuclear strike cruiser was omitted.

Still it was not clear if the heyday of the Navy had come to an end. After all, the "continental strategy" of the Carter administration could be seen as a stopgap measure taken in the hope that no more commitments will be called in to be honored, and in the knowledge that, in any case, Congress would likely restore some of the cuts.[6] As Edward R. Jayne, the ranking defense specialist at the Office of Management and Budget, told an audience at the Naval War College: "If you retain nothing else, I say to you, please remember this: . . . the present shipbuilding difficulties represent in my view the single most influential reason why President Carter chose not to accelerate navy ship purchases in the 1979 budget."[7] A bit later, Secretary Brown also seemed to allude to a hidden agenda of delay rather than substantial change in Carter's new budget. "Until the uncertainties regarding cost overruns and contract disputes" with the Newport News Shipyard, builders of aircraft carriers and other shipbuilders and yards (amounting to over 2.7 billion dollars) were settled, "it would be unwise—in my judgment—to plunge into a large shipbuilding and conversion plan,"[8] he told the House Subcommittee on Sea Power.

Cost overruns of 100% now make the Trident the most expensive weapon program ever begun. Current cost of the sub with its missiles is $1.5 billion an issue. If the Polaris and Poseidon submarines are to be replaced, a force of 28 Tridents would have to be built. The cost, the General Accounting Office reported, could be well over $50 billion.[9] But if the program is not funded then the Poseidons will have to be refitted and extended. How long the hull life of submarines might last beyond twenty years' service is problematic. Hence, by 1986, the deployment of the "ideal deterrent" and emerging counterforce weapon could be halved. The United States will have only 312 launchers underwater instead of 656 if current building and retirement schedules are followed. But it is hard to see how the United States can do without a large undersea deterrent and hold out, as the Carter administration has done, both the B-1 and the M-X ICBM as a "bargaining chip" for SALT. Thus, it seemed that the Carter administration, by its 1979 budget, was merely looking for temporary respite in the area of the defense budget.[10]

The dispute over the Navy role has been termed by some observers the biggest defense battle since Louis Johnson cancelled the supercarrier in 1949, arguing that it duplicated the mission of the Strategic Air Command.[11] The Navy, however, soon rallied its supporters: "brown shoe" aviators, nuclear advocates, labor union supporters and Capitol Hill sympathizers.[12] Moreover, support for defense spending in public opinion polls in recent years has actually risen under the twin impact of an information blitz by the national security lobby and a prolonged period of economic stagnation dating from 1971.

In terms of domestic politics and budgetary exigencies, then, the future of the Navy might not be as bright as it once was. But it is hard to see how contemporary commitments can be seriously honored or the supporters of large naval spending can be ignored. It is our guess that the Navy will continue to receive a disproportionate share of the defense budget for the foreseeable future. The salad days of the Navy might be over. It might have to gain a tighter control over its procurement processes and cost estimates and it may have to forego some increment of big ships. Still, the shape of the fleet is likely to remain hovering around 500 ships with, at its center, 12 carriers and some 600 intercontinental missile launchers based undersea.

U.S. Naval Power and World Politics in the Late Twentieth Century

The position of naval power as an instrument of American foreign and national security policy would seem, therefore, more secure than the most strident alarmists of the late 1970s feared. But such a position is surely a mixed blessing. For the U.S. Navy must serve a foreign policy the direction and scope of which are unclear, in a world moving rapidly away from the certainties of the bipolar Cold War era, but with a relatively unchangeable force structure predicated on the national security assumptions of the Cold War.

Although President Carter has emphasized Europe in military planning, he and administration spokesmen throughout 1978 remained insistent that our Asian "interests and commitments" remain "vital." In Thailand and Indonesia, Vice President Mondale reaffirmed American support of the 1954 Manila Pact and the Association of South East Asian Nations. In Korea, the American withdrawal of ground troops was slowed. Our top priority, the Vice

President told Asian leaders, "now that we have entered a new era in South East Asia,"[13] was to stand by our pledge to defend the region against Communist aggression.

Hence, the Carter administration not only retained, on the verbal level at least, the whole fabric of American commitments built up since World War II, but expanded them by adding the Persian Gulf as a region which deserved a military planning priority second only to Europe. But rhetoric seemed increasingly divorced from reality. There were, after every call to worldwide ramparts, voices stage-whispering from the State Department and elsewhere that all the sound was only for domestic consumption.[14] The fact that the Vice President—whose essential administration role was liaison with Congress—was picked to reaffirm the Asian theater in the midst of the emerging great debate about the Navy's future and in the wake of the harrowingly close vote on the Panama Canal Treaty brought further warrant to the suspicion that our far-flung commitments were to be supported only so that Mr. Carter could not be said to be capitulating to the Soviets in strategic issues and so that he could contend that American greatness remained undiminished. The administration's verbal assurances seemed, like a coin in an inflationary economy, of decreasing value. Yet Mr. Carter was probably right to fear that any liquidation might cause a run on the bank.

In the tenth century, foreign ambassadors used to be called to Constantinople in order that they might be impressed with the military splendor of an enervated empire. There were

> interminable reviews at which the same troops emerging from one of the gates and entering by another, came round and round again carrying different kinds of armour. In order to dazzle . . . [by] . . . glamour and mystery mechanical devices caused the steps of [the Emperor's] throne to roar terribly, while the throne itself worked up and down, so that the visiting ambassador, on rising from the kowtow . . . would notice that the Emperor had been miraculously elevated. . . .[15]

In the twentieth century, some observers had the feeling that the American Empire, like that of Byzantium, was increasingly held together with smoke and mirrors. Not that firepower to enforce commitments could not be had. It could. But the disposition to use it had become unbelievable.

The uncertainty surrounding any future contemplation of the use of force is in part attributable to the augmented naval and ground presence of Soviet forces and their Cuban surrogates. Furthermore, there is still sufficient competition in the Soviet-American relationship to merit the speculation that if, in an effort to reassure distant friends, an American naval force were sent to waters not customarily visited by either the Russians or ourselves, Soviet attention and a Soviet presence might be as likely to be attracted to such a spot as repelled. Hence, naval force would not necessarily either serve its purpose of soothing the anxieties of our associates (it might compound them), or dampen any level of engagement.

Moreover, any ambiguity as to the validity of our interests entertained by us or held by other relevant parties would vitiate the likelihood of success. The mere presence of the American Navy in distant reaches does not, after all, guarantee the validity or sincerity of our interests or intent to ourselves or others. In part, American naval force is discounted already merely because it is deployed globally. The appearance of American ships creates ambiguous impact; for they are presumed to have been near at hand in any case before most events were even contemplated. The Soviet Navy, on the other hand, is still not considered a ubiquitous phenomenon. The Soviets, having far fewer and less binding commitments to areas away from Russian frontiers, by just making an appearance, can have a disproportionate psychological impact, far beyond their combat capability. This is true no matter what the United States is likely to do.

For example, in 1976 the Soviets deployed a *Kresta* and one or more cruise-missile-armed submarines in a kind of blocking position for Cuban merchant vessels carrying men and equipment to Angola. The nature of the Soviet force was of no substantive menace to the United States. And the nature of Soviet interests in Angola could in no way justify the sinking of an American war vessel. But the political cost for the United States of "countering" Soviet ships would probably have been higher than the actual United States interest in Angola; for, at a minimum, it would have lent credence to the Gorshkov pleas for an expanded blue water navy. In any event, it would have gratuitously humiliated the Soviets and perhaps made them more truculent in areas where the stakes could be higher to both sides.

Thus the combination of growing parity but also fragility in the Soviet-American naval relationship will seriously complicate future interventionary calculations. Furthermore, the proliferation of sophisticated conventional weaponry and subsequently, perhaps, nuclear weapons, seems likely to heighten the risks associated with the projection of power against coastal states. Finally, these changes in the strategic framework of international politics will in time be reflected in an international legal regime for hydrospace which will complicate and perhaps constrain significantly the forward deployment and mobility of naval force.

A wager on naval power, therefore, like a bet on any form of military power, ultimately confronts the reality of what Edward L. Morse has called the "great transformation" of the foreign policy environment.[16] The "modernization of international society," Morse and others have pointed out, means that force is a necessarily discounted instrument of policy. The sources of our international "problems" are becoming less a zero-sum Soviet-American competition and more diffuse in origin. And as politics becomes "systemic" or "globalized," policy remedies become less apparent.

This does not mean that international military conflict or the use of naval power is about to disappear. It does mean that the ordering function of force for those who possess it—naval or otherwise—is less certain and, perhaps, less relevant. A world plagued by economic stagnation, rising demands on governmental structures, the emergence of fissiparous nationalism and subnationalisms, and nuclear proliferation will probably not be amenable to much order no matter how flexible the instrument, steadfast the will, or great the firepower. And when, in the end, only the quantity of firepower is certain, the future of the "regulatory phase" of international history, and the role of American naval power in it, remains clouded.

In such an international system, the nature of power may not change as much as some have suggested and the relationship of power to influence will undoubtedly remain recognizable. Nonetheless, it does seem plausible that a different mix of diplomatic and military instrumentalities could emerge. In the face of complex and uneven interdependence, a state's ability to "project influence" may be decreasingly a function of what that state can do *to* the target of its influence in a political and military sense, and increasingly a product of what it can do *for* the influence target in terms of the latter's political, economic and social needs. Obviously providing a "secure" politico-military environment is a service of considerable importance for a state beset by complex subnational and transnational forces. But in the Third and Fourth Worlds, and, indeed, throughout the international system, "neutralizing" Soviet influence projection will likely involve a great deal more than naval power.

Thus, the future of American naval power is in large measure a paradox: subnational and international conflict affecting American interests will likely persist and even increase. Yet, the apparent advantages of naval power may prove less and less appropriate to the ends of policy. Indeed, it is not clear that any military instrumentality promises comprehensive efficacy vis-à-vis conflict rooted in the political, economic, and racial inequities of a complexly interdependent world. In sum, Michael Howard's observation that the "quality of strategic thinking in the nuclear age is related to an understanding of international relations, on the one hand, and of weapons technology on the other,"[17] is no less applicable to the future of naval power. Planning the future of American naval power must ultimately entail more than a preoccupation with "operational problems" posed by Soviet power or changes in technology. The elements surveyed in this study are manifestations of a far more complex and, one suspects, dangerous transnational environment than experienced so far in this century. Naval power is clearly relevant.

But unless the future of American naval power is conceived in broader policy terms, then, notwithstanding the claims made for naval power, it may become what Clausewitz once feared war had become: "a thing unto itself" unrelated to the real purposes of foreign policy.

Appendixes

The following appendixes are supplementary to Chapters Two and Five. Appendixes A, B, and C survey current and projected aircraft deployment on the Navy's aircraft carriers, the types and capabilities of those aircraft, and an overview of the missiles currently deployed or under development. Appendixes D through I present the data from which the tables and indexes used in Chapter Five were developed.

Appendix A
Typical CV-CVN Aircraft Deployment, 1975–198?

1975			1985		
Number	Type	Designation and Name	Number	Type	Designation and Name
24	VF	F-4 Phantom II or F-14 Tomcat	24	VF	F-18 NACF F-14/F-4
24/36	VA(L)	A-7E (visual bombing) Corsair II	36	VA	A-7E A-6E
12	VA(H)	A-6E (all-weather) Intruder			(F-18 will adopt F-4 roles)
4	Tanker	KA-6D (Intruder with tanker facilities)	4	Tanker	(KS-3, S-3 tanker deriv.?) KA-6D
4	AEW	E-2C Hawkeye	4	AEW	E-2 (?)
4	ECM	EA-6B Prowler	4	ECM	EA-6 (or EVA-X)
3	Recon.	RA-5C Vigilante (phasing out) RA-7 (A-7 deriv.)	3	Recon.	(RF-18 [?]) RA-7
10	ASW	S-3 Viking	10	ASW	S-3
8	ASW	SH-3 Sea King Helo.	8	ASW	SH-3 (follow-on [CH-53H?] Helo)

VF = Fighter/Interceptor, VA = Attack, AEW = Airborne Early Warning, ECM = ElectroCounter Measures, Recon. = Reconnaissance, ASW = AntiSubmarine Warfare, NACF = Naval Air Combat Fighter, F-18.

Source: *Senate Authorization, 1976–197T: Part 9, Tactical Air Power*, p. 4905.

Appendix B

CV-Deployed Aircraft and Their Capabilities, 1975–1985

—**F-4 Phantom.** Mach 2.4; 4 Sparrow AAM, 16 thousand lbs. ordnance, 1000 mile radius. Rated one of the best fighters of the postwar era. First flown in middle 1950's. Replacement aircraft will be F-18.

—**F-18.** Mach 2. 4 AAM. 655 nm radius. Will weigh 20,000 lbs. less. Will carry up to 13,000 lbs. ordnance. Built-up version of YF-17 ACF which lost out to F-16. Will be more maneuverable than F-4, consume less fuel. Planned buy around 950 aircraft of both VF and VA configurations.

—**F-14 Tomcat.** Swing-wing. Mach 2.4. Can fire 6 Phoenix AAM at six separate targets and guide all six in. Long range fighter originally intended as replacement for F-4. High unit cost has resulted in the retention and modification of F-4's and their continued use into 1980's. F-14 said to be very agile. Major air-superiority fighter of 1980's.

—**A-7E Corsair II.** Burly, subsonic. Stores capcy. 19,000 pounds. Radius with 4,000 lbs. ordnance, 2 Sidewinder AAM, 20 mm cannon and external fuel = 820 nm. A-7E is updated version with computer to provide pilot with navigation and weapons delivery information. The Navy notes that the A-7 is "optimized for visual attack in strike and interdiction missions";[1] in this respect it differs from the A-6.

—**A-6E.** Subsonic. Long range (1920 sm with 4 Bullpup ASM and max. int'l fuel). All-weather, low-level attack. Chief attributes: High accuracy in foul weather. Avionics more sophisticated than A-7E.

—**E-2C Hawkeye.** Airborne Early Warning. Operates 100–150 miles from carrier. Can pick up and identify high and low level aircraft. Serves as command and control link. 2 turboprop engines. 3 hr. endurance at 100+ miles.

—**S-3 Viking.** AntiSubmarine Warfare. Replaces piston-engined S-2. 400+kn. speed. 6+ hours endurance. Can operate at 40,000 feet. "It contains and employs the most modern passive and active ASW search sensors . . . and integrates this data into general-purpose digital computer."[2] Can carry depth bombs, homing torpedoes, rockets, mines. Is being configured to carry Harpoon SSM. One of few weapons systems to come to the fleet on time and near estimated cost.

—**EA-6B Prowler.** ElectroCounter Measures. ". . . contains a fully integrated, computer-controlled electronic warfare system."[3] Can spook radars and communication. Used to protect fleet against attack or strike aircraft against interception.

—SH-3H Sea King. ASW helicopter. Also serves in Search and Rescue, light utility (with other designations). Similar duties to S-3. Less comprehensively outfitted, shorter range. Does not have facilities for interpreting data on-board to the same degree as S-3. CH-53E is a 3 engined heavy-lift helo, which some have suggested might be useful in the ASW role. Serving on "sea-control ships" as well as carrier, the CH-53E would be able to lift impressive amounts of ordnance as well as carry comprehensive avionics on-board.[4]

Notes

1. *Senate Authorization, 1976–197T, Part 7: Authorization,* p. 3749.
2. Ibid., p. 3763.
3. Ibid., p. 3747.
4. For details see LCDR R. H. Klippert, Jr., USN, "Sea Control Aircraft: The Case for the Chopper," *USNIP,* Vol. 101, No. 4 (April 1975), pp. 46–52.

Appendix C
USN Missiles

Missile Name	Designation	Speed (Mach)	Plat-form*	Range (NM)	Guidance System	Role
Brazo	–	NA	1	NA	Radar Homing	Air-Air ARM
Phoenix	AIM-54A	1.5+	1	50+	Semi-active Radar Homing (SAR)	AAM (Air to Air)
Sidewinder	AIM-9H/L	2	1	1.75	Infrared Homing (IR)	AAM
Sparrow III	AIM-7F	3.5+	1,2	24+	SAR	AAM
Bullpup A/B	AGM-12B/C	–	1	6/9	Command	ASM
Harpoon	AGM-84A	–1	1,2,3	55	Active radar	ASM/SSM
Shrike	AGM-45A	–	1	2.6+	Passive RH	ARM
Standard ARM	AGM-78C/D	–	1,2	13.5+	RH	ARM/SSM
Walleye	GW Mk. 2	–	1	depends on alt.	TV	Unpowered
Walleye II	GW Mk. 2	–	1	depends on alt.	TV/data link	ASM
ASROC	RUR-5A	1	2	1–6	Inertial	ASW
SUBROC	UUM-44A	–	3	20–25	Accoustic	ASW/Anti-Surface

Sea Sparrow	RIM-7H	—	2	7	SA-CW RH	SAM/SSM
Standard MR**	RIM-66A		2	10+	SAR	SAM/SSM
Standard ER**	RIM-67A	—	2	30+	SAR	SAM/SSM
Talos	RIM-8G/H/J	—	2	65+	SAR	SAM/SSM
Tartar	RIM-24B		2	10+	SAR	SAM
Terrier	RIM-2F		2	20+	SAR	SAM

*Platform Designation: 1 = Aircraft, 2 = Surface Combatant, 3 = Submarine

**Standard MR and ER are to replace Tartar and Terrier; Talos platforms diminishing in number.

Source: Derived from several sources: Jane's All the World Aircraft, Various Editors; International Institute for Strategic Studies, The Military Balance-1974-1975 (London: IISS, 1974), op. 84-87; Aviation Week and Space Technology, March 17, 1975; Dictionary of Weapons and Military Terms, John Quick (N.Y.: McGraw-Hill, 1973. Figures are approximations due to the disagreement among sources).

Appendix D
Congressional Changes in Presidential Budget
Requests 1971–1977, by Appropriation Title
(in Millions of Dollars)

	NOA Request	NOA Allowed	% Congressional Change
FY 1971			
Personnel	21,032.8	20,735.0	−1.416
O & M	18,300.1	18,188.9	−0.608
Procurement	17,309.1	15,990.2	−7.620
(Transfer Authority)		(+150.1)	(−6.753)
RDT & E	7,295.6	6,925.8	−5.069
TOTAL	63,937.6	61,839.9	−3.281
		(+150.1)	(−3.046)
FY 1972			
Personnel	21,291.8	21,024.7	−1.254
O & M	19,358.4	19,051.8	−1.584
Procurement	19,358.4	17,723.9	−9.642
(T.A.)	(+58.7)	(+780.0)	(−5.665)
RDT & E	7,899.3	7,469.0	−5.447
(T.A.)		(+101.9)	(−4.157)
TOTAL	68,164.6	65,269.4	−4.247
	(+58.7)	(+881.9)	(−2.954)
FY 1973			
Personnel	23,658.6	23,140.8	−2.189
O & M	20,270.9	19,789.2	−2.376
(T.A.)		(−200.0)	(−1.390)
Procurement	21,097.1	17,737.8	−15.923
(T.A.)		(+1,048.2)	(−10.955)
RDT & E	8,718.8	7,932.4	−9.020
(T.A.)		(+60.0)	(−8.331)
TOTAL	73,745.4	68,600.2	−6.977
		(+1,308.2)	(−5.203)
FY 1974			
Personnel	22,706.5	22,375.2	−1.459
O & M	21,431.8	20,830.9	−2.804

Appendix D (cont.)

	NOA Request	*NOA Allowed*	*% Congressional Change*
Procurement	15,299.4	16,159.8	−11.692
(T.A.)		(−499.8)	(−8.961)
RDT & E	8,475.7	8,063.8	−4.860
(T.A.)		(+3.5)	(−4.818)
TOTAL	70,913.4	67,429.7	−4.913
(T.A.)		(+503.3)	(−4.203)
FY 1975			
Personnel	24,774.5	24,214.2	−2.262
O & M	25,099.9	22,852.2	−8.955
Procurement	19,764.6	17,132.7	−13.316
(T.A.)		(+480.0)	(−10.888)
RDT & E	9,295.5	8,551.7	−8.002
TOTAL	78,934.5	72,750.8	−7.834
		(+480.0)	(7.226)
FY 1976			
Personnel	25,077.7	24,766.8	−1.240
O & M	26,534.1	25,393.7	−4.298
Procurement	24,351.2	21,000.1	−13.762
(T.A.)		(+99.3)	(−13.354)
RDT & E	10,150.4	9,150.4	−7.561
TOTAL	86,113.4	80,593.4	−6.468
			(−6.352)
FY 1977			
Personnel	25,498.0	25,418.4	−.003
O & M	29,073.2	28,630.3	−1.523
Procurement	30,336.5	28,166.2	−7.154
RDT & E	11,024.4	10,404.3	−5.625
TOTAL	95,932.1	92,619.2	−3.453

Source: U.S., Congress, Appropriation, Budget Estimates etc. for FY 1971 through 1975 and House and Senate Appropriations Bill *Reports* for 1976 and 1977.

Appendix E

Congressional Percentage Changes in Presidential
Budget Requests 1969–1977, by Appropriation Title

	Personnel	O & M	Procurement	RDT & E	DOD
1969	−1.92	−4.49	−14.07	−5.68	−6.75
1970	−3.31	−4.28	−14.58	−10.37	−7.49
1971 (T.A.)	−1.42	−0.61	−7.62 (−6.75)	−5.07	−3.28 (−3.05)
1972 (T.A.)	−1.25	−1.58	−9.64 (−5.67)	−5.45 (−4.16)	−4.25 (−2.95)
1973 (T.A.)	−2.19	−2.38 (−1.39)	−15.92 (−10.96)	−9.02 (8.33)	−6.98 (−5.20)
1974 (T.A.)	−1.46	−2.80	−11.69 (8.96)	−4.82 (−4.82)	−4.91 (−4.20)
1975 (T.A.)	−2.26	−8.96	−13.32 (−10.89)	−8.00	−7.83 (−7.23)
1976 (T.A.)	−1.24	−4.30	−13.76 (−13.35)	−7.56	−6.47 (−6.35)
1977	−.003	−1.52	−7.15	−5.63	−3.45

*Source: Kanter, "Congress and the Defense Budget: 1960–1970," Table 2, p. 132 and Table 2, *supra*.

Appendix F

Service Shares of Congressional NOA Appropriations, FY 1971–1977 (in billions of dollars)

	1971 Amt.	1971 %	1972 Amt.	1972 %	1973 Amt.	1973 %	1974 Amt.	1974 %	1975 Amt.	1975 %	1976 Amt.	1976 %	1977 Amt.	1977 %	CHANGE Amt.	CHANGE %
Army	19.6	31.7	20.1	30.8	20.4	29.7	19.2	28.5	20.1	27.6	22.5	28.0	25.4	27.6	+5.8	−4.1
(T.A.)			(20.5)	(31.0)	(20.8)	(29.8)	(19.4)	(28.6)	(20.3)	(27.7)						
Navy	18.3	29.6	20.6	31.5	22.2	32.4	22.5	33.4	24.5	33.7	27.3	33.9	33.0	35.9	+14.7	+6.3
(T.A.)	(18.4)	(29.7)	(20.9)	(31.6)	(22.5)	(32.2)	(22.7)	(33.4)	(24.6)	(33.6)	(27.7)					
Marine Corps	2.1	3.4	1.9	2.9	2.2	3.2	2.2	3.3	2.4	3.3	2.7	3.4	2.8	3.1	+.7	−.3
(T.A.)							(2.3)	(3.4)								
Air Force	21.4	34.6	22.2	34.1	23.4	34.1	23.1	34.6	25.2	34.6	27.4	34.0	30.7	33.4	+9.3	−1.2
(T.A.)			(22.5)	(34.0)	(24.0)	(34.3)	(23.2)	(34.2)	(25.4)	(34.7)	(27.5)	(34.1)				
Total	61.8		65.3		68.6		67.4		72.8		80.5		92.0		+30.2	
(T.A.)	(61.9)		(66.1)		(69.9)		(67.9)		(73.2)		(80.6)					

Source: *Appropriations and Budget Estimates, etc., 1971 through 1975 and Senate and House Appropriations Committee Report* for FY 1976 and FY 1977.

Appendix G

Service Shares of Congressional "Investment Authority" NOA Appropriations, FY 1971–1977

(in billions of dollars)

	1971 Amt.	1971 %	1972 Amt.	1972 %	1973 Amt.	1973 %	1974 Amt.	1974 %	1975 Amt.	1975 %	1976 Amt.	1976 %	1977 Amt.	1977 %
Procurement														
Army (T.A.)	2.9 (3.0)	18.1 (18.6)	3.1 (3.4)	17.5 (18.4)	2.7 (3.0)	15.3 (16.0)	2.1 (2.4)	13.0 (14.4)	2.4 (2.6)	14.0 (14.8)	3.2	15.2	4.4	15.6
Navy (T.A.)	7.0 (7.1)	43.8 (44.4)	8.5 (8.7)	48.0 (47.0)	8.8 (9.1)	49.7 (48.4)	8.2 (8.3)	50.6 (49.7)	8.1 (8.2)	47.4 (46.6)	9.8 (9.9)	46.4 (46.9)	13.2	47.0
Marine Corps (T.A.)	176M	1.3	103M (128M)	.6 (.5)	162M (183M)	1.1 (1.1)	174M (179M)	1.2 (1.2)	208M (218M)	1.2 (1.2)	281M	1.4	328M	1.2
Air Force (T.A.)	5.9	36.9	6.0 (6.3)	33.9 (34.1)	6.0 (6.5)	33.9 (34.6)	5.7 (5.9)	35.2 (34.7)	6.4 (6.5)	37.4 (38.0)	7.7	36.5	10.2	36.2
Total (T.A.)	16.0		17.7		17.7		16.2		17.1		21.1		28.2	
RDT & E														
Army	1.6	23.2	1.8	24.0	1.8	22.8	1.9	23.5	1.8	20.9	1.9	20.2	2.3	23.4
Navy	2.1	30.4	2.4	32.0	2.5	31.6	2.7	33.3	3.0	34.9	3.2	34.0	3.7	38.2
Marine Corps	—		—		—		—		—		—		—	
Air Force	2.7	39.1	2.9	38.7	3.1	39.2	3.0	37.5	3.3	38.4	3.6	38.3	3.8	38.4
Total	6.9		7.5		7.9		8.1		8.6		9.4		9.8	

Source: *Appropriations and Budget Estimates, etc., 1971 through 1975* and House and Senate Appropriations Committee, *Reports* for FY 1976 and FY 1977.

Appendix H

Congressional Changes in Presidential Budget
Requests 1971–1977 by Service Shares
(in millions of dollars)

	NOA Requested	NOA Appropriated	% Congressional Change
FY 1971			
Army	20,210.6	19,629.2	−2.87
(T.A.)		(+50.0/19,679.2)	(−2.629)
Navy	19,095.8	18,348.6	−3.913
(T.A.)		(+100.0/18,488.6)	(−3.389)
Marine Corps	2,104.9	2,057.4	−2.257
(T.A.)			
Air Force	22,055.6	21,361.1	−3.149
(T.A.)			
Total	63,937.6	61,839.9	−3.149
(T.A.)		(+150.0/61,989.9)	(−3.046)
FY 1972			
Army	21,257.1	20,112.9	−5.383
(T.A.)		(+351.9/20,464.8)	(−3.727)
Navy	21,459.3	20,617.2	−3.924
(T.A.)		(+235.0/20,852.2)	(−2.829)
Marine Corps	1,894.9	1,853.7	−2.174
(T.A.)		(+25.0/1,878.7)	(−0.855)
Air Force	23,053.9	22,244.5	−3.511
(T.A.)		(+265.0/22,509.5)	(−2.361)
Total	68,164.6	65,269.4	−4.247
(T.A.)		(881.9/66,151.3)	(−2.954)
FY 1973			
Army	22,027.1	20,402.0	−7.378
(T.A.)		(+441.0/20,834.0)	(−5.376)

Appendix H (cont.)

	NOA Requested	NOA Appropriated	% Congressional Change
Navy (T.A.)	23,964.2	22,185.6 (+295.0/22,480.6)	−7.422 (−6.191)
Marine Corps (T.A.)	2,190.4	2,157.4 (+21.0/2,178.4)	−1.507 (−0.539)
Air Force (T.A.)	25,043.6	23,419.9 (+551.2/23,971.1)	−6.483 (−4.283)
Total	73,745.4	68,600.2 (+1,308.2/69,908.4)	−6.977 (−5.203)
FY 1974			
Army (T.A.)	20,238.8	19,157.2 (+232.5/19,389.7)	−5.344 (−4.195)
Navy (T.A.)	23,617.7	22,504.1 (+151.8/22,655.9)	−4.715 (−4.072)
Marine Corps (T.A.)	2,231.7	2,203.7 (+5.0/2,208.7)	−1.255 (−1.031)
Air Force (T.A.)	24,345.8	23,106.8 (+114.0/23,220.8)	−5.089 (−4.621)
Total (T.A.)	70,913.4	67,429.7 (+503.3/67,933.0)	−4.913 (−4.203)
FY 1975			
Army (T.A.)	22,321.3	20,123.2 (+198.0/20,321.2)	−9.848 (−8.960)
Navy (T.A.)	26,287.8	24,484.9 (+100.8/24,585.8)	−6.858 (−6.476)
Marine Corps (T.A.)	2,503.1	2,431.1 (+10.0/2,411.1)	−2.477 (−2.477)
Air Force (T.A.)	27,293.5	25,220.5 (+171.2/25,391.7)	−7.595 (−6.968)
Total (T.A.)	78,934.5	72,750.8 (+480.0/73,230.8)	−7.834 (−7.226)

Appendix H (cont.)

	NOA Requested	NOA Appropriated	% Congressional Change
FY 1976			
Army (T.A.)	23,536.8	22,494.5	−4.428
Navy (T.A.)	29,861.3	27,328.3 (+75.0/27,403.3)	−8.483 (−8.231)
Marine Corps (T.A.)	2,706.2	2,667.2	−1.441
Air Force (T.A.)	29,411.0	23,449.1 (+24.3/27,473.4)	−6.671 (−6.588)
Total	86,113.4	80,543.5	−6.468
FY 1977			
Army	25,905.7	25,388.6	−1.996
Navy	34,958.2	33,024.4	−5.532
Marine Corps	2,893.7	2,845.0	−1.683
Air Force	31,508.3	30,707.0	−2.543
Total	95,265.9	91,965.0	−3.465

Source: *Appropriations and Budget Estimates, etc., 1971–1975,* and Appropriations *Reports FY 1976* and *FY 1977.*

Appendix I

Distribution and Relative Concentration of "No-Change"
Outcomes in New SCN Procurement, FY 1971–1977

	Total Decisions (%)		No Change Decisions (%)		Concen-tration
Strategic					
Trident	4	(8.2)	4	(11.8)	1.44
Sea Control					
A. Hi-Mix					
CVN	2	(4.1)	2	(5.9)	1.44
SSN-688	7	(14.3)	6	(27.6)	1.23
DLGN-38	4	(8.2)	2	(5.9)	.72
DD-963	5	(10.2)	4	(11.8)	1.16
DDG-47	1	(2.0)	1	(2.9)	1.45
Hi-Mix Subtotal	19	(38.8)	15	(44.1)	1.14
B. Lo-Mix					
FFG-7	4	(8.2)	2	(5.9)	.72
PHM	3	(6.1)	1	(2.9)	.48
PGM	1	(2.0)	0	—	.00
SCS	1	(2.0)	0	—	.00
LHA	1	(2.0)	1	(2.9)	1.45
Lo-Mix Subtotal	10	(20.4)	4	(11.8)	.58
Sea Control Subtotal	29	(59.2)	19	(55.9)	.99
Combatant Subtotal	33	(67.3)	23	(67.6)	1.00
Support & Misc.					
AS	3	(6.1)	2	(5.9)	.96
AD	4	(8.2)	3	(8.8)	1.07
AO	3	(6.1)	1	(2.9)	.48
ATS	1	(2.0)	1	(2.9)	1.45
T-ATF	4	(8.2)	3	(8.8)	1.07
AGOR	1	(2.0)	1	(2.9)	1.45
Noncombatant Subtotal	16	(32.7)	11	(32.4)	.99
TOTAL	49		34		

Source: Table 4

Notes

Introduction

1. See Warner R. Schilling, "The Politics of National Defense: Fiscal 1950," in Warner R. Schilling, Paul Y. Hammond, and Glenn H. Snyder, *Strategy, Politics, and Defense Budgets* (New York: Columbia University Press, 1962); George H. Quester, *Nuclear Diplomacy: The First Twenty-Five Years* (New York: Dunellen Co., 1970); Vincent Davis, *The Politics of Innovation*, Monograph Series in World Affairs, vol. 4, no. 3 (Denver, Col.: The Social Science Foundation and the Graduate School of International Studies, University of Denver, 1966–1967); and Paul Y. Hammond, "Super-Carriers and B-26 Bombers: Appropriations, Strategy and Politics," in Harold Stein, ed., *American Civil-Military Relations* (Tuscaloosa, Ala.: University of Alabama Press, 1963).

2. Harvey Sapolsky, *The Polaris System Development: Bureaucratic and Programmatic Success in Government* (Cambridge, Mass.: Harvard University Press, 1972).

3. See, for example, Michael MccGwire, and Ken Booth, eds., *Soviet Naval Policy: Objectives and Constraints* (New York: Praeger, 1975); MccGwire, "Western and Soviet Naval Building Programmes 1965–1976," *Survival* vol. XVIII, no. 5 (September/October 1976), pp. 204–209: and George E. Hudson, "Soviet Naval Doctrine and Soviet Politics, 1953–1975," *World Politics*, vol. XXIX, no. 1 (October 1976), pp. 90–113.

4. See, for example, Adm. James L. Holloway III, "The U.S. Navy: A Bicentennial Appraisal," United States Naval Institute *Proceedings*, vol. 102 (July 1976), pp. 18–24.

5. Ken Booth, "Navies and Foreign Policy," paper prepared for the International Studies Association Convention, St. Louis, 20–23 March 1974, pp. 2–3.

6. See, for example, "Power at Sea," *Adelphi Papers*, nos. 122–124; James Cable, *Gunboat Diplomacy: Political Applications of Limited Naval Force* (London: International Institute for Strategic Studies [hereafter cited as IISS], 1971); Edward N. Luttwak, *The Political Uses of Sea Power* (Baltimore: Johns Hopkins University Press, 1974); and Comm. Jonathan Howe (USN), *Multicrises* (Cambridge: MIT Press, 1971).

7. Hedley Bull, "Seapower and Political Influence," in "Power at Sea: Part I: The New Environment," *Adelphi Papers*, no. 122 (London: IISS, 1976), p. 6. In addition see Elizabeth Young, "New Laws for Old Navies: Military Implications of the Law of the Sea," *Survival*, vol. 16 (November/December 1974), pp. 262–267; Lt. Linton Wells, "Comments" in *Perspectives on Ocean Policy*, report of Conference on Conflict and Order in Ocean Relations, October 21–24, 1974, Airlie, Virginia, prepared for the National Science Foundation under Grant No. GI 39643 by Ocean Policy Project, Johns Hopkins University, Washington, D.C.; *Strategic Survey 1975*, pp. 21–26; and Robert Osgood, "U.S. Security Interests in Ocean Law," *Survival*, vol. 17 (May/June 1975), pp. 122–128.

8. The limited reload capacity of Soviet vessels is now generally recognized; see, for example, Johan Jorgen Holst, "The Navies of the Superpowers: Motives, Forces, Prospects," in "Power at Sea: Part II: Superpowers and Navies," *Adelphi Papers*, no. 123 (London: IISS, 1976), pp. 10–11.

9. See Osgood, "U.S. Security Interests in Ocean Law." The Soviet Union is likely to suffer more from such legal enclosure given her geographically enclosed global position.

1. Foreign Policy and Navy Power in the 1970s

1. "Power at Sea" is the title of one of the most recent attempts to survey the dimensions of modern seapower and its political and technological dimensions. In this case, the effort was undertaken by the prestigious International Institute for Strategic Studies. See "Power at Sea: Part I: The New Environment," *Adelphi Papers*, no. 122 (London: IISS, 1976); "Power at Sea: Part II: Super-powers and Navies," *Adelphi Papers*, no. 123 (London: IISS, 1976). An earlier assessment of "ocean technology" is John P. Craven's "Ocean Technology and Submarine War-

fare" in "The Implications of Military Technology in the 1970's," *Adelphi Papers*, no. 46 (London: IISS, 1968), pp. 38–46.

2. On sea power and foreign policy, see Laurence Martin, *The Sea in Modern Strategy* (London: Chatto and Windus for the IISS, 1967) and Ken Booth's paper "Navies and Foreign Policy," prepared for the International Studies Association Convention, St. Louis, Missouri, 20–23 March, 1974. On deterrence see, for example, Kosta Tsipis, Anne H. Cahn, and Bernard T. Feld, eds. *The Future of the Sea-Based Deterrent* (Cambridge, Mass.: MIT Press, 1973). Also Adm. Stansfield Turner (USN), "Missions of the U.S. Navy," *Naval War College Review*, vol. 26 (March–April 1974). On the presence mission, see: James Cable, *Gunboat Diplomacy: Political Applications of Limited Naval Force* (London: Institute for Strategic Studies, 1971); Comm. Jonathan Howe (USN), *Multicrises* (Cambridge, Mass.: MIT Press, 1971; and Edward N. Luttwak, *The Political Uses of Sea Power* (Baltimore: Johns Hopkins University Press, 1974). On technological change, see Stockholm International Peace Research Institute (SIPRI), *Tactical and Strategic Antisubmarine Warfare* (Cambridge, Mass.: MIT Press, 1974), also *Strategic Survey, 1975* (London: IISS, 1976), pp. 21–26. On Soviet naval power: Norman Polmar, *Soviet Naval Power: Challenge for the 1970's*, rev. ed. (New York: Crane, Russak & Company, Inc., 1974), Michael MccGwire, ed., *Soviet Naval Developments: Capability and Context* (New York: Praeger, 1973); Michael MccGwire and Ken Booth, eds., *Soviet Naval Policy: Objectives and Constraints* (New York: Praeger, 1975); Barry M. Blechman, *The Changing Soviet Navy* (Washington, D.C.: The Brookings Institution, 1973); and Robert W. Herrick, *Soviet Naval Strategy: Fifty years of Theory and Practice* (Annapolis, Md.: U.S. Naval Institute, 1968). On naval arms control see Blechman's *The Control of Naval Armaments* (Washington, D.C.: The Brookings Institution, 1975).

3. For a translation of Gorshkov's statements see the United States Naval Institute *Proceedings*, January–November 1974.

4. Polmar's assessments of Soviet naval power tend to emphasize the threatening nature of Soviet force structure change. Even more alarmed views can be found in almost any DOD assessment of the last decade, especially those of Admiral Elmo Zumwalt during his tenure as Chief of Naval Operations.

5. See especially, MccGwire, et al., *Soviet Naval Policy: Objectives and Constraints*; also his essay "Maritime Strategy and the Super-powers" in "Power at Sea: Part II: Super-powers and Navies," *Adelphi Papers*, no. 123.

6. For an important exception to this rule see Lawrence J. Korb, "The Defense Budget and Detente: Present Status, Assumptions and Future Possibilities," *Naval War College Review* (Summer 1975). See also Michael Klare, "Superpower Rivalry at Sea," *Foreign Policy*, no. 21 (Winter 1975–1976).

7. Korb, op. cit.

8. See especially "The Persistence of Force" in Robert E. Osgood and Robert W. Tucker, *Force, Order and Justice* (Baltimore: Johns Hopkins University Press, 1967), pp. 2–40.

9. Richard M. Nixon, *U.S. Foreign Policy for the 1970's: A New Strategy for Peace* (Washington: Congressional Printing Office, 1970), p. 2.

10. *Washington Post*, February 17, 1976.

11. *Washington Post*, February 14, 1976.

12. *New York Times*, March 12, 1976.

13. Ibid.

14. *New York Times*, January 17, 1974.

15. Text of background briefing, New Orleans, August 14, 1970, p. 16. Cited by David Landau, *Kissinger: The Uses of Power* (Boston: Houghton-Mifflin Company, 1973), p. 128.

16. Henry Kissinger, *Nuclear Weapons and Foreign Policy* (New York: W. W. Norton & Co., 1969), p. 54.

17. Ibid., p. 59.

18. Ibid., p. 247.

19. Daniel Ellsberg, *Papers on the War* (New York: Simon and Schuster, 1972), pp. 292–293.

20. It was not thought that in this matter there was any disagreement between Schlesinger and Kissinger, but for obvious tactical diplomatic reasons it was appropriate, and, since McNamara, it has been "traditional" that "new" substantive changes in strategic doctrine emanate from the Secretary of Defense.

21. *New York Times*, August 25, 1975.

22. *New York Times*, June 25, 1975.

23. Jack Anderson and Les Whitten, *Washington Post*, February 28, 1976.

24. "Deaths of American Military Personnel in the Korean Demilitarized Zone," *Hearings before the Sub-Committees on International Political and Military Affairs and on International Organizations*, 94th Cong., 2nd Sess. (Washington: Congressional Printing Office) September 1, 1976, p. 6. It turns out the North Korean attack on the tree cutters was preceded by two North Korean warnings so that when the U.S. party returned, three cameras were focused on the area because, in the words

of Assistant Secretary Abramowitz, "We were worried about [the primary operations]. . . . It was a concern, obviously," *Washington Post*, September 6, 1976.

25. James R. Schlesinger, "Now—A Tougher U.S.", *U.S. News and World Report*, February 28, 1976.

26. *Washington Post*, February 17, 1974.

27. *Washington Post*, February 28, 1976.

28. For story of the ailing Chairman's reception of Marcos, see the *Washington Post*, June 8, 1975. For the Chinese interest in Europe, see the *Washington Post*, June 2, 1975.

29. *Washington Post*, November 25, 1974.

30. Michael Pillsbury, "U.S.-Chinese Military Ties," *Foreign Policy*, no. 20, Fall 1975, p. 53.

31. James R. Schlesinger, "Face the Nation" transcript, Sunday, April 11, 1976, CBS, 524 W. 57th Street, New York, New York.

32. Pillsbury, op. cit., p. 58.

33. See Victor Zorza, "Clues to Kissinger's Peking Failure," *Washington Post*, December 5, 1974.

34. Victor Zorza, *Washington Post*, November 6, 1976.

35. Jonathan Pollack, "Peking's Nuclear Restraint," op. ed., *New York Times*, April 12, 1976.

36. Ibid.

37. *New York Times*, January 23, 1972.

38. Robert E. Osgood, *The Weary and the Wary* (Baltimore: Johns Hopkins University Press, 1972), p. 37.

39. Masataka Kosaka, "Options for Japan's Foreign Policy," *Adelphi Papers*, no. 97 (London: IISS, 1973), pp. 34–40, and esp. p. 36.

40. *New York Times*, April 1973.

41. *Washington Post*, February 9, 1974.

42. Hanns Maull, "Oil and Influence: The Oil Weapon Examined," *Adelphi Papers*, no. 117 (London: IISS, 1975), p. 9.

43. This phrase is from James Chace, *A World Elsewhere: The New American Foreign Policy* (New York: Charles Scribner's Sons, 1973).

44. Earl Ravenal, "The Nixon Doctrine and Our Asian Commitments," *Foreign Affairs*, vol. 49, (January, 1971), pp. 206–207.

45. Ibid., p. 209.

46. Richard M. Nixon, *U.S. Foreign Policy for the 1970's: Building for Peace* (Washington: Government Printing Office, 1971), p. 179.

47. Alain C. Enthoven and K. Wayne Smith, "What Forces for NATO? And From Whom?" *Foreign Affairs*, 48 (October, 1969), p. 82.

48. Richard Burt, "New Weapons Technologies: Debate and Directions," *Adelphi Papers*, no. 126 (London: IISS, 1976).

49. Hans J. Morgenthau, "Three Paradoxes," *The New Republic*, October 11, 1975, p. 20.

2. The "Official" View

1. Report of Secretary of Defense James R. Schlesinger to the Congress on the *FY 1976 and Transition Budgets, FY 1977 Authorization Request and FY 1976–1980 Defense Programs* (Washington: Government Printing Office, 1975), p. I-26 (hereafter cited as *Posture Statement, 1976–197T*).

2. Statement of Hon. J. William Middendorf II, Secretary of the Navy, U.S. Congress, Senate, Hearings before the Committee on Armed Services, *Fiscal Year 1976 and July-September 1976 Transition Period Authorization for Military Procurement, Research and Development, and Active Duty, Selected Reserve and Civilian Personnel Strengths, Part 2, Authorizations*, 94th Cong., 1st Sess., 1975, p. 574 (hereafter cited as *Sec/USN Posture Statement, 1976–197T*).

3. Ibid., pp. 574–575, and Statement of Adm. James L. Holloway III, Chief of Naval Operations, in Ibid., p. 640 (hereafter cited as *CNO Posture Statement, 1976–197T*) and Admiral Holloway's statement for fiscal year 1978 in U.S., Senate, Hearings before the Committee on Appropriations, *Department of Defense Appropriations, Fiscal Year 1978* Part 1. "Posture Statements," 95th Cong., 1st Sess., pp. 383–463 (hereafter cited as *CNO Posture Statement, 1978*), esp. p. 389.

4. Statement of Adm. James L. Holloway III in U.S., Congress, House Committee on Armed Services, Hearings on *Military Posture and H.R. 11500/H.R. 12438/Department of Defense Authorization for Appropriations for Fiscal Year 1977*. Part I, 94th Cong., 2nd Sess., 1976, p. 748, (hereafter cited as *CNO Posture Statement, 1977*).

5. *Sec/USN Posture Statement, 1976–197T*, passim and *CNO Posture Statement, 1976–197T*, pp. 645–653; also Adm. Stansfield Turner, "Missions of the U.S. Navy," *Naval War College Review*, September–October 1974, pp. 2–17. To some extent the presence category could be characterized as "peaceful presence." Presence short of the use of force might be lumped together with strategic deterrence to form a pair of "war-deterring missions" as opposed to the "war-fighting" missions of sea control and projection of power. Though of some analytical use, this bifurcation of the mission profile seems to break down in practice. As the weapons inventory available for use on all U.S. Navy platforms becomes

more diverse and flexible through the introduction of *Harpoon* the sea-launched cruise missile mission differentiation becomes more difficult. Moreover, the credibility of one mission—for example, "presence," ostensibly a "war-deterring" mission—is inevitably linked to other "war-fighting" missions, e.g., sea control or projection. Finally, these mission linkages are reinforced by the more or less simultaneous exercise of most if not all of these missions by a single platform such as an aircraft carrier or carrier task force. See Comm. James F. McNulty, "Naval Presence—The Misunderstood Mission," *Naval War College Review*, September–October 1974, pp. 21–31.

6. *CNO Posture Statement 1976–1977*, p. 401.

7. Robert S. McNamara, "The Dynamics of Nuclear Strategy," address made before the annual convention of United Press International editors and publishers at San Francisco, California, September 18, 1967. *Department of State Bulletin*. October 9, 1967, pp. 443–445.

8. *Sec/Def Posture Statement, 1976–1977*, p. II–3.

9. *Senate Authorization, 1976–1977*, p. 790.

10. Ibid., p. 789.

11. Ibid., p. 790.

12. See Malcolm Currie's comments concerning SSN modification in Ibid, p. 2700; see also *Sec/Def Posture Statement, 1976–1977*, p. II–39.

13. *Senate Authorization, 1976–1977*, pp. 738–739.

14. Drew Middleton, "Missile a Factor Before It's Ready," *New York Times*, October 15, 1975 and Lawrence Weiler, "Strategic Cruise Missiles and the Future of SALT," *Arms Control Today*, vol. 5, no. 10 (October 1975).

15. *CNO Posture Statement, 1978*, p. 408.

16. *CNO Posture Statement, 1977*, p. 768.

17. *CNO Posture Statement, 1978*, p. 408.

18. Middleton, op. cit., and Weiler, op. cit.

19. U.S. Congress, House, Committee on Armed Services, Hearings on *Military Posture and H.R. 12564, Department of Defense Authorizations for Fiscal Year 1975*, 93rd Cong., 2nd Sess., 1974, p. 14.

20. See H. Scoville, Jr., "Flexible Madness?" *Foreign Policy*, No. 14 (Spring 1974). See also W. K. H. Panofsky, "The Mutual-Hostage Relationship Between America and Russia," *Foreign Affairs*, vol. 52, no. 1 (October 1973) and T. Greenwood and M. L. Nacht, "The New Nuclear Debate: Sense or Nonsense?" *Foreign Affairs*, vol. 52, no. 4 (July 1974).

21. Middleton, op. cit., and Weiler, op. cit.

22. Middleton, op. cit.

23. *Senate Authorization, 1976–1977*, p. 790.

24. Turner, op. cit., p. 6.

25. *CNO Posture Statement, 1976–197T*, p. 646 and *CNO Posture Statement, 1978*, p. 391.

26. Turner, op. cit., p. 7.

27. *CNO Posture Statement, 1978*, p. 392; *CNO Posture Statement, 1976–197T*, p. 649; and Turner, op. cit., p. 10.

28. *Sec/Def Posture Statement, 1976–197T*, p. III-26; see also Martin Binkin and Jeffrey Record, *Where Does the Marine Corps Go from Here?* (Washington, D.C.: The Brookings Institution, 1976).

29. See Bernard Weinraub's two articles, "Clayton Criticizes Pentagon Aides on Plans to Reduce the Navy's Role," *New York Times*, March 28, 1978, p. 10 and "Dispute Over Navy Role Termed Biggest Defense Fight Since 1949," *New York Times*, April 4, 1978, p. 16.

30. Ibid.

31. *CNO Posture Statement, FY 1978*, p. 401.

32. For a review of these changes see "Congress Cancels Fifth Nuclear Aircraft Carrier," *Congressional Quarterly Weekly Report*, vol. XXXV. no. 12 (March 19, 1977), p. 478, "Panel Seeks Improved Combat Readiness," *CQWR*, vol. XXXV, no. 161 (April 16, 1977), pp. 719–722, and George C. Wilson, "New De-emphasis on Carriers Worrying Admirals," *Washington Post*, January 4, 1978.

33. Arnold Kuzmack, "Where Does the Navy Go from Here?" in George Quester, *Sea Power in the 1970s* (New York: Dunellen Press, 1975), pp. 47–51.

34. "Congress Cancels . . . Carrier," *CQWR*, op. cit. and Wilson, op. cit.

35. Testimony of Admiral Holloway in *Senate Authorization, 1976–197T*, p. 742.

36. "The Aircraft Carrier," documentation provided for the Seapower and Strategic and Critical Materials Subcommittee of the House Committee on Armed Services in Hearings on *Military Posture and H.R. 5068 and H.R. 1755, Department of Defense Authorization for Appropriations for Fiscal Year 1978*, Part 4, 95th Congress, 1st Sess., 1977, p. 280.

37. *Senate Authorization, 1976–197T: Part 9, Tactical Air Power*, pp. 4662–4663. For a sketch of the capabilities of these aircraft and their armament see Appendixes A, B, and C.

38. Ibid., pp. 4663–4664.

39. "Congress Cancels . . . Carrier," and "Panel Seeks . . . Readiness," esp. pp. 720–721.

40. *Senate Authorization, 1976–197T*, p. 787.

41. *Senate Authorization, 1976–197T: Part 9, Tactical Air Power*, pp. 4981–4982.

42. Michael Getler, "Navy Seeks More Fire Power," *Washington Post*, October 15, 1974, p. A2; and see U.S., Congress, Hearings before a Subcommittee of the House Committee on Appropriations, *Department of Defense Appropriations for 1978*, Part 4, 95th Cong., 1st Sess., 1977, p. 727.

43. *Report of Secretary of Defense Donald Rumsfeld to the Congress on The FY 1977 Budget and its Implications for the FY 1978 Authorization and the FY 1977–1981 Defense Programs* in U.S., Congress, Hearings before the Senate Committee on Armed Services, *Fiscal Year 1977 Authorization for Military Procurement, etc.* Part I, 94th Cong., 2nd Sess., 1976, p. 188 (hereafter, *Senate Posture Statement FY 1977*).

44. *Senate Authorization, 1976–197T*, p. 5057. This is expressed as an "opinion" by the Director of the Surface Warfare Weapons Group.

45. U.S., Congress, House, Committee on the Budget, Hearings before the Task Force on National Security Programs on *Force Structure and Long-Range Projections*, Part I, 94th Cong., 1st Sess., 1975, p. 108. See also the DDG-47-CSGN comparisons in the House Armed Services Seapower Subcommittee hearings, op. cit., p. 293.

46. For a discussion of congressional behavior regarding navy shipbuilding requests and proposals, see Chapter 5.

47. Hearings on *Force Structure and Long-Range Projections*, p. 110–111.

48. *Sec/Def Posture Statement, 1976–197T*, pp. III-26–III-27.

49. Ibid., p. III-27.

50. See Holloway's testimony in Hearings on *Military Posture and H.R. 5068 and H.R. 1755*, esp. pp. 906–913.

51. House Appropriations Committee, *DOD Appropriations for Fiscal 1978*, Part 4, pp. 722, 733, and 748.

52. Ibid., p. 748.

53. Ibid., p. 742.

54. See Holloway's response to a question put by Congresswoman Patricia Schroeder in Hearings on *Military Posture and H.R. 5068 and H.R. 1755*, p. 943.

55. Ibid., p. 907.

3. Naval Force: Changing Missions for a Changing World

1. Robert E. Osgood and Robert W. Tucker, *Force, Order and Justice* (Baltimore: Johns Hopkins University Press, 1967), passim.

2. Ibid., p. 42.

3. Inis Claude, *Power and International Relations* (New York: Random House, 1962), p. 88.

4. Ibid., p. 91.

5. Ibid.

6. See, for example, Walter Millis, *An End to Arms* (New York: Atheneum Press, 1964).

7. Osgood and Tucker, op. cit., p. 40.

8. Ibid.

9. Ibid., p. 26.

10. Robert M. Lawrence and Joel Larus, eds., *Nuclear Proliferation: Phase II* (Lawrence, Kansas: The University Press of Kansas, 1975) and Anne W. Marks, ed., *NPT: Paradoxes and Problems* (Washington, D.C.: Arms Control Association, 1975).

11. Tad Szulc, "Have We Been Had?" *The New Republic*, June 7, 1975, pp. 11–15. For an excellent review of Schlesinger's concept of "limited nuclear options" and the debate caused by it, see Lynn Etheridge Davis, "Limited Nuclear Options: Deterrence and the New American Doctrine," *Adelphi Papers*, no. 121 (London: IISS, 1976).

12. Osgood, op. cit., p. 26.

13. Ibid.

14. A. T. Mahan, *The Influence of Sea Power on History*, Little, Brown & Co., Boston, 1890, p. 138.

15. "Guidelines for the New Defense Budget," *The Defense Monitor*, vol. 4, January 1975, p. 8.

16. James A. Nathan and James K. Oliver, "Public Opinion and U.S. Security Policy," *Armed Forces and Society*, Fall, 1975, vol. 2, no. 2, pp. 46–63 and Chapter 6 below.

17. Comm. James F. McNulty, "Naval Presence—The Misunderstood Mission," *Naval War College Review*, September-October 1974, pp. 21–31.

18. U.S. Congress, Senate, *Hearings Before the Senate Committee on Appropriations*, 92 Cong., 2 Sess., 1972, Pt. 3—Navy, p. 67.

19. *Secretary of Defense's Posture Statement, FY 1976–197T*, p. III-27.

20. *CNO Posture Statement, 1976–197T*, p. 651.

21. See, for example, Lt. Comm. Kenneth R. McGruther, "The Role of Perception in Naval Diplomacy," *Naval War College Review*, September–October 1974, pp. 3–20, and Edward Luttwak, *The Political Uses of Sea Power* (Baltimore: Johns Hopkins University Press, 1974).

22. *CNO Posture Statement, 1976–197T*, p. 652.

23. Adm. Stansfield Turner, "Missions of the U.S. Navy," *Naval War College Review*, September–October 1974, p. 14.

24. *Sec/Def Posture Statement, 1976–197T*, p. III-27.

25. Turner, op. cit.

26. *CNO Posture Statement, 1976–197T*, pp. 651–652.

27. See *Naval War College Second Annual Report to the President*, 9 August 1974, Newport, R.I., "Educational Innovation at the Naval War College 1972–1974: A Case Study," p. 70.

28. Turner, "Designing a Modern Navy: A Workshop Discussion," in "Power at Sea: Part II: Super-powers and Navies," *Adelphi Papers*, no. 123, p. 28.

29. Ken Booth, "Navies and Foreign Policy," paper prepared for the International Studies Association, St. Louis, 20–23 March 1974, p. 29.

30. James Cable, *Gunboat Diplomacy: Political Applications of Limited Naval Force* (London: IISS, 1971), p. 20.

31. See Booth's critique in op. cit., p. 29.

32. Comm. Jonathan Howe (USN), *Multicrises* (Cambridge: MIT Press, 1971).

33. Although some official skepticism has emerged (though tainted perhaps with election-year overtones). See "Mayaguez Operation Criticized in Report," *New York Times*, Oct. 6, 1976, pp. 1 and 10.

34. McGruther, "The Role of Perception in Naval Diplomacy," p. 11.

35. Ibid.

36. Luttwak, *The Political Uses of Sea Power*, and Ken Booth, *Navies and Foreign Policy* (New York: Crane, Russak, 1977).

37. See, for example, Luttwak, p. 1, and Booth, chap. 2.

38. *CNO Posture Statement, FY 1978*, p. 394.

39. Ibid.

40. Barry M. Blechman and Stephen S. Kaplan, "Armed Forces as a Political Instrument," *Survival*, vol. 19 (July/Aug. 1977), v., pp. 168–174.

41. Ibid., p. 171.

42. McGruther, op. cit., p. 17.

43. Luttwak, op. cit., p. 17.

44. McNulty, p. 29.

45. Blechman and Kaplan, pp. 172–173.

46. Ibid., p. 172.

47. Turner, "Missions of the U.S. Navy," p. 16.

48. McGruther, pp. 12–13.

49. Luttwak, pp. 39–40 (emphasis in the original).

50. Ibid., p. 47.

51. Adm. James L. Holloway III, "The U.S. Navy: A Bicentennial Appraisal," United States Naval Institute *Proceedings*, vol. 102 (July 1976), pp. 20–21.

52. Turner, "Designing a Modern Navy," Ibid., p. 23.

53. Dean Acheson, *Present at the Creation* (New York: W. W. Norton, 1969), p. 405.

54. See Luttwak, pp. 49–52.

55. Holloway, "The U.S. Navy: A Bicentennial Appraisal," p. 23.

56. Turner, "Designing a Modern Navy," pp. 26–27, esp. figures 2 and 3.

57. Holloway paraphrasing Title X of the U.S. code in "The U.S. Navy: A Bicentennial Appraisal," p. 18.

58. George C. Wilson, "New U.S. Military Plan: European, Persian Focus," *Washington Post*, January 27, 1978, p. A17.

59. Holloway, "The U.S. Navy: A Bicentennial Appraisal," p. 19.

60. Wilson, op. cit.

61. William Safire, "The Battle of Whizkid Gulf," *New York Times*, February 9, 1978 and Weinraub, op. cit.

62. McNulty, op. cit., p. 29.

63. We are indebted to Francis West and Ken McGruther for pointing out this nuance of the bureaucratic politics of naval planning.

64. See, for example, the papers presented at the Eighteenth Annual Conference of the IISS at Baden bei Wien, Austria, September 1976: "The Diffusion of Power I: Proliferation of Force," *Adelphi Papers*, no. 133 and "The Diffusion of Power II: Conflict and its Control," *Adelphi Papers*, no. 134 (London: IISS, 1977).

4. An Uncertain International Future

1. For example, Robert W. Herrick's *Soviet Naval Strategy: Fifty Years of Theory and Practice* (Annapolis, Md.: U.S. Naval Institute, 1968); David Fairhill, *Russian Sea Power* (Boston: Gambit, 1971); Norman Polmar, *Soviet Naval Power: Challenge for the 1970's*, rev. ed. (New York: Crane, Russak and Co., Inc., 1974); Michael MccGwire and Ken Booth, eds., *Soviet Naval Policy: Objections and Constraints* (New York: Praeger, 1975); MccGwire, ed., *Soviet Naval Developments: Capability and Context* (New York: Praeger Publishers, 1973); Barry M. Blechman, *The Changing Soviet Navy* (Washington, D.C.: The Brookings Institution, 1973); Barry M. Blechman, *The Control of Naval Armaments: Prospects and Possibilities* (Washington, D.C.: The Brookings Institution, 1975).

2. Polmar, p. 1.

3. Ibid., p. 107.

4. Adm. Worth Bagley, "Superpowers at Sea: A Debate," *International Security*, vol. 1, #1 (Summer, 1976), p. 67.

5. Adm. James L. Holloway III, "The U.S. Navy: A Bicentennial Appraisal," United States Naval Institute *Proceedings*, vol. 102 (July 1970), p. 21.

6. MccGwire and Booth, eds., *Soviet Naval Policy*, passim.

7. Ibid., esp. MccGwire, "Current Soviet Warship Construction and Naval Weapons Development," pp. 424–451; MccGwire, "The Evolution of Soviet Naval Policy; 1960–1974," pp. 505–541; and Robert Weinland, "Analysis of Admiral Gorshkov's 'Navies in War and Peace,'" pp. 547–572.

8. Text published in January through November 1974 issues of the U.S. Naval Institute *Proceedings*.

9. MccGwire, "The Evolution of Soviet Naval Policy: 1960–1974," in *Soviet Naval Policy*, p. 540.

10. John W. Finney, "Data Shows Navy Leads in Big Ships," *New York Times*, May 3, 1976, p. 4.

11. Finney, "Aging Fleet Called A Soviet Handicap," *New York Times*, May 20, 1974, and Finney, "Study Finds a Decline in Shipbuilding for Soviet Navy," *New York Times*, May 4, 1976, p. 12.

12. Ibid.

13. *U.S. Department of Defense, Annual Defense Department Report, FY 76 and FY 77*, Washington, GPO, 1975, p. I-21.

14. Ibid., p. I-22.

15. Ibid., p. I-21–22. Recent posture statements reach similar conclusions; see U.S. Department of Defense, *Annual Defense Department Report, FY 77*, (Washington: GPO, 1976), pp. 99–100.

16. Testimony of Adm. James L. Holloway III in U.S., Congress, Hearings before a Subcommittee of the House Committee on Appropriations, *Department of Defense Appropriations for 1978*, 95th Cong., 1st Sess., 1977, p. 726.

17. CNO's Posture Statement, FY 1978, U.S., Congress, Senate Committee on Appropriations, *Department of Defense Appropriations, Fiscal Year 1978*, 95th Cong., 1st Sess., 1977, p. 422.

18. Blechman, *The Changing Soviet Navy*, p. 36.

19. *Annual Report, FY 76 and FY 7T*, p. I-22.

20. Blechman, *The Control of Naval Armaments*, esp. 47–63.

21. See, for example, *Annual Report, FY 76 and FY 77*, p. I-22.

22. U.S. Congress, Hearings before the Senate Committee on Armed Services on S. 920, *FY 76 and July–September 1976 Transition Period*

Authorization for Military Procurement, Research and Development and Active Duty, Selected Reserve and Civilian Personnel Strengths, Part 2, Authorizations, 94th Congress, 1st Sess., 1975, p. 744.

23. Drew Middleton, "Study Says Navy's Anti-submarine Warfare Spending Will Rise From $2.5 Billion to $4.5 Billion by '75," *New York Times*, October 20, 1972, p. 15.

24. Kosta Tsipis, *Tactical and Strategic Anti-submarine Warfare* (Cambridge, Mass.: MIT Press for the Stockholm International Peace Research Institute, 1974), p. 15.

25. Ibid., p. 44.

26. George C. Wilson, "Soviets Change Sub Tactics," *Washington Post*, April 28, 1975.

27. Tsipis, op. cit., p. 47.

28. Ibid.

29. John P. Craven, "The Future of the Sea-Based Deterrent" in "Power at Sea: Part III: Competition and Conflict," *Adelphi Papers* no. 124 (London: IISS, 1976), p. 11.

30. Adm. Sergei G. Gorshkov, *Red Star Rising at Sea* (Annapolis, Md.: U.S. Naval Institute, 1974), pp. 131–132, also cited by Johan Jorgen Holst, "The Navies of the Super-Powers—Motives, Forces, Prospects," in "Power at Sea: Part II: Super-powers and Navies," *Adelphi Papers*, no. 123.

31. "The Feasibility of a 600-ship Fleet," Members of Congress for Peace through Law, *Congressional Record*, House, vol. 121, no. 147 (October 2, 1975), pp. H9451FF.

32. Ibid.

33. Testimony of R. Adm. Alfred J. Whittle, Jr., Director, General Planning and Programming Division, Office of the CNO, in U.S. Congress, House Committee on the Budget, Hearings before the Task Force on National Security Programs, *Force Structure and Long-Range Projections*, 94th Cong., 1st Sess., 1975, p. 101.

34. *Adelphi Papers*, no. 123, p. 1.

35. Seyom Brown, *New Forces in World Politics* (Washington, D.C.: The Brookings Institution, 1974), p. 3.

36. Holloway, "The U.S. Navy: A Bicentennial Appraisal," p. 20.

37. Elizabeth Young, "New Laws for Old Navies: Military Implications of the Law of the Sea," *Survival*, vol. 16 (November–December 1974), pp. 262–267. See also *Survival*, vol. 17 (March–April 1975), pp. 69–72.

38. Young, op. cit., p. 265.

39. Testimony of John Norton Moore before the Subcommittee on Oceans and International Environment of the Senate Committee on Foreign Relations, *Law of the Sea Conference*, 94th Cong., 1st Sess., May 22, 1975, pp. 21–23.

40. Ibid., p. 9 and Jonathan V. Charney, "Law of the Sea: Breaking the Deadlock," *Foreign Affairs*, vol. 55, no. 3 (April 1977), pp. 598–629.

41. See Richard G. Darman, "The Law of the Sea: Rethinking U.S. Interests," *Foreign Affairs*, vol. 56, no. 2 (January 1978), pp. 373–395 and Ann Pelhan, "Harvesting the Rocks: Investment Guarantees are Key Issue in Proposals to Promote Seabed Mining," *Congressional Quarterly Weekly Report*, vol. 36, no. 3 (January 21, 1978), pp. 121–126.

42. Darman, op. cit.

43. Charney, p. 614.

44. See Robert Osgood, "U.S. Security Interests in Ocean Law," *Ocean Development and International Law*, Spring, 1974.

45. Robert W. Tucker, "A New International Order?" *Commentary*, vol. 59 (February 1975), pp. 38–50.

46. Ibid., p. 46.

47. Laurence Martin, "The Role of Force in the Ocean," in *Perspectives on Ocean Policy*, report of Conference on Conflict and Order in Ocean Relations, October 21–24, 1974, Airlie, Virginia, prepared for National Science Foundation under Grant No. GI 39643 by Ocean Policy Project, Johns Hopkins University, Washington, pp. 33–44.

48. *Strategic Survey, 1975* (London: IISS, 1976), p. 25.

49. James Digby, "Precision-Guided Weapons," *Adelphi Papers*, no. 118 (London: IISS, 1975), p. 1.

50. Lt. Linton Wells, "Comments," in *Perspectives on Ocean Policy*, p. 47.

51. "U.S. Arms to the Persian Gulf: $10 Billion Since 1973," *The Defense Monitor*, vol. 4, May 1975, p. 5.

52. Wells, op. cit.

53. Kenneth R. McGruther, "The Role of Perception in Naval Diplomacy," *Naval War College Review*, September–October 1974, p. 11.

54. Martin Binken and Jeffrey Record, *Where Does the Marine Corps Go from Here?* (Washington, D.C.: The Brookings Institution, 1976), p. 12.

55. Ibid., p. 12.

56. *Report of Secretary of Defense James R. Schlesinger to the Congress on the FY 1976 and Transitional Budgets FY 197T, Authorization Request and FY 1976–1980 Defense Programs*, Feb. 5, 1975, pp. 111–126.

57. Ibid.

58. "New Naval Technologies," *Strategic Survey 1975*, p. 25.

59. *New York Times*, April 26, 1976.

60. Statement of Adm. James L. Holloway III, Chief of Naval Operations in U.S. Congress, Senate Hearings before the Committee on Armed Services, *Fiscal Year 1976 and July–September, 1976, Transition Period Authorization for Military Procurement, Research and Development, and Active Duty, Selected Reserve and Civilian Personnel Strengths*, Part 2, Authorizations, 94th Cong., 1st Sess., 1975, pp. 11 and 12.

61. *Encyclopaedia Britannica*, 1970, vol. 21, p. 343.

62. George P. Steele, "A Fleet to Match Our Real Needs," *Outlook, Washington Post*, May 16, 1976, p. 30.

63. Geoffrey Kemp, "Threats from the Sea: Sources for Asian Maritime Conflict," *Orbis*, Fall, 1975, vol. XIX, no. 3, pp. 1954–1965.

64. John W. Finney, "Dreadnought or Dinosaur," *New York Times Magazine*, January 18, 1976, p. 30.

65. Schlesinger, op. cit., pp. 111, 125–126.

66. "Navy Cool to Land-Based Aircraft Study," *Aviation Week and Space Technology*, October 18, 1976, p. 91.

67. David Fromkin, "The Strategy of Terrorism," *Foreign Affairs*, vol. 53, no. 4 (July 1975), pp. 692–693.

68. Binkin and Record, op. cit., p. 33.

69. See James A. Nathan and James K. Oliver, "The Diplomacy of Violence," *Society/Transaction*, vol. 11 (September/October 1974), pp. 32–34.

70. Michael Klare, "Superpower Rivalry at Sea," *Foreign Policy*, no. 21 (Winter 1975–1976), p. 167.

71. Young, op. cit., p. 263.

72. See J. R. Hill, "Maritime Power and the Law of the Sea," *Survival*, vol. 17 (March–April 1975), pp. 69–72, for such a view.

73. Tucker, "A New International Order?" op. cit.

74. For an elaboration of an international system of mutual deterrence or a "unit veto" system see: Morton Kaplan, *System and Process in International Politics* (New York: John Wiley, 1957).

5. Congress and the Future of American Sea Power

1. See Aaron Wildavsky, *The Politics of the Budgetary Process* (Boston: Little, Brown Co., 1975).

2. Inasmuch as this chapter focuses on the Nixon-Ford years we have chosen the fiscal year 1971 through 1977 budgets as our data base. The

fiscal 1970 budget requests are noted but exclude from detailed analysis because the peculiar confluence of presidential terms, fiscal years and budgetary planning cycles means that the first two budgets under which an incoming president operates are largely the product of his predecessor's planning and priorities. Thus, the first six months of Richard Nixon's first administration were carried out under the fiscal 1969 budget and the next twelve months under the fiscal 1970 budget, both of which were prepared under President Johnson's direction and submitted to Congress before Nixon was inaugurated. Nixon submitted a series of amendments to Johnson's fiscal 1970 budget, but by and large they were marginal adjustments. On balance, therefore, the fiscal 1971 and subsequent budgets are better indicators of the two Republican administrations' priorities and the congressional reaction to them. The FY 1978 budget is considered but falls into the same category as FY 1970.

3. Alton Frye, *A Responsible Congress: The Politics of National Security* (New York: McGraw-Hill Book Co., 1975), p. 98.

4. Lewis Dexter, "Congressmen and the Making of Foreign Policy," in *Components of Defense Policy*, edited by Davis B. Bobrow (Chicago: Rand McNally & Co., 1965), p. 101. See also Raymond H. Dawson, "Congressional Innovation and Intervention in Defense Policy," *American Political Science Review*, vol. 56 (March 1962), p. 44.

5. Samuel Huntington, *The Soldier and the State* (Cambridge: Harvard University Press, 1959), p. 409.

6. See Huntington, "Strategy Planning and the Political Process," *Foreign Affairs*, vol. 38 (January 1960), p. 285–299.

7. Frye, op. cit., p. 98.

8. Ibid., p. 99.

9. Arnold Kanter, "Congress and the Defense Budget: 1960–1970," *The American Political Science Review*, vol. 66, no. 1 (March 1972), p. 131.

10. Ibid.

11. Ibid., p. 133. Kanter describes the index and the procedure for its derivation as follows:

The absolute value of the difference between the President's budget request and the Congressional appropriations (computed as a percentage of the President's request) is one measure of the distribution of Congressional activity. The mean annual absolute difference between the President's request and Congress' appropriations supplies a useful summary index of Congressional activity for the period under consideration. If Congress made no changes in a particular budget category in the eleven year period, the index of activity = 0.000. Large or infrequent Congressional changes in the President's requests (either increases or decreases) will yield larger indexes for the index.

12. Ibid., p. 135. Kanter's correlation figure was r = 0.006.

13. Ibid.

14. For a detailed treatment of the 1971–1977 period see Appendixes D and E and, for the 1960–1970 period, Kanter, Tables 1 and 2. The computations in this section are based on these sources.

15. Determining the magnitude of cuts for the 1971–1977 period is complicated by the fact that in many instances where voted by Congress these were offset by the provision of often significant levels of transfer authority especially for the Procurement and RDT & E titles. Louis Fisher in his *Presidential Spending Power* (Princeton, N.J.: Princeton University Press, 1975), pp. 104–122, has concluded that much of this authority was used by the Nixon administration in Vietnam and Cambodia.

How such funds should be treated in analysis of the sort undertaken here is not evident. The following description of transfer authority taken from a Senate Appropriations Committee Report indicates the ambiguous nature of transfer authority, i.e., simultaneously a *reduction* in *total* Department of Defense total obligational authority but an *increase* in the given fiscal year's obligational authority:

> Attention is called to the fact that in addition to the appropriations recommended the committee has recommended provisions that provide for the transfer to appropriations in this bill approximately $945 million from other appropriations revolving funds. While these transfers do reflect conditions in the total new obligational authority recommended, they do not reflect reductions in budget programs. However, the utilization of these funds for fiscal 1972 programs does constitute a reduction in the total funds available to the Department of Defense for obligation (U.S., Congress, Senate Committee on Appropriations, *DOD Appropriation Bill, 1972*, Senate Report 92–498, 92nd Cong., 1st Sess., p. 5).

In the following sections NOA is reported both with and without the inclusion of transfer authority. In only a few instances does the inclusion of transfer authority significantly affect the total NOA levels.

16. Lawrence J. Korb, "The Defense Budget and Detente: Present Status, Assumptions, and Future Possibilities," *Naval War College Review* (Summer 1975), pp. 19–27 and Appendix F.

17. See Appendix G.

18. See Appendix H.

19. See the FY 1977 *Conference Report* of the House and Senate Armed Services Committees, H. Rpt. No. 94–1305, 94th Cong., 2nd Sess., 1976, p. 23.

20. Hearings, *Authorization for Fiscal Year 1976 and 197T*, pp. 569 and 585.

21. See "Shipbuilding Claims Settlement Scored," *Washington Post*, June 2, 1976, p. A3: John W. Finney, "Rickover Warns of a Ship 'Rip-off,'" *New York Times*, June 8, 1976, p. 43; and Dan Morgan, "Admirals Dispute Pentagon on Shipbuilding Claims," *Washington Post*, June 26, 1976, p. 42.

22. U.S., Congress, Senate Committee on Armed Services, Hearings on *Military Posture and H.R. 12564: Department of Defense Authorization for Appropriations for Fiscal Year 1975*, 93rd Cong., 2nd Sess., 1974, pp. 1043–1056.

23. U.S., Congress, Senate Committee on Armed Services, Hearings on *Fiscal Year 1977 Authorization for Military Procurement, Research and Development, etc.*, 94th Cong., 2nd Sess., 1976, pp. 183–184.

24. See, for example, Michael Klare, "Superpower Rivalry at Sea," *Foreign Policy*, no. 21 (Winter 1975–1976).

25. Complicating the picture, however, is the fact that average percentage reductions as an indicator are influenced by the size of the base upon which they are calculated. This limitation is especially relevant to the analysis of new SCN requests and congressional action because those items or groups of items displaying the largest percentage changes are also those ships or classes of ships that were, until recently, requested in small numbers: no more than four support vessels in any year; in the case of the Lo-Mix ships no significant force numbers requested until fiscal 1975. Moreover, while the unit cost of these ships is lower than in the case of a CGN or a DD-963 class destroyer, it is nonetheless significant (see Table 7). Accordingly, if even one vessel is cut from an appropriation request, the resulting percentage change from the request can be quite large. In comparing force level decisions by line item, care must be exercised to determine whether the incidence of "no change" decisions observed for a particular item or class of items is indeed "significant" vis-à-vis the proportion of the total budget represented by the item as well as the incidence of "no change" decisions on other items or groups of items. Kanter proposes an index of "relative concentration" of "no change" outcomes based on a simple weighted proportion of "no change" and total decisions as a test of "significance." With minor changes in his language appropriate to the problem at hand, Kanter suggests the following procedure:

> Since each [SCN item] includes a different number of [decision points], a measure of relative concentration of "No Change" outcomes . . . is obtained by taking (1) the incidence of "No Changes" (for an SCN item) as

a percentage of the total number of "No Change" outcomes, (2) the number of [SCN item] budget decisions as a percentage of the total number of budget decisions, and (3) dividing the former by the latter. If the incidence of "No Change" outcomes were distributed in the same proportion as the total [decision points], the relative concentration would equal 1.00. Index values greater than 1.00 indicate a greater than expected incidence of "No Change" and values less than 1.00 indicate a fewer than expected number of cases . . . (Kanter, op. cit., p. 132, n. 10).

Appendix I arrays the proportions and the index of relative concentration of "no change" outcomes in force level decision.

26. U.S., Congress, House Appropriations Committee Report on *Defense Department Authorization for Fiscal Year 1973*, H. Rpt. No. 92–1389, 93rd Cong. 1st Sess., 1972, p. 174.

27. See, for example, the Senate Armed Services Committee's *Report on Defense Department Authorization for Fiscal 1976 and 197T*, S. Rpt. 94–146, 94th Cong., 1st Sess., 1975, p. 56.

28. Senate Armed Services Committee Report No. 94–146, pp. 56–57.

29. Senate Armed Services Committee, *Report Authorizing Defense Appropriations for FY 1972*, S. Rpt. No. 92–359, 92nd Cong., 1st Sess., 1971, p. 69.

30. House Appropriations Committee, *Defense Department Appropriations for FY 1973*, H. Rpt. No. 92–1389, pp. 142–143.

31. Senate Armed Services Committee, *Report Authorizing Appropriations for the Department of Defense for FY 1975*, S. Rpt. No. 93–884.

32. Senate, *Fiscal Year 1977 Authorization Hearings*, p. 184.

33. Letter from Congressman Melvin Price to Deputy Secretary of Defense William P. Clements, Jr., in House, Armed Services Committee, Hearings on *Military Posture and H.R. 11500/H.R. 12438/Department of Defense Authorization for Appropriations for Fiscal Year 1977*, Part 4.

34. House Appropriations Committee, *Department of Defense Appropriations for FY 1974*, H. Rpt. No. 93–662, 93rd Cong., 1st Sess., 1973, p. 173.

35. House Report No. 94–1305.

36. See Senator John Stennis's speech before the Senate on "U.S. Naval Power," *Congressional Record*, September 19, 1974, S17132–34.

37. House Report No. 94–1805, p. 22.

38. Ibid., p. 54.

39. Charles Mohr, "Carter Tells Crowds in Jersey He'd Move to Strengthen Navy," *New York Times*, June 6, 1976, p. 32.

40. For a summary of Ford requests and Carter revisions for FY 1978 see "Panel Seeks Improved Combat Readiness," *Congressional Quarterly*

Weekly Report, vol. XXXV, no. 16 (April 16, 1977), pp. 719–722, esp. p. 720.

41. "Congress Cancels Fifth Nuclear Aircraft Carrier," *Congressional Quarterly Weekly Report*, vol. XXXV, no. 12 (March 19, 1977), p. 478.

42. Quoted in "Panel Seeks Improved Readiness," op. cit., p. 721.

43. See Bernard Weinraub, "House Approves $36 Billion Plan for the Military," *New York Times*, April 26, 1977, pp. 1 & 16.

44. See Pat Towell, "Carter Defense Policies Challenged," *Congressional Quarterly Weekly Report*, vol. 36, no. 20 (May 20, 1978), pp. 1251–1262; Towell, "Liberals Defeated in Efforts to Cut Defense Arms Bill," *Congressional Quarterly Weekly Report*, vol. 36, no. 21 (May 27, 1978), pp. 1295–1298; Towell, "Panel Cautious on New Navy Technology," *Congressional Quarterly Weekly Report*, vol. 36, no. 23, (June 10, 1978), pp. 1471–1475; Towell, "Senate Gives Mixed Signals on Navy Future," *Congressional Quarterly Weekly Report*, vol. 36, no. 28 (July 15, 1978), pp. 1817–1820; "Fiscal '79 Appropriations," *Congressional Quarterly Weekly Report*, vol. 36, no. 30 (July 29, 1978), p. 1970; and B. Drummond Ayres, Jr., "Move to End Funds for Atomic Carrier Rejected by House," *New York Times*, August 8, 1978, pp. A1, A16.

45. A recent assessment of the degree to which the Carter administration proposes to change the priorities of previous administrations can be found in Lawrence J. Korb, "The Arms Control Implications of the Carter Defense Budget," *Naval War College Review* (Fall 1978), pp. 3–16.

6. Public Opinion and Naval Power: An Ambiguous Relationship

1. V.O. Key, *Public Opinion and American Democracy* (New York: Knopf, 1961), p. 97.

2. Bernard C. Cohen, *The Public's Impact on Foreign Policy*, (Boston: Little, Brown & Co., 1973), p. 11.

3. Cohen, *The Political Process and Foreign Policy: The Making of the Japanese Peace Settlement* (Princeton, N.J.: Princeton University Press, 1957), p. 29.

4. Among the more useful recent analyses of the climate of American public opinion as it relates to foreign and defense policy are: William Watts and Lloyd A. Free, *State of the Nation* (Washington, D.C.: Potomac Associates, 1973); Free, "The International Attitudes of Americans" and "The International Attitudes of Americans," in Donald R. Lesh, ed., *A Nation Observed: Perspectives on America's World Role* (Washington, D.C.: Potomac Associates, 1974); Watts and Free, "Na-

tionalism, Not Isolationism," *Foreign Policy*, no. 24 (Fall 1976), pp. 3–26; Louis Harris, *The Anguish of Change* (New York: W. W. Norton and Company, 1974): and U.S., Congress, Senate, Hearings before the Committee on Foreign Relations, *Foreign Policy Choices for the Seventies and Eighties*, vol. 1, 94th Congress, 1st and 2nd sess., 1975–1976, pp. 1–129.

5. Ole R. Holsti and James N. Rosenau, "The Meaning of Vietnam: Belief Systems of American Leaders," mimeo, Duke University, April 1977.

6. Gabriel Almond, *The American People and American Foreign Policy* (New York: Praeger, 1960), esp. Chapter 1. The classic statement of the "mood theory" of American foreign policy is that of Frank L. Klingberg, "The Historical Alteration of Moods in American Foreign Policy," *World Politics*, vol. IV (January 1952), pp. 239–273. A more recent statement of this thesis is that of Jack E. Holmes, "A Mood/Interest Theory of American Foreign Policy," a paper prepared for delivery at the 17th Annual Convention of the International Studies Association, Toronto, Canada, February 25, 1976. It should be noted that both Klingberg and Holmes encompass a good deal more than public opinion in their conceptions of alternating "moods" in American foreign policy.

7. William R. Caspey, "The Mood Theory: A Study in Public Opinion and Foreign Policy," *American Political Science Review*, vol. 64, June 1970, pp. 536–547; Watts and Free, "Nationalism, Not Isolationism"; and *Foreign Policy Choices for the Seventies and Eighties*.

8. See, for example, the discussion of John P. Robinson and John D. Holm, *The Public Looks at Foreign Policy: A Report from Five Cities*, pp. 16–18, and *Hard Choices: The American Public and U.S. Foreign Policy*, p. 8. Both reports were published by the Kettering Foundation of Dayton, Ohio in 1978—the latter under Department of State auspices.

9. James Nathan, "A Comparison of Columnists and Public Opinion, 1953–1960," unpublished paper, Washington Center for Foreign Policy Research, Johns Hopkins School of Advanced International Studies, 1965.

10. See, for example, Hazel Gaudet Erskine, "The Polls: Textbook Knowledge," *Public Opinion Quarterly*, vol. 27, no. 4 (Spring 1963) and "The Polls: The Informed Public," *Public Opinion Quarterly*, vol. 26, no. 4 (Winter 1962).

11. Bruce Russett, "The Revolt of the Masses: Public Opinion on Military Expenditures," in Russett, ed., *Peace, War and Numbers* (Beverly Hills, Calif.: Sage Publications, 1972), p. 103.

12. Louis Harris, *The Anguish of Change*, pp. 12 and 13; "Harris Survey for the Senate Committee on Intergovernmental Relations, 1973," *New York Times*, October 13, 1974, p. 1.

13. "Social Pressures Put Chemical Industry Under Fire," *Management Bulletin*, vol. 7, no. 1 (January-February 1978), pp. 1–2. The *Management Bulletin* is a DuPont Corporation publication.

14. Louis Harris in *Foreign Policy Choices for the Seventies and Eighties*, vol. 1, p. 112.

15. Testimony of Mervin D. Field in ibid., p. 71. Field found in response to the question, "Who do you believe should have the strongest voice in foreign policy—the President or Congress?":

	Percent
The President	28
Congress	54
Both equal	12
No opinion	6

16. Testimony of Daniel Yankelovich in ibid., p. 76.

17. Louis Harris, *The Anguish of Change*, p. 57.

18. Jong R. Lee, 'Rallying Around the Flag: Foreign Policy Events and Presidential Popularity," *Presidential Studies Quarterly*, vol. 7, no. 4 (Fall 1977), p. 253.

19. Ibid., p. 256.

20. Gabriel A. Almond and Sidney Verba, *The Civic Culture: Political Attitudes and Democracy in Five Countries* (Princeton, N.J.: Princeton University Press, 1963), p. 102.

21. *New York Times*, December 3, 1973, p. 34.

22. "Hard Choices," p. 10.

23. Henry Kissinger, "Preface to the Third Edition," *American Foreign Policy*, 3rd ed. (New York: W. W. Norton, 1977), p. 7.

24. "Hard Choices," p. 2.

25. Harris, *The Anguish of Change*, pp. 229–257.

26. Watts and Free, "Nationalism, Not Isolationism," pp. 19–20.

27. Ibid., pp. 19–20.

28. Ibid., pp. 11–16.

29. Harris, *The Anguish of Change*, p. 76.

30. *Time*, May 2, 1969.

31. Free, "The International Attitudes of Americans," pp. 143–144.

32. Watts and Free, *State of the Nation*, p. 217, and the *New York Times* June 16, 1974. Regarding the latter response it is interesting to

note that this sentiment is not entirely new, for in 1964, 59% of the public agreed with the proposition and 60% in 1968.

33. Robinson and Holm, *The Public Looks at Foreign Policy*, Table 4, p. 12.

34. Ibid., p. 13. Similarly, 60% of the public was found in the Kettering study to favor "Making sure the U.S. is the most powerful country in the world." However, the conditions "at all costs, even going to the very brink of war if necessary" posed in early polls was not included. "Hard Choices," p. 10.

35. Russett, "The Revolt of the Masses, pp. 313–315.

36. "Hard Choices," p. 11.

37. Ibid.

38. Harris in *Foreign Policy Choices for the Seventies and Eighties* pp. 14 and 15 and Watts and Free, "Nationalism, Not Isolationism," pp. 10, 11, 13, and 16.

39. Ibid.

40. Harris, *Foreign Policy Choices for the Seventies and Eighties*, pp. 15 and 16.

41. Ibid., p. 16.

42. Ibid.

43. Watts and Free, "Nationalism, Not Isolationism," passim.

44. Harris, op. cit., p. 17.

45. Watts and Free, op. cit., p. 9.

46. See, for example, George F. Kennan, *American Diplomacy, 1900–1950* (New York: New American Library, 1959); Kennan notes:

> But I sometimes wonder whether in this respect a democracy is not uncomfortably similar to one of those prehistoric monsters with a body as long as this room and the brain the size of a pin: he lies there in his comfortable primeval mud and pays little attention to his environment; he is slow to wrath—in fact you practically have to whack his tail off to make him aware that his interests are being disturbed; but once he grasps this, he lays about him with such blind determination that he not only destroys his adversary but largely wrecks his native habitat. You wonder whether it would not have been wiser for him to have taken a little more interest in what was going on at an earlier date and to have seen whether he could not have prevented some of these situations from arising instead of proceeding from an indiscriminating indifference to a holy wrath equally indiscriminating (p. 59).

47. *Foreign Policy Choices for the Seventies and Eighties*, p. 78.

48. Ibid., pp. 13 and 17.

49. "An Inward-Looking Nation," *New York Times*, February 25, 1978, p. 20.

50. "The Consensus That Died at Tet," *New York Times*, February 19, 1978, p. 20.

51. "An Inward-Looking Nation," op. cit.

52. *New York Times*, June 16, 1974.

53. Bruce Russett and Betty C. Hanson, "How Corporate Executives See America's Role in the World," *Fortune*, May 1974, p. 165, and Russett, "The American's Retreat From World Power," mimeo, n.d., pp. 7–9.

54. "The American's Retreat," op. cit.

55. Russett and Hanson, p. 168.

56. Ibid., p. 165.

57. Robinson and Holm, op. cit., pp. 16 and 17.

58. Ibid., p. 17.

59. "Hard Choices," p. 6.

60. "The Meaning of Vietnam: Belief Systems of American Leaders," op. cit.

61. Ibid., p. 13.

62. Ibid., pp. 13–14.

63. Ibid., p. 14.

64. Ibid., p. 15.

65. See, for example, the report on a conference held at the University of North Carolina to assess, a decade later, the impact of the Tet Offensive. Charles Mohr, "Hawks and Doves Refight Tet Offensive at Symposium," *New York Times*. February 27, 1978, p. A2.

66. *New York Times*, June 16, 1974. In 1964, "internationalist" sentiment stood at 70%.

67. "A New Generation of Isolationists," *Foreign Affairs* 49, no. 1, p. 143.

68. Graham Allison, "Cool It: The Foreign Policy of Young Americans," *Foreign Policy*, no. 1 (Winter 1970–71), pp. 144–160. (Although surveyed in a particularly turbulent time, Allison's analysis seems likely to be not far from the mark.)

69. Roger Handberg, Jr., "The Vietnam Analogy: Student Attitudes on War," *Public Opinion Quarterly*, Winter, 1972–1973, p. 612.

70. Ibid., p. 615.

71. Robinson and Holm, op. cit., p. 16.

72. William P. Bundy, Transcript of Remarks, October 16, 1973, University of Delaware, Newark, Delaware, quoted in James A. Nathan and James K. Oliver, *United States Foreign Policy and World Order* (Boston: Little, Brown and Co., 1976), pp. 7 and 8.

73. Watts and Free, "Nationalism, Not Isolationism," p. 26.

74. Ibid., pp. 25–26.

75. Holsti and Rosenau, p. 14.
76. Robinson and Holm, p. 16, n. 2.
77. Ibid., p. 16.

7. The Future of the United States Navy

1. *The Defense Monitor* vol. 1, no. 1 (January 1976), p. 3.
2. Laurence Martin, "The Role of Force in the Ocean," in *Perspectives on Ocean Policy: Conference on Conflict and Order in Ocean Relations,* October 21–24, 1974, Arlie, Va., NSF Report, Grant No. GI-39643.
3. *New York Times*, March 18, 1978.
4. *New York Times*, May 8, 1978.
5. Ibid.
6. *New York Times*, March 24, 1978.
7. *New York Times*, March 24, 1978.
8. *New York Times*, May 8, 1978; *Washington Post*, April 10, 1978.
9. *Washington Post*, April 13, 1978.
10. Indeed, the current budget provides almost 3 billion dollars for Trident. The projected number in FY79 is 14; but it is likely the production run will be extended as the Poseidon boats age and as some economies of scale are realized.
11. *New York Times*, April 4, 1978; *New York Times*, May 8, 1978.
12. *Washington Post*, March 21, 1978.
13. *Wilmington Evening Journal*, May 4, 1978.
14. *New York Times*, May 6, 1978.
15. Harold Nicolson, *The Evaluation of the Diplomatic Method* (New York: Collier Books, 1954) p. 41.
16. Edward L. Morse, *The Modernization of International Society* (New York: Free Press, 1977).
17. Michael Howard, "The Classical Strategists" in Alistair Buchan, ed., *Problems of Modern Strategy* (London: Praeger Publishers, for the International Institute for Strategic Studies, 1970), p. 75.

Index